Designing Learning Experiences for Inclusivity and Diversity: Advice for Learning Designers

Designing Learning Experiences for Inclusivity and Diversity: Advice for Learning Designers

KEITH HEGGART; MAIS FATAYER; CAMILLE DICKSON-DEANE; PUVANESWARI P ARUMUGAM; KATRINA THORPE; SHAUN BELL; SUSAN PAGE; JOHN VULIC; NHUNG NGUYEN; KATIE DUNCAN; AND BRUNA CONTRO PRETERO

UTS EPRESS
SYDNEY

Designing Learning Experiences for Inclusivity and Diversity: Advice for Learning Designers Copyright © 2024 by the Authors is licensed under a Creative Commons Attribution-NonCommercial 4.0 International License, except where otherwise noted.

This book was published by UTS ePress at the University of Technology Sydney via the Council of Australian University Librarians Open Educational Resources Collective. The online version is available at https://oercollective.caul.edu.au/designing-learning-experiences.

Disclaimer

Note that corporate logos, branding and images captioned as All Rights Reserved are specifically excluded from the Creative Commons Attribution Noncommercial Licence of this work, and may not be reproduced under any circumstances without the express written permission of the copyright holders.

Recommended citation

Heggart, K., Fatayer, M., Dickson-Deane, C., Arumugam, P.P., Thorpe, K., Page, S. Bell, S, Vulic, J., Nguyen, N., Duncan, K., Hall, R., & Pretero, B.C., (2024). *Designing Learning Experiences for Inclusivity and Diversity: Advice for Learning Designers.* UTS ePress. https://oercollective.caul.edu.au/designing-learning-experiences.

Recommended attribution

Designing Learning Experiences for Inclusivity and Diversity: Advice for Learning Designers by Keith Heggart, Mais Fatayer, Puvaneswari P. Arumugam, Katrina Thorpe, Susan Page, Shaun Bell, John Vulic and Katie Duncan is licensed under a Creative Commons Attribution Noncommercial 4.0 Licence.

Cover (illustration) by UTS ePress is licensed under a Creative Commons Attribution 4.0 International Licence.

Contents

Acknowledgement of Country — vii
Accessibility Information — viii
Acknowledgements — xiii
About the authors — xiv
Foreword — xxii
Royce Kimmons

Part I. Chapters

1. Introduction — 1
   Keith Heggart
2. Making socially just pedagogy a reality — 11
   Keith Heggart and Camille Dickson-Deane
3. Designing inclusive learning experience through Open Educational Practices — 39
   Mais Fatayer
4. Negotiating the assumptions and identity tensions surrounding third space academics/professionals — 103
   Puvaneswari P Arumugam
5. Indigenous-led learning design: Reimagining the teaching team — 142
   Katrina Thorpe; Shaun Bell; and Susan Page
6. Designing for equity in learning — 175
   John Vulic

7. Designing for cultural responsiveness — 206
   Nhung Nguyen
8. Working with students with lived experience of disability to enhance inclusive and accessible learning — 251
   Katie Duncan and Rhiannon Hall
9. Baking a cake: Engaging staff in inclusive learning design — 282
   Bruna Contro Pretero
10. Conclusion — 319
    Mais Fatayer

Versioning History — 329

Review Statement — 330

Feedback and corrections — 331

Glossary — 332

Acknowledgement of Country

The authors gratefully acknowledge the Aboriginal and Torres Strait Islander peoples of this nation. We extend our deepest respect to the traditional custodians of the country throughout Australia, recognising their enduring connection to the land, culture, and community.

We specifically recognise the Gadigal People of the Eora Nation and the Boorooberongal People of the Dharug Nation, upon whose ancestral lands the campus of the University of Technology Sydney (UTS) now stands. We honour the Elders, past and present, as the custodians of knowledge for these lands.

In writing this book, we acknowledge the traditional custodians of the lands where we live and work, and where this book was created. We pay our respects to the cultural diversity of all Aboriginal and Torres Strait Islander peoples, and express our gratitude for their enduring contributions to Australian society.

Furthermore, we celebrate the rich and resilient cultures of First Nations Australians, acknowledging their profound impact on shaping our collective identity and heritage. We commit ourselves to fostering understanding, reconciliation, and mutual respect as we continue to learn from and alongside Aboriginal and Torres Strait Islander communities. We also pay our respect to the traditional lands of the First Nations from where our authors are coming. We honour their ancestors, present communities, and future generations.

Accessibility Information

University of Technology Sydney believes that education needs to be available to everyone, which means supporting the creation of free, open, and accessible educational resources. We are actively committed to increasing the **accessibility** and usability of the textbooks we produce.

Accessibility of This Resource

The web version of this resource has been designed to meet Web Content Accessibility Guidelines 2.0, level AA. In addition, it follows all guidelines in Appendix A: Checklist for Accessibility of the *Accessibility Toolkit – 2nd Edition*. It includes:

- **Easy navigation**. This resource has a linked table of contents and uses headings in each chapter to make navigation easy.
- **Accessible videos**. All videos in this resource have captions.
- **Accessible images**. All images in this resource that convey information have alternative text. Images that are decorative have empty alternative text.
- **Accessible links**. All links use descriptive link text.
- **Interactive H5P**. All H5P interactive content has been modified to be accessible for screen readers.
- **Podcast**. Transcripts are available for all podcasts in this resource

Accessibility Checklist

Element	Requirements	Pass?
Headings	Content is organized under headings and subheadings that are used sequentially.	Yes
Images	Images that convey information include alternative text descriptions. These descriptions are provided in the alt text field, in the surrounding text, or linked to as a long description.	Yes
Images	Images and text do not rely on colour to convey information.	Yes
Images	Images that are purely decorative or are already described in the surrounding text contain empty alternative text descriptions. (Descriptive text is unnecessary if the image doesn't convey contextual content information.)	Yes
Tables	Tables include row and/or column headers that have the correct scope assigned.	Yes
Tables	Tables include a title or caption.	Yes
Tables	Tables do not have merged or split cells.	Yes
Tables	Tables have adequate cell padding.	Yes
Links	The link text describes the destination of the link.	Yes
Links	Links do not open new windows or tabs. If they do, a textual reference is included in the link text.	Yes
Links	Links to files include the file type in the link text.	Not applicable
Audio	All audio content includes a transcript that includes all speech content and relevant descriptions of non-speech audio and speaker names/headings where necessary.	Yes

Video	All videos include high-quality (i.e., not machine generated) captions of all speech content and relevant non-speech content.	Yes
Video	All videos with contextual visuals (graphs, charts, etc.) are described audibly in the video.	Not applicable
H5P	All H5P activities have been tested for accessibility by the H5P team and have passed their testing.	Partial (see below)
H5P	All H5P activities that include images, videos, and/or audio content meet the accessibility requirements for those media types.	Partial (see below)
Formulas	Formulas have been created using LaTeX and are rendered with MathJax.	Not applicable
Formulas	If LaTeX is not an option, formulas are images with alternative text descriptions.	Not applicable
Font	Font size is 12 point or higher for body text.	Yes
Font	Font size is 9 point for footnotes or endnotes.	Yes
Font	Font size can be zoomed to 200% in the webbook or eBook formats.	Yes

Known Accessibility Issues and Areas for Improvement

In Chapter 3, there is an H5P interactive titled 'OER Development Model' that utilises the Interactive Book format. It's worth noting that this particular H5P element is known to be inaccessible, highlighting an area that requires improvement.

Accessibility features of the web version of this resource

The web version of this resource has been designed with accessibility in mind by incorporating the following features:

- It has been optimized for people who use screen-reader technology.
    - all content can be navigated using a keyboard
    - links, headings, and tables are formatted to work with screen readers
    - images have alt tags
- Information is not conveyed by colour alone.

Other file formats available

In addition to the web version, this book is available in a number of file formats including PDF, EPUB (for eReaders), and various editable files. Choose from the selection of available file types from the 'Download this book' drop-down menu. This option appears below the book cover image on the eBook's landing page.

Third-Party Content

In some cases, our open text includes third-party content. In these cases, it is often not possible to ensure accessibility of this content.

Let Us Know if You are Having Problems Accessing This Book

We are always looking for ways to make our resources more accessible. If you have problems accessing this resource, please contact us to let us know so we can fix the issue.

Please include the following information:

- The name of the resource
- The location of the problem by providing a web address or page description.
- A description of the problem
- The computer, software, browser, and any assistive technology you are using that can help us diagnose and solve your issue (e.g., Windows 10, Google Chrome (Version 65.0.3325.181), NVDA screen reader)

Here is how you can contact us: mais.fatayer@uts.edu.au, keith.heggart@uts.edu.au, utsepress@uts.edu.au.

This statement was last updated on 30 August 2024.

The Accessibility Checklist table was adapted by from one originally created by the Rebus Community and shared under a CC BY 4.0 licence.

Acknowledgements

In this journey, we would like to acknowledge the invaluable contributions of our colleagues who supported us along the way. We extend our appreciation to the UTS Library staff, with a special mention of Helen Chan, whose collaboration was instrumental.

We would also like to thank other UTS Library staff, including Matthew Noble (Lead, Copyright, Open Scholarship and Copyright) for his valuable advice on copyright; Megan Wong (Specialist, Identity and Design, User Experience) for the book cover; Marie-Louise Taylor (Editor, Open Scholarship and Copyright) for copyediting; Patrick Tooth (Lead, Copyright, Open Scholarship and Copyright) for thorough review of publishing approvals and copyright permissions; and Ria Hamblett (acting Manager, Open Scholarship and Copyright) for managing the final stage of this journey.

Furthermore, we recognise and thank the team at Council of Australian University Librarians (CAUL), for their support through Open Educational Resources Collective initiative, advancing open education within the learning and teaching sector, and for providing a platform for collaboration among academics and professionals in scholarly pursuits.

We are also thankful to our academic peers who generously dedicated their time to review the book and provide valuable feedback. We extend our gratitude to Associate Professor Henk Huijser from QUT (Queensland University of Technology), Associate Professor Leanne Ngo from La Trobe University, and Associate Professor Royce Kimmons from Brigham Young University, who graciously contributed the foreword to the book.

About the authors

Keith Heggart is the academic lead for the Graduate Certificate in Learning Design at UTS. He designed and developed this brand-new and innovative course that combines microcredentials and work-integrated learning in order to meet the needs of a diverse and busy student body. This course was recognised for its approach internationally, receiving the Learning Innovation Award from AECT in 2022. It has also received a UTS Teaching and Learning Citation. Keith's research interests lie at the intersection of social justice and learning design. He has won numerous awards for his research, including a Best Publication for his paper on Learning Design for Social Justice from the Culture, Learning and Technology SIG in AECT, and the Early Career Researcher award from ASCILITE in 2021. In 2022, Keith won an ASCILITE/D2L grant to investigate learning design and microcredentials. Keith has more than 20 publications to his name, including two books. Before becoming an academic, Keith worked as a learning designer and developer in three different universities, and also for not-for-profit organisations. Keith is also an Apple Distinguished Educator.

Mais Fatayer is an educational technology specialist, learning designer and early career researcher. She has been working in higher education since 2008, during which she worked in several capacities at higher educational institutions including the Open University and Western Sydney University. At the time of publishing this book, she was the Learner Experience Design Manager at University of Technology Sydney (UTS).

Mais specialises in designing and co-designing engaging learning materials, implementing open learning strategies and resources, leading transformative learning projects, and creating award-winning technology-enhanced learning environments. She received UTS Vice Chancellor's Professional Staff Excellence Awards for High Performing Professional Staff in 2023 in recognition of her achievement to the work of open education at UTS. She was also awarded Blackboard 2018 Catalyst Awards for Australia and New Zealand in the Student Success category. Mais received her PhD from the School of Computing, Engineering and Mathematics in 2016 from the University of Western Sydney. Her thesis is titled 'Towards a sustainable OER model: Tapping into the cognitive surplus of student-generated content'.

Camille Dickson-Deane is a Senior Lecturer at the University of Technology Sydney, Australia. She is a Fulbright and Organization of American States (OAS) scholar with her research focusing on pedagogical usability, individual differences and contextualised online learning designs. Camille serves on two Q1 editorial boards – Educational Technology Research and Development and Internet and Higher Education – along with serving as an advisor for the open science publishing project EdTechnica and an Associate Editor for the *Journal of Computing in Higher Education*. She is also an Australian representative on the EDUCAUSE Horizon Report panel of experts, having served since 2021.

Puvaneswari P Arumugam (Puva) is a third space academic (Lecturer, Learning Futures) at Deakin University's Faculty of Business and Law Learning Innovations team. Her research interests include studying the perceptions and identity issues relating to third space academics/professionals together with stakeholder perspectives of digital literacy. Puva is also a Senior Fellow of the Higher Education Academy.

In her current role, Puva leads the academic development of programmatic course redevelopment across the faculty, ensuring that the courses are aligned and fit for integrated teaching and learning. At Deakin, Puva has also been a valued team member over the past six years, providing stakeholder and SoTL input to several university-wide projects such as CloudFirst project, FutureLearn MOOC/ Microcredentials and Deakin Design Principles. Apart from being an Advance Higher Education Fellowship Mentor and Assessor at Deakin, she has also been a mentor at ASCILITE Community Mentorship Program for the past four years, where she has presented conference papers and won an award for a poster she co-created with her mentee. She is an Executive Committee (Communication) member for Higher Education Research and Development Society of Australasia (HERDSA) at the Victoria Branch. Puva co-published a book (with a publication grant from Singapore National Heritage Board) in 2017 depicting the cultural identity of an Indian minority group in Singapore. Her recent publications include an ASCILITE Conference paper in 2019 and being a co-author on ASCILITE's Horizon Report 2022. Puva is currently working on an autoethnographic research project conducted by herself and two colleagues studying the assumptions that third space academics bring to their roles and how these assumptions impact the work that they do.

Katrina Thorpe (Worimi) is the Academic Lead at Nura Gili: Centre for Indigenous Programs at the University of New South Wales. At the time of writing this book, Katrina was a Senior Lecturer at the Centre for the Advancement of Indigenous Knowledges and School of International Studies and Education, UTS. She has over two decades experience teaching Indigenous Studies within the fields of education, social work, nursing, health and community development. Katrina's teaching and research focuses on developing culturally responsive pedagogies that facilitate connections between students and Aboriginal people, communities and Country. Katrina has received several teaching awards including the Faculty of Education and Social Work's Teaching Excellence Award at the University of Sydney, the Faculty of Arts and Social Sciences – University of Sydney, Unit of Study Commendation for teaching *KOCR2013 Indigenous Health and Communities* and the Faculty of Arts and Social Sciences – UTS, Learning and Teaching Award for Integration of Indigenous Professional Capabilities into Curriculum. Her co-authored paper '*Learning from Country to conceptualise what an Aboriginal curriculum narrative might look like in education*' received the Australian Curriculum Studies Association's *2023 Colin Marsh Award* for the best journal article.

Susan Page is a national teaching award-winning Aboriginal educator and Indigenous higher education specialist who is currently the Director of Indigenous Learning and Teaching at Western Sydney University. Susan's research focuses on Indigenous Australian experiences of learning and academic work in higher education and student learning in Indigenous Studies. She has collaborated on multiple competitive research grants and is well published in Indigenous Higher Education. Susan has held several leadership positions including Associate Dean (Indigenous Leadership and Engagement), Centre Director and Head of the Department, and she is currently an appointed Indigenous representative for the Universities Australia Deputy Vice-Chancellor (Academic) Committee.

Shaun Bell is a learning designer at UTS' Postgraduate Learning Design unit, working in partnership with experts to co-design innovative digital learning. They hold a PhD in Literature from UNSW and have published reviews and award-winning essays on literary culture and the teaching of English in *JASAL*, *Southerly* and *TESOL Quarterly*. Shaun has taught in the English Program at UNSW and has several years of experience designing learning materials for eLearning and distance education.

John Vulic is an academic for the Graduate Certificate in Learning Design at UTS. Prior to this role, John was a Senior Learning Designer at UTS. In this role he managed a team of learning designers who designed and developed a suite of online and blended learning products at UTS. These included microcredentials, short courses, tasters, enterprise learning and traditional enrolled, and online program management (OPM) courses. John was a co-recipient of the AECT Learner Engagement Division's 2022 Excellence in Innovation Award for the Graduate Certificate in Learning Design Program at UTS. John has over 25 years' experience in various education, teaching and training and development roles. These roles have encompassed positions across tertiary, government and private sectors. As an early career educational researcher (H index of 2), John's PhD focused on a comparison of learning designs that promote learning transfer.

As a researcher, John has been involved in an international 21st Century Partnership for STEM Education project titled Mathematical Thinkers Like Me (MLM). This project seeks to support Black, Latinx, and low-income students in the United States with an online collaborative problem-solving and storytelling context that helps develop their identity and strength as mathematical thinkers.

Nhung Nguyen is a highly respected and passionate educator with over 19 years of experience in learning design, digital technologies in education, and science education. She is a Senior Lecturer in Learning and Teaching at the University of Tasmania. Previously, she worked as a Senior Lecturer and Learning and Teaching Consultant at Auckland University of Technology – Learning Transformation LAB (New Zealand), where she plays a key role in helping to transform the way that students learn and engage with education. Throughout her career, Nhung has been committed to creating learning experiences that are inclusive and responsive to the needs of diverse learners. She has received awards at conferences, been invited as a keynote speaker and given speeches at conferences and universities.

Nhung has published more than 25 titles, one of which has 4,582 accesses and was the most highly accessed article published in *Asia-Pacific Science Education* at the time Springer ranked it.

Katie Duncan is an advocate for inclusivity in higher education. She likes finding practical and sustainable ways to help academics make their subjects accessible for all students, including those with disabilities and access requirements, such as using assistive technology like screen readers.

In 2021, she established the Inclusive Practices team in the LX.lab (Learner Experience Lab) at the University of Technology Sydney (UTS). During her leadership, the team has won two Accessibility in Action Award from the Australian Disability Clearinghouse on Education and Training (ADCET). The first award for their inclusive practice review – a framework for assessing how learning and teaching tools can be used in accessible ways. The second for their collaborative support for Subject Coordinators implementing complex access requirement for a student to ensure they have an inclusive experience. The team has also partnered with ADCET to adapt their own accessibility resources for the Australian and New Zealand tertiary sector.

Katie brings the student voice into the work that she does, by advocating for and implementing paid opportunities for co-design. Examples of this include the *Students Explain Digital Accessibility* video series, where five UTS students draw on their lived experiences of disability to explain why academics need accessibility for their subjects. Most recently, Katie has led SLAC (Student Learning Advisory Committee) with the UTS Accessibility Services, a group of 14 students in paid roles who meet once a month to provide insights into improving the student experience through the lens of accessibility – named by students as a way of reclaiming the idea students who require adjustments are "slackers".

Rhiannon Hall writes and edits content for LX at UTS, the digital home of the University of Technology Sydney's Education Portfolio. Rhiannon works across content on all aspects of learning and teaching, and has a particular interest in accessibility, social equity and collaborating with students. She is passionate about educating the learning and teaching community on accessible practices, and has co-facilitated a number of projects working with students as partners. Rhiannon has a Bachelor of Communication from the University of Newcastle and a Master of Cultural Studies from the University of Sydney.

Bruna Contro Pretero. Being queer and disabled, Bruna has devoted her life to making a positive impact on society. In terms of education, she has undertaken extensive studies in her field, achieving Bachelor's degrees in Sciences and Teaching, as well as in Translation and Interpreting Services with a specialisation in English and Portuguese. She later focused on education, diversity and accessibility studies, earning a range of postgraduate diplomas in Higher Education Learning and Teaching, Inclusive Learning and Teaching Practices, and Education Psychology, as well as gaining certification in Web Accessibility Compliance.

Over the last 15 years, Bruna has worked in various educational settings, from primary to tertiary levels, and has held a variety of roles including education specialist, education designer/technologist and learning technologist. At the time of writing this book, she was employed as a Digital Accessibility Specialist at the Australian National University.

Bruna's areas of expertise include Technology-Enhanced Learning (TEL), Critical Pedagogy, Diversity and Inclusion, Digital Accessibility, and Care and Trauma-Informed Pedagogy. As a lifelong learner, she firmly believes that education has the power to transform people and enable them to drive positive change in society.

Foreword

ROYCE KIMMONS

Educational systems are social systems. That shouldn't be an earth-shattering thing to say, but it's amazing how often those doing education-adjacent work view education as something that is inherently non-social (i.e. non-human). Near the end of a recent class about universal design for learning, one of my students who was preparing to become a secondary science teacher raised his hand. "You mean," he said, with exasperation in his voice, "that we're expected to teach every student in our classes?" "Well, yes," I replied, unsuccessfully hiding some shock, "of course!".

Yet, it's not always obvious that education should actually involve teaching someone at all, let alone everyone. A charitable interpretation of this student's reaction may be found in teachers' motivations to enter the field. Secondary and tertiary teachers especially are drawn to education because they love their subjects, with their hearts focused on Shakespeare, cellular mitosis, the Renaissance, or the quadratic formula, and though there is nothing wrong with such a love of knowledge, per se, this focus can quickly warp into a view of education as being merely "teaching something" rather than "teaching someone something." Perhaps that's why classroom management is the biggest reason teachers in my own country are quitting in droves. We attract and train teachers by focusing on the something of teaching, but those pesky someones keep getting in the way, and when our teachers can't deliver on the something, they feel unappreciated and unfulfilled, and they become the someones we blame.

As industrialized nations grapple with perceived failures in their education systems, they have historically taken this basic misunderstanding to an extreme: focusing even more firmly on the something rather than the someone. In the U.S., the "Johnny can't read" crisis led us to focus on the abstract something of "reading," rather than the someone of "Johnny," and altogether ignoring the someones of "Isabella," "Ahmed," and others. Worldwide, university faculty are hired and evaluated on their publishing and grant-seeking prowess rather than their teaching skill. Secondary teachers are hired with decreasing pedagogical training in favor of more subject-area coursework. Initiatives and policies are enacted to "raise standards" rather than to "raise students." And designers are trained to think first, foremost, and always about their objectives (the somethings), as their work is packaged and delivered to unseen and unknown someones at ever-increasing scale.

I'm obviously painting in broad strokes here, but do you see any of these patterns in your spheres of experience? Do you sense education ever being approached in lieu of (or at times in spite of) the someones being taught? Do you ever sense the someone of the learner being sacrificed to the something being taught? And if so, what in the world can we possibly do about it as learning designers?

This book, *Designing Learning Experiences for Inclusivity and Diversity*, provides a useful leap in the right direction by helping us to first understand the depth and nuances of this problem and then providing practical guidance for moving forward. The authors provide a simple and approachable definition of "inclusivity" in design as "the practice of creating an environment where everyone feels welcome, respected and valued" (Chapter 1), and "diversity" is framed as a simple reality that the someones involved in learning are actually very different from one another in ways that really matter. Rather than overlooking, minimizing, or altogether ignoring the social nature of education, such an emphasis can help us move away from the reductionistic and doomed view of education as merely "teaching something" to a more complete and inspiring view that seeks to

> Teach everyone
> as they really are
> things that matter
> in ways that matter.

In my mind, that's the heart of the inclusive learning designer. It aligns deeply with the tenets and practices of openness and social justice (Chapters 2 & 3) and represents the only morally sustainable and also the most effective way to design learning environments in a diverse social world.

Beyond moral posturing or ideological hand wringing, championing inclusivity and diversity in design is a very practical way to become a great designer as it helps us to avoid three of the most common and limiting pitfalls designers face. Let's call these pitfalls (a) Me Design, (b) Median Design, and (c) Meaningless Design.

Me Design. The first mistake of a designer in any field, ranging from architecture to software design to learning, is to design for the designer rather than the target audience of the design. This is rarely intentional but reflects the reality that if we do not clearly and consistently think about our audience in our design work, then we will subconsciously fill in any gaps with ourselves. If I'm a sports guy, then I may use baseball metaphors to teach about the criminal justice system even if my audience has no idea what a "run," "ball," or "three strikes" is in this context, thereby introducing extraneous cognitive load and confusion. If I'm a native English speaker, then I may use colloquialisms like "bite the bullet," "break a leg," or "beat around the bush" that English speakers in other countries have never heard of, thereby yielding misunderstandings. And if I'm food secure, I might create an entire unit about learning fractions from cutting up pizzas without ever hearing the grumbling stomachs of my food insecure students, who are now even more distracted by their hunger. In learning design, this pitfall historically has occurred as white, male, middle-class, Western, English-speaking, etc. designers created learning experiences that they assumed were for everyone simply because they made them for no one in particular. However, it turns out that all designs are for someone. Designs made for "no one in particular" are designs made for the designer, and the designer can never escape designing for themselves until they first understand the true diversity of their audience and inclusively seek to make their designs spaces "where everyone feels welcome, respected and valued" (Chapter 1).

Median Design. The second mistake that plagues designers is creating for an "average" or "typical" learner. As a young designer, a faculty member boasted to me "I don't care about my students individually; only in aggregate," suggesting that designers should plot learners along a bell curve and aim to meet the needs of a dot at the top middle peak, ignoring all else. This median learner, however, is a faceless apparition that doesn't exist, and by focusing on it, we ignore our actual learners (particularly those on the perceived margins). It also reductionistically classifies learners on performance and treats this as an inherent trait rather than a byproduct of the design. The result is design work that artificially views learners unidimensionally and only seeks to meet their needs on a single dimension. The alternative that an inclusive approach to design proposes is to intentionally design for the greatest diversity of learners as possible and recognize that any bell curve of performance is a byproduct of design decisions, not an inherent trait. Richly understanding and designing for a few dots on the edges of the bell curve, such as by attending to cultural responsiveness (Chapters 5 & 6) and the needs of students experiencing disability (Chapter 7), helps the designer to meet the needs of everyone (including the imagined median). It also helps the designer to break away from morally and philosophically problematic roots of the bell curve mentality, which is based on an attempt to sort people and an assumption that not everyone will be able to learn equally.

Meaningless Design. And a third common pitfall that learning designers face emerges from doing work that is so disconnected from actual learners that it ends up feeling empty and meaningless. I think most learning designers enter the field out of a desire to teach and to help people, but as learning design as a discipline becomes increasingly distanced from learners and focuses on delivering learning experiences at increasing scale, designers may find themselves in a crisis of meaning as they ply their efforts to help people but can never see the results. They create learning experiences but don't see students engaging in them nor see the effects on students' lives. This is especially true when working as third-space academics (Chapter 4) and would be like a nurse attending to patients through a veil, a chef delivering all their entrees to a black box, or a musician who never left the recording studio. At some point, we would rightly ask ourselves "what's the point?" and "am I even doing any good in my work?" Focusing on inclusivity and diversity has the potential to rehumanize these efforts, because though we might still be working behind a computer in an office away from our learners, our mental and emotional energies become invested in understanding our actual learners as people, building teams to meet their needs (Chapters 5 & 8), and experiencing learning with them. Rather than focusing entirely on tools, processes, or frameworks, we become reinvested in and refocused on people, the someones of learning. From my own experience, this breathes life into our careers and improves our designs, making us happier, more effective, and more fulfilled in our work.

The problem of practice that this book seeks to address, then, is a critical (perhaps existential) problem for learning design: "How do we design for inclusivity and diversity?" Like the problems faced in education broadly, this problem can only be effectively approached as a social problem as designers seek to understand the someone component of their mandate to "teach someone something." Proposed practices, solutions, or guides to learning design that ignore or minimize inclusivity and diversity fundamentally misunderstand the purpose of the field and are akin to attempting to solve medical problems by pretending that patients do not exist. Rather, the future of learning design should be a future that is increasingly human-centered, by inclusively focusing on people and their true (diverse) selves. As such, I can't think of a topic that should merit the attention of learning designers more than that of this book. Its guidance can practically help novice and experienced designers alike to avoid some of the most common pitfalls in the field, and its vision of a world of learning that is more inclusive for everyone is the only one worth having.

About the author

Associate Professor Royce Kimmons
BRIGHAM YOUNG UNIVERSITY
https://education.byu.edu

Dr. Kimmons is an Associate Professor of Instructional Psychology and Technology at Brigham Young University where he studies technology integration in K-12/higher education, open education, and social media.

1. Introduction

KEITH HEGGART

Why this textbook, and why now?

Academia in Australasia and globally is increasingly a challenging environment as universities seek to come to terms with limited funding opportunities, more constrained regulatory requirements, reduced staffing budgets and new relationships with external communities. As more students attend universities, either commencing their studies or renewing them under the guise of lifelong and life-wide learning, institutions are required to find ways to adapt traditional approaches to more modern methods that meet the demands of diverse student bodies in cost-effective ways.

The role of the learning designer is central to this; they are often described as either third space professionals or third space academics, working as they do in the interstitial spaces between the traditional designations of professional and academic staff. The role of learning designer (however it is defined) is vital to the development, implementation and maintenance of online and blended learning approaches. This has seen a rapid rise in the need for well-trained and experienced learning designers, and a concomitant need for courses that offer learning design qualifications. Numerous Australian universities now offer these qualifications in both microcredential and postgraduate format.

As a result, learning designers are often involved in efforts to ensure that courses incorporate inclusivity and accessibility. This involves technical knowledge on digital accessibility, so that learning management systems (LMSs) are accessible and comply with the latest version of the Web Content Accessibility Guidelines (WCAG), to ensure they are perceivable, operable, understandable and robust for all students including those with disabilities, access requirements or who use assistive technology like screen readers. This is related to the increasing diversity of the student cohort. Subjects, courses and programs at universities are beginning to recognise that diversity and tailor their educational offerings in such a way as to ensure that all students feel welcome. The notion of belonging, especially among first-year students, is an important aspect of students' ongoing success at university – and learning designers have a role to play in engendering that.

It is for this reason that this textbook has been developed. While there are similar textbooks available in other geographical locations (although few are Open Educational Resources), this book is unashamedly Australasian in its focus. This is because the Australasian tertiary education system has unique features. These includes the diversity of students, but also there is a need to consider the funding arrangements, the role of governments and the broader sociocultural context within the Australasian context. A key aspect of addressing this diversity is designing learning experiences that meet the needs of all students, regardless of their language, culture, accessibility needs, family or other commitments.

This textbook will equip learning designers and related professionals with the knowledge and skills to deal efficiently and effectively with that diversity. It provides detailed and comprehensive accounts of the ways that learning designers can work within their institutions to ensure that students' learning experiences are accessible and inclusive. It provides thoughtful and thorough case studies highlighting the need for learning design practices that privilege accessibility and inclusivity, in a variety of settings and from several different institutions.

This book is unusual in that it seeks to combine the perspectives of academics researching inclusivity and learning design with those of practising learning designers and similar roles. In some cases, this takes place in separate chapters, but in others, learning designers and academics have worked together to combine their expertise into a single chapter. This means that some chapters have more of a research or conceptual focus, while others are more practice-focused. We encourage readers to engage with all of the chapters. By combining the perspectives of academics with those of learning designers, this textbook provides learning designers with both a firm theoretical foundation for their practice and a helpful guide to implementing those practices in current university environments.

The greatest strength of this book lies in its diverse authorship, as it was thoughtfully written and developed by a diverse group. The authorial team represents a rich tapestry of culture, language, ethnicity and abilities, bringing unique perspectives to the chapters and the book as a whole. We also possess a wide range of expertise in primary, secondary and tertiary education, Australian Indigenous communities, immigrant experiences with education, adult learning and, of course, learning design.

Key terms

This section addresses the key ideas related to social justice, accessibility and inclusivity in learning design throughout the book, and authors will refer to these terms in order to explain the design choices they made and the reasons why they adopted those. With that in mind, a basic definition is presented here for each of these terms, although readers should keep in mind that these definitions are only a starting point for understanding these terms and how they intersect with learning design.

Social justice is the fair and just treatment of all people, regardless of their race, ethnicity, gender, sexual orientation, disability or other personal characteristics. It is about ensuring that everyone has the same opportunities to succeed in life.

Inclusivity is the practice of creating an environment where everyone feels welcome, respected and valued. It is about recognising and celebrating the diversity of people and ensuring that everyone has the opportunity to participate fully in all aspects of society.

Accessibility is the ability of people with disabilities to access and use goods, services and facilities. It is about making sure that everyone can participate in society on an equal basis, regardless of their disability.

Topics covered in this book

The development and implementation of inclusive and diverse learning experiences is a vital consideration for educators in higher education. Increasingly, learning designers play a significant role in this process. This textbook offers postgraduate students a comprehensive guide to designing learning experiences that are accessible, equitable and inclusive. It provides advice, principles and practical strategies to help learning designers create a learning environment that recognises and celebrates diversity while promoting equitable learning outcomes. Through detailed accounts of theory and practice, it will canvas the following topics:

1. **Diversity and inclusion in learning:** Concepts of diversity and inclusion and their impact on the design of learning

experiences are discussed. Theories and concepts related to diversity and inclusion, such as cultural competence, intersectionality and social justice, are considered. The chapter also highlights the importance of recognising cultural differences and creating learning experiences that celebrate and embrace these.

2. **The role of learning designers in promoting diversity and inclusion:** Attention will be paid to the roles and responsibilities of learning designers in creating inclusive and equitable learning experiences. Both theorists and designers can use their skills and knowledge to create accessible and culturally responsive learning environments. This topic also covers the ethical and legal obligations of learning designers in creating inclusive learning experiences.

3. **Designing for accessibility:** This textbook will also focus on the importance of designing for accessibility to ensure that all learners can access and engage with the learning material. It will provide practical strategies for designing learning experiences that are accessible, such as using clear and concise language, providing alternative text for images and videos, and creating content that is compatible with assistive technologies.

4. **Designing for equity:** Learning designers are also required to design experiences that promote equitable learning outcomes. This book will consider how to design in this way, with a focus on assessments that are fair and inclusive, such as using multiple forms of assessment and providing opportunities for feedback and revision. Attention will also be paid to creating a learning environment that is supportive and fosters a sense of belonging for all learners.

5. **Designing for cultural responsiveness:** This topic provides practical strategies for learning designers to design learning experiences that are culturally responsive. It

explores the importance of acknowledging cultural differences and creating learning experiences that are relevant to diverse learners. It covers strategies for incorporating cultural responsiveness into the learning design process, such as incorporating culturally relevant examples and incorporating the learners' cultural background into the learning experience.
6. **Implementation and evaluation:** This theme will address the implementation and evaluation of inclusive learning design. Strategies for implementing inclusive learning design, such as providing training to educators and using feedback from learners to improve the learning experience, will be examined. Strategies for evaluating the effectiveness of inclusive learning design, such as using formative and summative evaluation methods and collecting feedback from learners, will also be explored.

About the chapters

Chapter 1: Introduction (Keith Heggart)

This chapter begins by considering why there is a need for a book such as this, especially in the Australasian context. It recognises the increasing diversity and expectations within and upon universities, including the need to cater for a more diverse student cohort. The central role played by learning designers and similar is then presented, and their importance is discussed. The chapter concludes with an outline of the structure of the book and a brief biography of each of the contributors.

Chapter 2: Making socially just pedagogy a reality (Keith Heggart and Camille Dickson-Deane)

This chapter examines the concept of socially just learning

design. It begins by describing both how and why socially just learning design is important in the current higher education context, before suggesting a framework that learning designers can adopt in order to ensure that their work is socially just. This framework combines elements of Universal Design for Learning, Nancy Fraser's three dimensions of social justice and David Wiley's ideas about open education into a cohesive approach to designing learning experiences that are socially just. In the final section of this chapter, a number of examples that make use of the framework are presented.

Chapter 3: Designing inclusive learning experience through Open Educational Practices (Mais Fatayer)

This chapter serves as a guide for learning designers seeking to integrate Open Educational Practices (OEP) into their work. Drawing on both theoretical frameworks and practical insights, the chapter emphasises the role of OEP in advancing social justice within higher education. Through extensive experience in learning design and open education, the author outlines how OEP can reduce barriers, democratise education, foster community, and enhance the student learning experience. Despite the potential benefits, the chapter acknowledges prevalent challenges hindering the widespread adoption of OEP in learning design practices, including lack of awareness, concerns about quality and intellectual property, and inadequate infrastructure. However, the chapter elaborates on the argument that learning designers, equipped with their unique skills and positions, play a pivotal role in driving the integration of OEP into educational settings.

Chapter 4: Negotiating the assumptions and identity tensions surrounding third space academics/professionals (Puva P Arumugam)

This chapter outlines the perceptions of identity and assumptions surrounding the role of third space academics/

professionals. It also considers the tensions and challenges faced by third space academics/professionals. It concludes by discussing the adaptations and adjustments made by third space academics/professionals.

Chapter 5: Indigenous-led learning design: Reimagining the teaching team (Katrina Thorpe, Shaun Bell and Susan Page)

This chapter outlines the authors' approach to developing a highly successful Indigenous-led microcredential, *Supervising Indigenous Higher Degree Research*. It highlights the role of collaboration, which hinges on three key factors: (1) the importance of trust; (2) the value of conversation and iteration; and (3) the strength of a multidisciplinary team. Through reflecting on the creative synergy which propelled the teaching development, the authors have reimagined the composition of a teaching team beyond the traditional academic model. The authors offer recommendations for educators/learning designers undertaking work in Indigenous-led learning design collaborations.

Chapter 6: Designing for equity in learning (John Vulic)

This chapter highlights Indigenous disadvantage across the subjects of Math and Science, a common disadvantage that occurs in many countries. In response to this, it introduces ways learning designers can create well-designed learning environments to provide students opportunities to learn the skills and abilities that will set them up for success in school, career and life. The chapter documents a case study of teachers redesigning their Math curriculum with a focus on promoting executive function skills to allow students to take control of their own learning. Finally, the chapter unpacks practical ways learning designers can design and promote the development of skill sets, including the ability to pay attention and ignore distractions, keep track of ideas in one's head and think flexibly to solve problems.

Chapter 7: Designing for cultural responsiveness (Nhung Nguyen)

This chapter discusses cultural responsiveness in education. It explores practical strategies to design for cultural responsiveness (e.g., incorporating culturally relevant examples and incorporating the learners' cultural background into the learning experience) and provides specific examples of incorporating cultural responsiveness into the learning design process such as designing learning materials using artefacts that reflect cultural diversity and/or inviting Māori and Pacific/Indigenous experts to get involved in different stages of the learning design process. The experts can work collaboratively with the team to brainstorm a course plan (an outline of the content, assessment and learning activities), writing some sections of a course, design some learning activities and assessment tasks and/or review content and assessments.

Chapter 8: Working with students with lived experience of disability to enhance inclusive and accessible learning (Katie Duncan and Rhiannon Hall)

This chapter documents the importance of working with students to understand their requirements. The chapter uses the *Students Explain Digital Accessibility* video project as an example of how to use co-design to engage with students. The chapter also looks at other inclusive design approaches that aim to improve the experience for all students and ensure that no one is disadvantaged.

Chapter 9: Baking a cake: Engaging staff in inclusive learning design (Bruna Contro Pretero)

This chapter examines how learning designers and associated professionals can work more productively with other members of the course teams. It uses the analogy of baking a cake to show the importance of planning, preparing different materials, consulting all stakeholders and then serving the finished cake – and highlights examples of how each of these contributes to the successful implementation of a course.

Chapter 10: Conclusion (Mais Fatayer)

The final chapter draws together the various case studies into advice for developing learning designers to adopt in their practice.

About the author

Dr Keith Heggart
UNIVERSITY OF TECHNOLOGY SYDNEY
https://www.uts.edu.au

Keith Heggart is the academic lead for the Graduate Certificate in Learning Design at UTS, where he developed an innovative course combining microcredentials and work-integrated learning. This course received the AECT Learning Innovation Award in 2022 and a UTS Teaching and Learning Citation. Keith's research focuses on social justice and learning design, earning him awards such as the Best Publication from AECT and the Early Career Researcher award from ASCILITE. He has over 20 publications, including two books, and is an Apple Distinguished Educator.

2. Making socially just pedagogy a reality

KEITH HEGGART AND CAMILLE DICKSON-DEANE

The authors would like to acknowledge the assistance of Kae Novak in developing this chapter.

The following chapter is a development of ideas presented in the post by Heggart, K., Dickson-Deane, C. & Novak, K. (2020, September 7). The path towards a socially just learning design. The Society of Research in Higher Education Blog. Retrieved September 12, 2020, from https://srheblog.com/2020/09/07/the-path-towards-a-socially-just-learning-design/. We as authors see this as an ongoing project.

Introduction

Being socially just has different connotations and meanings for every individual and institution. Higher education institutions, which often have as part of their mission the promotion of social good, are required to consider their own systems and practices and how they intersect with social justice, while at the same time they struggle with residual challenges from the pandemic. These challenges include ongoing questions about how universities are funded, precarious employment within those universities, and a student demographic that is increasingly demanding – and increasing diverse. Amidst these challenges, universities are also required (by government and industry) to demonstrate their connection to the workforce, and by other parts of society to commit to widening pathways to participation, especially from groups that have previously been marginalised and prevented from attending higher education.

Perhaps heightened by the growing awareness of educational injustices in the past (especially in the form of exclusion, marginalisation and systemic oppression), there have been calls for educational practice to adapt so that it is more inclusive (Bradley et al., 2008; Collins et al., 2019). This path has by no means been straightforward: arguments in the United States and even in Australia about the place of Critical Race Theory and its relevance to higher education are one example of the challenges faced by those who advocate for greater inclusivity (Bargallie & Lentin, 2022; Morgan, 2022). Nevertheless, many universities have made significant strides and implemented programs that are intended to make universities, and learning within them, more accessible and inclusive. In some cases, this focuses on entry into university (Devlin et al., 2023). Another element is to ensure that students feel like they belong at university and are therefore less likely to drop out (Mahoney et al., 2022). These initiatives are often branded as a commitment to social justice, but that term suffers from a frustrating vagueness.

This chapter works towards resolving that vagueness by bringing some clarity to the discussion around social justice within higher education. Specifically, it is an attempt to explore what that term might look like within educational practice, and specifically within the design of learning ecosystems at the tertiary level. In doing so, it is important to distinguish between teaching *about* social justice and *socially just pedagogy*. Both are important within educational settings, but there is a difference: teaching about social justice refers to content and learning activities related to equality, equity and similar topics. Socially just pedagogy, however, refers to the practice of education; that is, the principles that inform pedagogy, which ensure that the context, including tools, techniques, mindsets and behaviour, include elements such as fairness, equity, equality and inclusivity as major contributors to a holistic ecosystem that embodies diverse beings – students of the world.

This chapter examines just one aspect of that educational ecosystem: the design of learning. Learning and instructional design is still considered a developing field, even though it has been in existence for more than a century (Reiser, 2001). As recognition of the field continues to grow, learning designers are increasingly required to ensure that their designs meet both legal and institutional requirements. This is often captured under the broad umbrella of the term accessibility, whereby learning designers need to be mindful about features like font types and size, contrast, the availability of transcripts and interactive elements. However, this is a necessary but not sufficient part of socially just pedagogy. In addition to a focus on **accessibility**, there is a need to examine **inclusivity** – how it is actioned and what it means to those who experience it. This is in keeping with recent work that considers inclusivity as a rightful presence within courses (Calabrese Barton & Tan, 2020). This chapter seeks to identify ways in which learning designers can do just that. In doing so, it builds upon previous work by the authors in this field (Heggart et al., 2020).

Socially just pedagogy

Learning design, and imply by association that learning designers are becoming an integral part of the Australian higher education landscape (Heggart & Dickson-Deane, 2022). This is apparent in the increasing numbers of courses that seek to train individuals to become learning designers, as well as the numbers of advertisements for learning designers (Heggart

& Dickson-Deane, 2022). Learning designers and those in similarly situated spaces are expected to liaise with academics to ensure that course materials are accessible to all students. This is becoming more important as many university courses make use of educational technologies to offer learning opportunities in different modalities. To be able to use and learn in such environments (Dickson-Deane & Chen, 2018), makes accessibility a key factor but it is not the only factor that should be considered. While it is vital that, for example, students with vision impairment can engage with course material, it is also vital that these students be seamlessly included in the learning ecosystem whilst at the same time accommodating students from differing characteristics. This is often overlooked despite calls for the decolonisation of curriculum (Tuitt et al., 2023). As the cohort of higher education students becomes increasingly diverse, there is a need to ensure that the curriculum, its content and, indeed, the entire learning ecosystem, reflects the target audience.

Achieving this can be difficult as the field commercialises core learning design processes (Traxler, 2018) At first glance, balancing time to delivery, costs and implementation with the ongoing worldly challenges is difficult for all institutions. Thus, we ask: how can learning designers cater for all the different characteristics and needs within a student cohort? This may lead to a focus on one group over another (for example a focus on accessibility via captions but ignoring inclusivity of students from diverse backgrounds) to meet institutional requirements, and it also ignores the compounding challenges presented by the intersectional nature of disadvantage (Heggart et al., 2020).

Nancy Fraser (2007) has suggested that there are ways in which this might be done. In her view, the answer lies in providing more opportunities for students to take an active part in the development of the course, rather than the learning designer and/or academic seeking to cover every eventuality.

To do this, Fraser (2007) proposed three principles that could inform the design of learning experiences. The first is *redistribution*. This principle is about economics and in educational terms it seeks to ensure that more people have access to education (and in this case, higher education) through varying allocations – designs. Simply by increasing the opportunities for access for diverse groups of society, including those that have previously been marginalised, higher education will become more socially just. This is something that many universities are already taking seriously, via various programs and policies. Such programs are often implemented at a level beyond the remit of the individual learning designer and hence this principle will not be discussed at length in this chapter.

The second principle, however, is very much within the domain of learning designers. This is the principle of *recognition*. This principle encourages designers to reconsider the content of higher education, with a view to making it more diverse and representative. Pedagogical approaches that have adopted this idea include culturally relevant (Ladson-Billings, 2021) and culturally sustaining (Alim & Paris, 2017) pedagogies. There have been significant strides made in this area over recent years, with efforts to decolonise the curriculum (for an example, see Zembylas, 2018) and to include scholars who are women or gender diverse, from the Global South, or from non-dominant cultures.

The final principle espoused by Fraser is *representation*. This principle is perhaps the hardest to realise, even if it is the most important. Representation is best described as politically developing authentic partnerships between students and teachers in the decision-making process (Casey et al., 2022). Representation can invite learning designers to consider students less as objects, and more as active participants in the learning ecosystem, who might take a more active role in determining the what and the how of that experience – a shared design and ultimately a learning ecosystem. In doing so, it requires academics and learning designers to relinquish, in part, their control over the learning ecosystem, and instead embrace the complex and 'messy' nature of student-centred learning.

Clare Hocking (2010, p. 2) argues that a truly socially just education is one that 'embraces a wide range of differences and explores their effects on individual learning' – basically a positive acknowledgement of individual differences (Cronbach & Snow, 1969; Heggart et al., 2020; Jonassen & Grabowski, 1993). Hocking proposes that the relationships between participants be fair and just, measured by choice, distribution, opportunities, privileges, and indeed, any form of activity (Boyles et al., 2009) .

Adopting these principals signals a more in-depth approach to pedagogical activities. In the past, many attempts at inclusivity or accessibility have necessitated a focus on a particular group or learning requirement. In some cases, especially around accessibility, this will continue to be important. However, a truly socially just pedagogy requires a shift in attention away from the group or individual, to the learning ecosystem as a whole. In other words, through a careful understanding of what comprises learning ecosystems, it should be possible to incorporate the principles of redistribution, recognition and representation for all. The term learning ecosystem (Huijser et al., 2022) is used deliberately here to mark a difference between it and the more commonly used term 'teaching and learning'. This is important because a student's experience incorporates much more than just the 'in-class' time, and learning designers should be mindful of that.

The question of educational technology

While these principles are important, even more important is the practice of how these might be implemented within learning ecosystems. This is where the challenge lies: after all, what does redistribution or recognition actually look like, in Chemistry, or Accounting, or Law? And how might these principles be implemented effectively, considering the challenges involved in changing academic practice, and the limited time and budgets available to many universities?

Educational technology may answer some of these questions, especially when it is considered in conjunction with the ideas of universal design, and especially **Universal Design for Learning (UDL)**. The usual caveats apply when it comes to educational technology: the field is littered with disappointing applications and unfulfilled promises, and this must be kept in mind in the context of developing a socially just pedagogical framework (Watters, 2023). Attention must be paid to specific learning goals, rather than the tools themselves (de Alvarez & Dickson-Deane, 2018; Dickson-Deane & Asino, 2018; Watters, 2023) – using needs to frame behaviour (Dickson-Deane & Edwards, 2021).

As described above, shifting the focus away from the student towards the learning ecosystem is something that is central to UDL (Meyer et al., 2014). Indeed, the broader universal design movement calls for a change from an individual deficit model (i.e., there is something wrong or missing with a person) towards a recognition that the deficit or problem is a societal one – which is where the problem should be addressed. It is this line of thought that has led to accessible buildings, for example. However, what does that look like in the learning context? In short, it means that, once a student has enrolled in a course or program, the learning ecosystem should be relevant to them (Dickson-Deane, 2023). For example, a student from a low socio-economic background should not face barriers due to their status, such as required access to paid content. Instead, the course should be adaptable so that these 'deficits' are not an imposition. Some examples might help to illustrate this point. One of the key principles of UDL is that the alterations to learning design are essential for some students, but they are of benefit for many, if not all (Fornauf & Erickson, 2020). Students with hearing impairments might require captions or transcripts on video content. Yet captions are also useful for students with no hearing difficulties or students for whom the language used to teach is not their first language. Furthermore, this is an accommodation where those who prefer to watch course materials while traveling, and do not want to disturb those around them, can prosper. This principle of multiple means of representation thus has value far beyond the students who might expressly need it.

A second principle of UDL focuses on providing multiple means of engagement for all learners. This is potentially a powerful tool, and aligns well with Fraser's ideas of representation, in that engagement between learners and educators suggests the start of a partnership. Yet, such opportunities for engagement are often limited. This is understandable as many academics and learning designers are dealing with tight timelines and institutional inertia, and as such the learning environments may not be conducive to experimentation. In this case, interaction might be limited to some form of asynchronous activity. There is nothing wrong with asynchronous forms of interaction in and of themselves, and they definitely have a place in a course or program. However, they fail to recognise that many students, especially those entering higher education, have grown up in a world where the formalised environment is being merged with the societal environment (informal learning spaces) whereby online and interaction means something very different to them (Bennett, 2008). Students are expecting to be able to have some ownership over the course material, and to be able to adjust the content (Dickson-Deane et al., 2023). In order to leverage this predilection, learning designers can make use of David Wiley's (2014) **5 Rs** of open educational infrastructure (Table 1). These 5 Rs provide clear guidance for how learners might interact with the course material in new and interesting ways. Clearly, the ideas of remixing and redistributing, to name a few examples, go far beyond online discussion boards and opinion polls.

R	Explanation
Retain material	make, own and control a copy of the resource (e.g., download and keep your own copy)
Revise material	edit, adapt and modify your copy of the resource (e.g., translate into another language)
Remix material	combine an original or revised copy of the resource with other existing material to create something new (e.g., make a mashup)
Reuse material	use your original, revised or remixed copy of the resource publicly (e.g., on a website, in a presentation, in a class)
Redistribute material	share copies of your original, revised or remixed copy of the resource with others (e.g., post a copy online or give one to a friend)

Table 1: David Wiley's 5Rs (Wiley, 2014)
Text-based version of Table 1

> This table lists the 5Rs that define the principles of open content according to David Wiley. Each R is paired with a brief description of the rights it encompasses, emphasising the freedoms provided to users regarding **open educational resources**.

The 5Rs are not without significant challenges to the current higher education ecosystem. Principally, there are questions about ownership and intellectual copyright that need to be carefully negotiated, as well as issues of trust, control and management. It might prove to be confronting for academics to be expected to give permission for their course content to be remixed and distributed by students, for example. Such cases will need to be carefully considered. Nevertheless, we would propose that this shift in the locus of control is part of a wider movement in higher education, where courses are becoming less the domain of an individual course or subject coordinator and instead the product of a group of individuals, which includes academics, learning designers, analysts, media producers and so on. There are two further possible extensions of this idea of openness. Firstly, the development of a course could be made dynamic – that is, ongoing for the duration of the course – as it responds to changing ideas and discussions within the cohort. Secondly, the learners could be included as partners within the design and development of the course.

Putting it all together: Developing iterations

Taken together, the three concepts (**Fraser's 3Rs**, **Wiley's 5Rs** and **UDL**) described above provide learning designers with a framework to use in their work to ensure that they are designing socially just learning ecosystems. There is significant overlap between some of the ideas. For example, allowing students to demonstrate their learning via multiple means of expression has something in common with the notion of remixing course material by students. Equally, there is a connection between recognising diverse learners (from Fraser's three dimensions of social justice) and multiple means of representation. And, of course, by allowing students to reuse and redistribute course materials, students are becoming partners in the learning process and thus are more likely to be represented (although this is not an automatic process and needs to be carefully designed for and resourced if it is to occur). These connections are depicted in Figure 1.

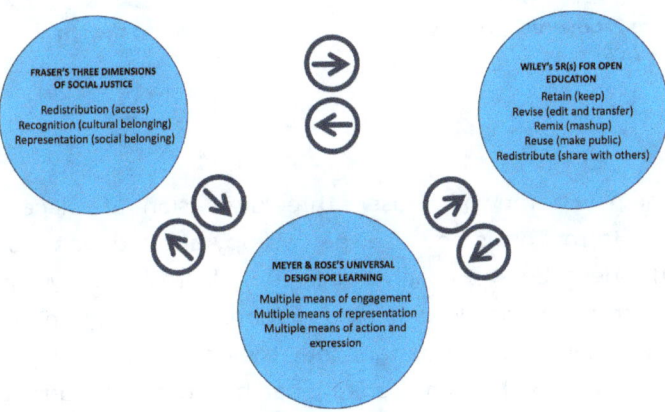

Figure 1: One-dimensional framework for socially just learning design activities

Figure 1 shows the original conception of a framework for socially just learning design (Heggart et al., 2020). It captures the connections between the different elements discussed above. However, it fails to fully articulate the nature of the relationships between the different elements, and specifically the ways in which they influence one another. The more carefully theorised depiction (Figure 2) has been developed by the authors to address this and explains the more complex relationship between the different elements of the framework.

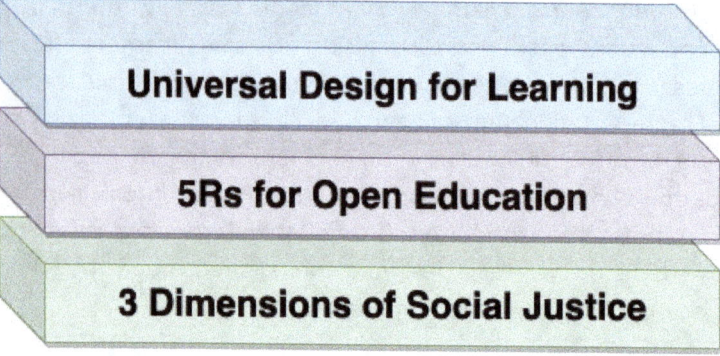

Figure 2: *Layered framework for socially just learning design activities*

In the new framework, Fraser's three dimensions are placed at the bottom. This is because they occupy a foundational part of the described approach to designing learning ecosystems. The three principles of recognition, redistribution and representation are important, but they are aspirational and wide-ranging. They are aspirational because they describe what a socially just learning environment should look like: it should be accessible to all, and all should feel like they belong within the environment and they should be able to 'see' that belonging through representation. However, what Fraser's dimensions do not do is provide advice or guidance (except in the most general terms) on how learning designers might create such an environment that does this: this is where the next two levels come into play.

Wiley's 5Rs of Open Education provide actionable structures to re-envision what a contemporary learning ecosystem might look like. Recognising the fundamental shift in both resource availability and possible interaction that technological change has provided, Wiley describes ways in which the traditional learning ecosystem can be altered in order to make the most of it. The 5Rs of Open Education point out how the three dimensions of social justice might be realised in the classroom.

The final level of this revised framework belongs to Universal Design for Learning (UDL). A broad conception of UDL offers the best description of how to employ the 5Rs in a classroom setting – and, crucially, to what end they should be employed. This is worth some further explanation: the 5Rs themselves do not necessarily constitute an approach to socially just learning design. While not necessarily Wiley's intention, it would be theoretically possible, for example, to redistribute or remix materials in a way that makes them less accessible than previously. More likely, however, the 5Rs can be used in such a way that they have little impact on the learning process. Clearly, this is not desirable for educators. By placing UDL at the highest layer, learning designers are prioritising the student experience over the technological affordances. In the next section, some examples of what this might look like in practice are explored, as well as how they align to the framework described above.

What it looks like in practice

Example 1: Creating a culture that values inclusivity

The use of the word culture can be unclear to many as it is typically used to reference the characteristics of an individual or group. The formalised processes used in designing for learning are not separate from who participates in the activity, and through self-reflection of those contributing to the outcome, there is positivity/success. Designers, instructors, administrators and (eventually) students need to cohesively contribute to the process of design and implementation knowing that without their individual interactions, understandings, discussions and perceived-positionalities, the process will have less successful outcomes. By always iteratively thinking of the next step of who will be contributing with what knowledge, and that the current knowledge is not all that can be shared in the space at that specific time, it basically shows that the design process is not only dynamic but a living process and is the key to developing an inclusive culture. This kind of activity is not easily portrayed. It requires boundaries to be relaxed, powers to be relinquished and reflections to act as a partial guide to how the learning design occurs. It allows for less formalisation of what is assumed to be known, leading to an iterative process whereby the cognitive power used to guide intentional designs leaves doors open for contextual interpretation and subjective value-making.

An example of what this may look like is not making conclusive design decisions but instead leaving enough wriggle room for students to explore the what-ifs in their learning process.

For example:

- asking students to contribute steps 3 and 4 of a guided activity which they believe will contribute to the learning goal
- allowing students to introduce ideas which they think are relevant to their understanding of the topic and then be assessed on that same topic
- going off script with one of the topics – loosely designing spaces to fill the gaps in student knowledge.

Each of these examples introduces unstructured designs that may leave everyone uneasy. Yet, this also creates a space for students to breathe and restate what they do understand with a new path as to where they would like to go with their knowledge. This can be seen as retracting the lifelong learning back into the formalised learning environment.

Example 2: Creating relevance by adding context to an existing OER

In order to increase representation, learning designers and other educators can encourage students to contribute to the development of course materials. One effective way of doing this could be in the form of an **Open Educational Resource (OER)**. In this example, rather than the course materials or textbooks being sacrosanct and provided by the lecturer or subject coordinator (or worse, having to be purchased by the students), they could instead become open and 'living' documents that are being updated and developed by both the students and the academic staff.

For example, students in an Initial Teacher Education course (a program of study for students learning to be teachers) might find and share exemplars and resources on a particular topic, which are then curated into a resource that all students can use. The academic's role in this case is to be a curator of the examples provided by the student, rather than a content producer. The learning designer, then, must provide the structure or mechanism that is required in order to make the sharing of resources as seamless as possible.

In more advanced iterations, students and the academic could use this platform as a mechanism to comment on the shared resources and to engage in a critical discussion of their usefulness and validity in various settings. Simple tools can be used by teachers and students to undertake this task. This approach is a powerful one; it reframes students less as consumers of pre-generated material and instead casts them as equal partners in the learning process. This meets the criterion of representation, as educators and students are now working as partners. It also allows students to retain, revise and remix the finished textbook or resource – and the fact that it is likely to be of immediate use in their practice will probably lead to higher levels of engagement.

Example 3: Adjusting rubrics to accommodate for different media

Rubrics are becoming an increasingly common aspect of assessment in many higher education institutions. While the development of rubrics is an area of expertise in and of itself, the use of rubrics can sometimes be restrictive. This is often the case in higher education, where there is (still) a preponderance of written assignments, reports and essays in assessment. Of course, this is appropriate in some settings, but it should be recognised that firstly, these assignments are not constructively aligned (Biggs, 1996) with the outcomes of the learning ecosystem, and secondly, such approaches privilege students who have more experience with those forms of assessment. Fortunately, the solution is relatively simple and involves redesigning the assessment in such a way as to allow students to submit their assessment task in multiple different forms.

For example, students in a nursing course might previously have been expected to write an essay about culturally safe approaches to nursing. This is clearly an important topic, and one that nurses should be expected to know about. However, there is no requirement for such an assessment task to have to be submitted in written form. Why shouldn't students have the opportunity to record a video, or create an infographic, or even make a presentation? This allows students to choose a form that they think best suits their work. Incidentally, it might also address some concerns regarding academic integrity. Of course, such an approach might lead to some concerns about the rigour or validity of the assessment; an essay is not necessarily any more rigorous than a video presentation. For example, in some nursing courses, students recording assessment tasks is becoming more common as it is seen as more relevant than a written essay due to the advent of telemedicine. More recent advances in generative artificial intelligence have also troubled this area. The key to rigour doesn't necessarily lie in the format but rather in the task itself, and the rubric that guides the students.

This example demonstrates aspects of all parts of the socially just learning design framework. Firstly, it adopts the UDL principle of multiple means of expression by allowing students to determine how best to meet the assessment task requirements instead of mandating them to demonstrate their learning in a particular fashion. This, in and of itself, is also an example of recognition: it recognises that students have different backgrounds and expertise and they should be able to make use of these to present their learning in the best possible setting. Broadly speaking, this is also an example of remixing: students are remixing the traditional assessment task into something that is more familiar to them.

Example 4: Providing more contextual choice in assessments

The final example also pertains to assessment. It is not particularly surprising that there is such a focus on assessment in terms of socially just learning design. As others have noted (Biggs, 1996), it is often the case that assessment drives the learning, regardless of whether that should be the case or not. In this example, assessments can be restructured or even entirely redesigned in order to provide more opportunity for students to contextualise their learning to the assessment task. This works especially well when students are asked to respond to a brief, or to take part in a scenario-type assessment. Normally, students are presented with a brief upon which to base their assessment task. However, such an approach can be exclusive, rather than inclusive, because the content of the brief will include elements of assumed or 'hidden' knowledge that not all students will be privy to, and thus students might be marginalised.

A better approach allows students to develop their own brief, tailored to their unique contexts and experiences. For example, in a Learning Design Program, students are often asked to develop a high-level learning design plan in response to a brief. In the past, the course coordinator has provided them with a generic brief based on a small enterprise seeking to train its facilitators in online learning practices. All students had to make use of the same brief. As explained above, this kind of context might be very familiar to some students in the course, especially those who have undertaken work in the corporate world. Yet, it might also be very unfamiliar to those who have come into the course from an educational background.

In order to improve this task, the students could be required to develop their own brief, based on their own experience. A generic brief could still be provided for those students who want it, but it would be far more effective in terms of engagement and motivation for students to consider a learning design problem to resolve that is directly related to their own context and experience. This approach necessitates extra work from learning designers; who must create a framework for students to draft their own briefs and provide several exemplars, but the increased engagement and likely higher quality outcomes would be a payoff for the additional work.

Again, this approach draws on the framework. Fraser's (2007) notions of recognition and representation are both present: by changing the curriculum to one that is more inclusive, recognition is addressed; and allowing students to choose their own brief is an example of the development of an authentic partnership between educators and students. Students will have the opportunity to remix the exemplar brief to suit their own circumstances, and they will also have the chance to engage in the topic in multiple ways, by virtue of the choice element of the assessment task.

Conclusion

Designing for inclusivity is challenging but vitally important for learning designers. A learning designer's first instinct might be to design learning materials that cater to everyone, but this is quickly revealed to be impossible. Some features of accessibility are not negotiable and need to be included in all course materials. However, in order to truly develop a feeling of inclusivity and belonging in a course, rather than focusing on individuals or specific groups, learning designers would be better placed to consider how they can incorporate students as active and authentic partners in the learning ecosystem. One way of doing this is by adopting the framework described in this chapter, which combines Fraser's (2007) three dimensions of social justice with the principles of UDL and also with David Wiley's (2014) 5Rs of Open Educational Practices.

References

Alim, H. S., & Paris, D. (2017). What is culturally sustaining pedagogy and why does it matter? In D. Paris & H. S. Alim (Eds.), *Culturally sustaining pedagogies: Teaching and learning for justice in a changing world* (pp. 1–21). Teachers College Press.

Bargallie, D., & Lentin, A. (2022). Beyond convergence and divergence: Towards a 'both and' approach to critical race and critical Indigenous studies in Australia. *Current Sociology*, *70*(5), 665–681. https://doi.org/10.1177/00113921211024701

Bennett, W. L. (2008). *Civic life online: Learning how digital media can engage youth.* MIT Press.

Biggs, J. (1996). Enhancing teaching through constructive alignment. *Higher Education*, *32*(3), 347–364. https://doi.org/10.1007/BF00138871

Boyles, D., Carusi, T., & Attick, D. (2009). Historical and critical interpretations of social justice. In W. Ayers, T. Quinn, & D. Stovall (Eds.), *Handbook of social justice in education* (pp. 30–42). Routledge.

Bradley, D., Noonan, P., Nugent, H., & Scales, B. (2008). *Review of*

Australian higher education: Discussion paper. Department of Education, Employment and Workplace Relations.

Calabrese Barton, A., & Tan, E. (2020). Beyond equity as inclusion: A framework of 'Rightful presence' for guiding justice-oriented studies in teaching and learning. *Educational Researcher*, 49(6), 433–440. https://doi.org/10.3102/0013189X20927363

Casey, C. C., Goodsett, M., Hoover, J. K., Robertson, S., & Whitchurch, M. (2022). Open pedagogy. *EdTechnica: The open encyclopedia of educational technology*. https://dx.doi.org/10.59668/371.8682

Collins, A., Azmat, F., & Rentschler, R. (2019). 'Bringing everyone on the same journey': Revisiting inclusion in higher education. *Studies in Higher Education*, 44(8), 1475–1487. https://doi.org/10.1080/03075079.2018.1450852

Cronbach, L. J., & Snow, R. E. (1969). *Individual differences in learning ability as a function of instructional variables. Final report*. School of Education, Stanford.

Devlin, M., Zhang, L. C., Edwards, D., Withers, G., McMillan, J., Vernon, L., & Trinidad, S. (2023). The costs of and economies of scale in supporting students from low socioeconomic status backgrounds in Australian higher education. *Higher Education Research & Development*, 42(2), 290–305. https://doi.org/10.1080/07294360.2022.2057450

Dickson-Deane, C. (2023). Learning within context [Case study]. In V. Rossi, *Inclusive learning design in higher education: A practical guide to creating equitable learning experiences* (pp. 207-210). Routledge.

Dickson-Deane, C., & Asino, T. I. (2018). Don't forget, instructional design is about problem solving. *EDUCAUSE Review*.

https://er.educause.edu/blogs/2018/3/dont-forget-instructional-design-is-about-problem-solving

Dickson-Deane, C., & Chen, H. L. O. (2018). Understanding user experience. In M. Khosrow-Pour (Ed.), *Encyclopedia of information science and technology* (pp. 7599–7608). IGI Global.

Dickson-Deane, C., & Edwards, M. (2021). Transcribing accounting lectures: Enhancing the pedagogical practice by acknowledging student behaviour. *Journal of Accounting Education, 54*, 100709.

Dickson-Deane, C., Heggart, K., & Vanderburg, R. (2023). Designing learning design pedagogy: Proactively integrating work-integrated learning to meet expectations. In M. J. Lehtonen, T. Kauppinen, & L. Sivula (Eds.), *Design education across disciplines: Transformative learning experiences for the 21st century* (pp. 125–142). Springer International Publishing.

Fornauf, B. S., & Erickson, J. D. (2020). Toward an inclusive pedagogy through universal design for learning in higher education: A review of the literature. *Journal of Postsecondary Education and Disability, 33*(2), 183–199.

Fraser, N. (2007). Reframing justice in a globalizing world. In D. Held & A. Kaya (Eds.), *Global inequality: Patterns and explanations* (pp. 252–272). Polity.

Heggart, K., & Dickson-Deane, C. (2022). What should learning designers learn? *Journal of Computing in Higher Education, 34*(2), 281–296.

Heggart, K., Dickson-Deane, C., & Novak, K. (2020, September 7). The path towards a socially just learning design. *SRHE Blog.* https://srheblog.com/2020/09/07/the-path-towards-a-socially-just-learning-design/

Hocking, C. (2010). *Inclusive learning and teaching in higher education: A synthesis of research*. Higher Education Academy.

Huijser, H., Kek, M. Y. C. A., Padró, F. F. (2022). Introduction: Student support services in an overall ecology for learning. In H. Huijser, M. Kek, & F. F. Padró (Eds.), *Student support services*. University Development and Administration. Springer, Singapore. https://doi.org/10.1007/978-981-13-3364-4_49-1

Jonassen, D. H., & Grabowski, B. (1993). *Individual differences and instruction*. Allen and Bacon.

Ladson-Billings, G. (2021). *Culturally relevant pedagogy: Asking a different question*. Teachers College Press.

Mahoney, B., Kumar, J., & Sabsabi, M. (2022). Strategies for student belonging: The nexus of policy and practice in higher education. *Student Success, 13*(3), 54–62. https://doi.org/10.5204/ssj.2479

Meyer, A., Rose, D. H., & Gordon, D. T. (2014). *Universal design for learning: Theory and practice*. CAST Professional Publishing.

Morgan, H. (2022). Resisting the movement to ban critical race theory from schools. *The Clearing House: A Journal of Educational Strategies, Issues and Ideas, 95*(1), 35–41. https://doi.org/10.1080/00098655.2021.2025023

Reiser, R. A. (2001). A history of instructional design and technology: Part I: A history of instructional media. *Educational Technology Research and Development, 49*(1), 53–64. https://doi.org/10.1007/BF02504506

Sulecio de Alvarez, M., & Dickson-Deane, C. (2018). Avoiding educational technology pitfalls for inclusion and equity.

TechTrends, 62(4), 345–353. https://doi.org/10.1007/s11528-018-0270-0

Traxler, J. (2018). Distance learning – Predictions and possibilities. *Education Sciences*, 8(1), 35. https://doi.org/10.3390/educsci8010035

Tuitt, F., Haynes, C., & Stewart, S. (Eds.). (2023). *Race, equity, and the learning environment: The global relevance of critical and inclusive pedagogies in higher education*. Routledge.

Watters, A. (2023). *Teaching machines: The history of personalized learning*. MIT Press.

Wiley, D. (2014). The access compromise and the 5th R. In D. Wiley (Ed.), *An open education reader*. https://openedreader.org/chapter/the-access-compromise-and-the-5th-r/

Zembylas, M. (2018). Decolonial possibilities in South African higher education: Reconfiguring humanising pedagogies as/with decolonising pedagogies. *South African Journal of Education*, 38(4), 1–11. https://doi.org/10.15700/saje.v38n4a1699

Media Attributions

- Figure 1: One-dimensional framework for socially just learning design activities
- Figure 2: Layered framework for socially just learning design activities

About the authors

Dr Keith Heggart
UNIVERSITY OF TECHNOLOGY SYDNEY
https://www.uts.edu.au

Keith Heggart is the academic lead for the Graduate Certificate in Learning Design at UTS, where he developed an innovative course combining microcredentials and work-integrated learning. This course received the AECT Learning Innovation Award in 2022 and a UTS Teaching and Learning Citation. Keith's research focuses on social justice and learning design, earning him awards such as the Best Publication from AECT and the Early Career Researcher award from ASCILITE. He has over 20 publications, including two books, and is an Apple Distinguished Educator.

Dr Camille Dickson-Deane
UNIVERSITY OF TECHNOLOGY SYDNEY
https://www.uts.edu.au

Camille Dickson-Deane is a Senior Lecturer at the University of Technology Sydney and a Fulbright and OAS scholar. Her research focuses on pedagogical usability, individual differences, and contextualised online learning designs. Camille serves on the editorial boards of Educational Technology Research and Development and Internet and

Higher Education, is an advisor for EdTechnica, and is an Associate Editor for the Journal of Computing in Higher Education. She also represents Australia on the EDUCAUSE Horizon Report panel of experts.

3. Designing inclusive learning experience through Open Educational Practices

MAIS FATAYER

Introduction

I wrote this chapter to equip learning designers with both theoretical insights and practical guidance on integrating **Open Educational Practices (OEP)** into learning design practice. Along the chapter, I provide advice that helps learning designers understand how OEP contribute to the advancement of social justice in higher education, drawing on my experience in learning design and open education.

For higher educational institutions, OEP hold the potential to reduce educational barriers for students, thereby expanding learning opportunities and democratising education, promoting a connected academic community and enhancing student learning experience. In the field of educational technology, OEP benefit from leveraging current technologies to develop content that is both accessible and inclusive. In the learning design sphere, OEP offer innovative methods and techniques to enhance interaction and active participation in the learning process, fostering a more dynamic and collaborative approach to knowledge acquisition as an integral part of pedagogy (Paskevicius & Irvine, 2019). However, drawing from over a decade of experience in both formal and informal leadership roles as a learning designer, I have frequently observed the hesitant and fragile incorporation of OEP into daily learning design practices is. These instances occur due to many barriers such as lack of awareness of the role of open education in advancing learning, concerns about the quality of Open Educational Resources (OER), time constraints for either creating or reviewing OER, lack of clarity about intellectual property issues, lack of recognition of OEP and lack of adequate infrastructure for hosting OER. Existing literature is also in alignment with of all these barriers (Atenas et al., 2022; Morgan, 2019), which highlights evidence of similar barriers from institutions around the world.

Even with the previous challenges, learning design is a significant area to advance open education in higher education. In this chapter, I reinforce the prevailing call for the involvement of learning designers in open education, as advocated by Roberts at al. (2022). Additionally, I extend this appeal by calling for intentional steps toward adopting OEP in learning design practice. The aim here is to help learning designers to seamlessly integrate OEP into their learning design practice in order to enhance student learning experiences. Further, the advice provided in this chapter offers a pathway to make OEP more visible through practical approaches so learning designers will be able to take concrete steps towards socially just education.

But why is open education important to learning designers? Why does it matter, and why should learning designers care? In response to these underlying questions, I pose three key broad responses that I'll elaborate on throughout the chapter:

1. **Learning designers possess the skills to develop OER:** These skills are integral in learning design practice and are deployed consistently in building educational materials.
2. **The open education movement in higher education is**

advancing slowly: Learning designers are urged to utilise their relationships and leadership skills to raise awareness and encourage greater engagement among faculties and senior management.
3. **Learning design is rooted in human-centred approaches:** As learning designers, our core commitment is to design for the betterment of people to enable socially just education. This ethical responsibility aligns strongly with the values of open education.

As a final note, over the past two decades the open education movement has made substantial advances in various parts of the world, notably in the United States and Canada. While Australia has been perceived as a late adopter, it has increasingly begun to make significant contributions to the field, signaling a promising emergence in open education initiatives. Throughout the chapter, I will be borrowing examples from existing projects and initiatives in Australia and globally to illustrate the growing impact of OEP on higher education in different places.

Understanding Open Educational Practices (OEP)

This section offers a concise chronological exploration of key concepts in open education. It begins with a historical overview of open education and open pedagogy, encompassing contemporary perspectives, and concludes with an exploration of Open Educational Practices (OEP). The section concludes with highlighting the role of open education as a catalyst for social justice.

Before delving into OEP, it is vital to highlight the more general concept of open education. As a pedagogical approach, open education advocates for increased participation, democracy, and social inclusion within the educational sphere. Lambert (2018, p. 239) introduced a conceptualisation of open education wherein social justice stands as its overarching objective:

> *"Open Education is the development of free digitally enabled learning materials and experiences primarily by and for the benefit and empowerment of non-privileged learners who may be under-represented in education systems or marginalised in their global context. Success of social justice aligned programs can be measured not by any particular technical feature or format, but instead by the extent to which they enact redistributive justice, recognitive justice and/or representational justice."*

For learning designers who are usually immersed in the design process (i.e., co-creation, constructive alignment between content and outcomes, developing inclusive and accessible material, etc), this definition holds significance for two key reasons. Firstly, it transitions the perspective of open education from being perceived merely as a collection of pedagogies applicable to all learners, to encompassing both processes and artefacts tailored for and co-created with marginalised learners. Secondly, it establishes a quality assurance mechanism, ensuring that both the process and artefacts are responsive to the existing needs of the learners involved.

The evolution of open education has unfolded gradually, shaped by various influences and developments over time. The historical timeline of open education spans decades, from the introduction of the Open University in the 1960s (Open University, 2010), as an advocate for openness and socially just education, to the early mention of open education in the 1970s by Elliot (1973) and Mai (1978), describing tensions between 'closed' and 'open' pedagogies. In 1998 David Wiley coined the term 'open content' working on the premise that educational content should be developed and shared freely and openly similar to the free software philosophy (DiBiase, 2011). Moving into the 21st century, the emergence of Web 2.0 technologies contributed significantly to the rise of OER. In 2001, the OpenCourseWare of Massachusetts Institute of Technology (MIT) marked a milestone, when MIT academics made course materials freely available online. This was followed by the introduction of Creative Commons licenses in 2001, enabling legal sharing and remixing of content.

Following the efforts of MIT and Creative Commons, in 2002 the William and Flora Hewlett Foundation, the Western Cooperative for Educational Telecommunications, and global education leaders met at UNESCO headquarters for the OER Forum. The group explored the impact of open courseware in higher education and concluded with a declaration

> 'At the conclusion of the Forum on the Impact of Open Courseware for Higher Education in Developing Countries, organized by UNESCO, the participants express their satisfaction and their wish to develop together a universal educational resource available for the whole of humanity, to be referred to henceforth as Open Educational Resources.' (UNESCO, 2002, p. 28)

This forum represents a significant milestone in the open education movement's journey. Additionally, international organisations, including UNESCO, OECD, and ICDE, played a significant role in initiatives such as 'open educational quality initiatives' (OPAL) to promote OER adoption globally (Falconer et al., 2013). Since that time, there was a projection of a substantial increase in demand for open learning innovations, encompassing OER, open textbooks, and Massive Open Online Courses (MOOCs) (Jacobi et al., 2013).

In February 2011, with UNESCO funding, an open meeting

aimed to establish the OERu, a project building a parallel learning universe for more affordable education. Now a global initiative, OERu includes institutions from five continents, collaborating to broaden access and is a formal project of the UNESCO-Commonwealth of Learning (COL) OER Chair network (Open Educational Resources University, n.d.).

At this stage, the term OEP began to take clearer shape as introduced by OPAL (Open Educational Quality Initiative, 2011) as 'a set of activities around instructional design and implementation of events and processes intended to support learning. They also include the creation, use and repurposing of Open Educational Resources (OER) and their adaptation to the contextual setting. They are documented in a portable format and made openly available' (p. 13). As the concept of OEP gained momentum, Cronin (2017) introduced OEP by encompassing OER, pedagogies, and the sharing of teaching practices. Cronin's work is noteworthy as it highlights that academics integrating OEP into their teaching do so in four dimensions:

- **Balancing privacy and openness:** This dimension involves managing digital identity boundaries and carefully considering teacher-student interactions in online spaces.
- **Developing digital literacies:** This involves academics developing proficiency in social media use and encouraging students to cultivate digital identities, fostering overall digital literacy.
- **Recognising the importance of social learning:** This requires understanding of theories of social learning such as social constructivism and sociocultural theory that emphasise the importance of learners being actively involved in the learning process.
- **Challenging conventional expectations associated with the traditional teaching role:** This involves academics embracing broader identities, viewing themselves as

learners, dismantling lecturer-student barriers, and demonstrating care for students such as creating different communication channels (e.g., communicating with students via X previously known as Twitter) (Cronin, 2017).

Meanwhile, scholars like Weller (2014) and Wiley (2013) emphasised the term 'open pedagogy' that became closely associated with OEP. Both Weller and Wiley contributed significantly to expanding on integrating OEP into learning activities and teaching practices. For instance, Wiley's significant contribution lies in defining the practical set of five activities in using OER or what is now known as the 5R activities—retain, revise, remix, reuse and redistribute (Wiley, n.d.). These activities provide a foundation for designing learning approaches for integrating OEP in learning and teaching. Wiley and Hilton (2018) further defined open pedagogy as a shift towards student-centred, flexible learning experiences, emphasising trust in students and adaptability based on learner needs.

UTS Learning Design Meetup community: Adopting OEP with David Wiley

Back in March 2021, I invited David Wiley to share his thoughts with the "UTS Learning Design Meetup community" about adopting OEP. Demonstrating through a couple of examples, David showed how the 5R's enable students to engage in content through collaboratively creating an enhanced version of an existing open textbook and students reusing videos to create a debate of 'wikis vs blogs' by imitating the voices of Kennedy and Nixon. The following video is a 15-minute snippet from the meetup where David elaborates on those ideas.

 One or more interactive elements has been excluded from this version of the text. You can view them online here: https://oercollective.caul.edu.au/designing-learning-experiences/?p=56#oembed-1

Open Education in Australian higher education

The initial phases of open education in Australia were predominantly government-led initiatives that were committed to demonstrating transparency, information sharing, and access to publicly funded research projects. This is demonstrated by government-focused initiatives such as Australian Government Policy on Open-Source Software, Government 2.0 and Australian Government Open Access and Licensing Framework (AusGOAL), which paved the way for the Australian higher education sector to follow (Bossu, 2016, pp. 15-16).

Australian higher education institutions are positioned towards the late majority of what is known as Rogers' innovation-adoption curve (Rogers, 2003, pp. 35-36), particularly in joining the open education movement. However, over the last two decades, there have been considerable efforts across Australian universities towards OEP, where innovative projects and initiatives take place. The following are some of the examples of OEP in the Australian higher education sector:

1. The Open textbooks at La Trobe project demonstrates the value of modern curriculum in providing flexibility in developing educational resources and enhancing affordability for students. Dr David Walker from La Trobe's School of Business highlighted that 'this [adopting open textbook] has also enabled me to structure the content and frame the questions and topics more precisely to the things we want to cover'. Associate Professor Tanya Serry, School of Education, also emphasised the contribution to students' wellbeing as she mentions that 'the open textbook for this core 1st year subject has generated up to $45,650 of student cost savings by replacing a traditional commercial text'.
2. University of South Australia (UniSA) Textbook Minimisation Project: Between 2020 and 2022, the Library and the Teaching Innovation Unit at UniSA implemented a pilot project with the aim of minimising course material costs for students. The university is actively working to reduce the number of textbooks students need to purchase during their program of study by transitioning certain courses from traditional textbooks to high-quality research-driven resources. This significant initiative has already saved UniSA students a total of $9 million in textbook costs. Two crucial outcomes have emerged from this effort: firstly, the integration of this initiative into Action Item 2.7 of the University's Academic Enterprise

Plan 2021-2025 as a strategic priority, and secondly, under the direction of the Academic Strategy, Standards, and Quality Committee (ASSQC), the Library is now incorporating the minimisation of student textbook costs as a 'business as usual' activity.

3. University of Southern Queensland OEP Grants: Learning and Teaching Staff Scholarships provide grants to aid a USQ staff member or a team in enhancing their leadership in and approaches to advancing students' educational experiences and graduate outcomes. Several academics shared their experience about this initiative, stating that these scholarships empower them to enhance their pedagogical skills, leading to publications, presentations, and increased impact while concurrently engaging in projects including developing renewable assessments and open textbooks.

4. The Council of Australian University Librarians (CAUL) and the OER Collective: an organisation representing the university librarians or library directors of Australian universities. CAUL is committed to advancing open access within the sector, helping institutions implement, communicate, deliver, and evaluate their open access initiatives. CAUL is also committed to raise awareness of OER with government and higher education sector stakeholders through professional development programs. The CAUL OER Collective initiative has also been introduced to develop capacity for publishing open textbooks and other educational resources, working collaboratively to promote OER within the broader agenda of OEP across Australian higher educational institutions and offering a publishing platform for authors from the Australian universities.

It is important to note that the creation of the textbook you're reading was made possible through a CAUL grant awarded to the authors. This grant has allowed us to offer learning designers in the Australasian context a comprehensive resource that aligns with the distinctive aspects of the learning design profession, both in theory and practice.

This brief exploration underscores the evolution of the OEP concept and its proliferation in Australian higher education, forming a starting point for considering their relevance in the context of socially just learning design. As learning designers, we stand at a strategic vantage point to actively contribute to the realisation of the overarching objectives of OE. Our engagement can take the form of implementing and cultivating OEP to expand access, as well as advocating for **inclusivity** through the incorporation of OEP principles in higher education.

OEP and learning designers

Nowadays, open education definitions are often amalgamated into OER; therefore, it is crucial for learning designers to use these terms accurately when communicating with stakeholders. Clear understanding of applications of OEP is vital when incorporating them into the learning design practice, whether through content creation, developing activities and assessments, use of technology, communication or faculties relationships.

As learning designers, we play a pivotal role in advancing OEP in higher educational institutions. Delving into the opportunities within learning design requires thoughtful consideration, deep reflection on the potential impact, and careful decision-making to effectively embrace and implement OEP. The following activity provides a short list of just a few practices in which learning designers can actively engage to promote OEP.

Exercises

As you read through these, consider which practices you can promptly incorporate into your work. Reflect on areas within your workplace that may have gaps, and identify how one of the OEP below can address them. Also, consider evaluating which of these practices are inherent to your learning design role. Finally, think about whether there are practices that you will be incorporating into your work over the long term.

- **Creation and adaptation of OER:** Learning designers are inherently capable of developing OER or adapting existing resources to suit specific educational needs. For example, through utilising Wiley's 5 Rs, you can consider developing interactive H5P content and sharing in H5P OERHub, sharing videos in Kaltura, learning elements in Canvas Commons or enhancing accessibility of existing OER. Nevertheless, this may entail the challenge of navigating tension when collaborating with academics and senior management who may not embrace OEP (Roberts et al., 2022).

- **Integration of OEP into learning design**: Embedding principles of OEP into the instructional design process ensures that courses and learning materials are designed with openness in mind. This includes using content that is published under **open licenses**, ensuring proper attribution of materials published under open licenses and public domain, adopting open learning design models such as ABC Learning Design, and developing reusable teaching resources such as the UTS Adaptable Resources for Teaching with Technology resource collection and Equity Unbound online community.
- **Promotion of open pedagogy:** Learning designers can advocate for and incorporate open pedagogical practices, which involve engaging students in the creation and sharing of knowledge. This might include collaborative projects for creating OER, student-generated content, and renewable assessments. As learning designers, our approach to engaging academics in open pedagogy involves presenting practical examples for adoption of approaches to open pedagogy, rather than offering a theoretical overview. For example, the Open Pedagogy Notebook curates valuable resources for educators and learning designers who are seeking to delve deeper into open pedagogy, offering a range of evidence based examples from classroom practices.
- **Training and professional development:** Providing training and professional development

opportunities for academics on OEP ensures that the broader educational community is aware of and skilled in implementing open approaches. This can be through running workshops and generating instructional resources such as the UTS resource collection Integrating Open Education Resources into your teaching.

- **Advocacy for OEP:** This can involve encouraging academics to share learning materials, raising awareness of the benefits of OEP in teaching and learning, and engaging in conversations with senior management and key stakeholders in higher educational institutions. It is important to ensure that these efforts align with institutional strategic goals, emphasising the value that OEP brings to the overall educational mission. For example, the OER Advocacy Toolkit, developed under the CAUL Enabling a Modern Curriculum OER Advocacy Project, serves as a comprehensive reference for advocates of OEP in higher educational institutions. The Toolkit includes information, resources, checklists, and practical ideas for effectively communicating with various stakeholders, including academics, librarians, teaching and learning committees, and university executives.
- **Accessibility and inclusivity:** As learning designers, we weave inclusivity into our work. OER hold the potential for ensuring accessible and inclusive learning. The fact that OER allow for adaptation, reuse, remix, and repurpose means we can use any OER to translate, create subtitles,

and enhance content by adding alt text to images, among other improvements. This signifies that OEP help us cater to different learning styles, provide alternative formats, and ensure content is usable by individuals with various abilities. As a good practice, checking accessibility of H5P elements can be vital given the popularity of the tool. A good example is the H5P Accessibility tool by Libre Studio, which helps assessing and evaluating accessibility of H5P activities.
- **Community engagement:** Actively participating in the open education community such as Open Education Global, and special interest groups such as Australasian Open Educational Practices Special Interest Group allows librarians and learning designers to share insights, collaborate on projects, and stay informed about best practices and emerging trends in the field.

OEP encompasses skills and approaches that are inherent in learning design. As learning designers working directly with faculties, we can deliberately integrate these strategies into our practice. This will enable us to make meaningful contributions to the learning and teaching ecosystem, fostering collaboration, accessibility, and the widespread sharing of knowledge.

Open pedagogy: From theory to practice

The term open pedagogy has been introduced in the literature as a concept that revolves around making educational resources freely available, encouraging collaboration, and involving students in the creation and sharing of knowledge (Tietjen & Asino, 2021). Open pedagogy goes beyond that, as it entails not only making resources accessible but also influencing and transforming the methods and approaches used in teaching.

DeRosa and Jhangiani (2017) define open pedagogy as a dynamic and 'contested site of praxis', where theories of learning, teaching, technology, and social justice intersect, guiding the ongoing development of educational practices and structures. It embodies an access-oriented commitment to learner-driven education, involving the intentional design of architectures and the use of tools that empower students to actively contribute to and shape the public knowledge commons in which they participate.

Wiley and Hilton (2018) underscore the idea that students learn best through hands-on experiences. They argue that copyright laws restrict various educational activities (like copying or creating derivative works without permission), limiting students' learning options. OER with their permissions for the 5R activities (retain, revise, remix, reuse and redistribute), remove these limitations. The advantages of using open licenses extend to facilitating pedagogical approaches that are otherwise unattainable when working with copyrighted materials (DeRosa & Robison, 2017). Therefore, when using OER instead of traditional copyrighted resources, students have the freedom to engage in a wider range of activities and, consequently, to learn in more diverse ways. Further, Fatayer and Tualaulelei (2023) have argued that learning activities should take place in socially relevant settings that allow knowledge to be cognitively mediated between two or more people. In the context of renewable assessments, defined by David Wiley as assessments that produce meaningful and valuable artifacts that contribute positively to the world and can be extended, revised, and improved upon by future students and others, the process of learning becomes more explicit as students engage in the negotiation of knowledge with academics, fellow students, and professionals, concurrently contributing to the development of student-generated OER. Students may then share their growing knowledge with people other than those who are assessing their assignments and they become a member of a learning community (Fatayer & Tualaulelei, 2023). It is important to point out that such inclusive practice of engaging students with different stakeholders in the knowledge development process is core to OEP and a result of openness as a pedagogical approach. Importantly, OEP are recognised for their economic advantages in terms of cost savings for students. An additional and often overlooked benefit is the engagement of students in the learning process.

The following H5P element is adapted from 'Attributes of Open Pedagogy' by Bronwyn Hegarty, originally licensed under CC BY 3.0. The new derivative is an H5P accordion redesigned for accessibility, incorporating resources and tools specifically intended for learning designers and redesigned to include examples of each attribute.

 An interactive H5P element has been excluded from this version of the text. You can view it online here:

> https://oercollective.caul.edu.au/designing-learning-experiences/?p=56#h5p-1

Adapted from *Attributes of Open Pedagogy* by Bronwyn Hegarty, licensed under CC BY 3.0.

Paskevicius and Irvine (2019) suggest that OEP constitute a developing approach to learning design, incorporating elements from established models of constructivist and networked pedagogy. This involves leveraging open software tools and content to innovate the creation and dissemination of learning materials and assessments.

The previous section introduced different tools for adopting open pedagogy and suggested tools that can be utilised by learning designers to develop activities that are informed by open pedagogy. Among the impactful approaches is utilising renewable assessments. Renewable assessment, as exemplified by Wiley's concept of "renewable assignments," (Wiley & Hilton, 2018) is a pedagogical approach that integrates constructionism and openness within OER-enabled teaching. In contrast to "disposable assignments," where the work is understood to be temporary and discarded after grading, renewable assignments aim to serve dual purposes. They not only facilitate individual student learning but also contribute to the creation or enhancement of OER that can benefit the wider learning community. This approach underscores the idea that assessments can be valuable beyond their immediate use, providing lasting educational value by producing resources that are shared and reused by others.

As learning designers, embracing a model for renewable assessment is in line with principles of co-creation, student agency, and ownership of learning, contributing to the development of valuable, reusable educational resources. The following section provides an evidence-based approach for constructing an OER development model. This model aims to sustain OER in higher education by leveraging renewable assessments.

OER development model

The concept of student-generated content, originating from user-generated content, has gained prominence in formal learning environments. The term 'student-generated content' was first used by Sener (2007) and encompasses various terms such as 'learner-generated content' (Pérez-Mateo et al., 2011) and 'student as producer' (Neary, 2010) and is utilised in teaching approaches like project-based learning and group work. When students work together on assignments, they generate extra brainpower called 'cognitive surplus'. This term, coined by Shirky (2010) in his book *The Cognitive Surplus*, describes the abundance of content created through activities that people generate when they collaborate online. This surplus leads to creative outcomes through activities like Wikipedia.

The proliferation of content generation tools, such as blogs, wikis, and social networking sites, has made it easier to design collaborative learning activities. Importantly, these technologies enhance the learning experience, promote digital literacy, and support active learning (Mason & Rennie, 2008; Sener, 2007).

Crafting effective learning design models is crucial for successful teaching with technology in today's educational landscape. This section presents a learning design model that offers clear instructions and adaptable resources, catering to various disciplines.

Three-stage model for student-generated OER

At the outset, a model was proposed where students and academics developed OER as learning artefacts through a three-step process: creating, evaluating and publishing (Fatayer, 2016). The following H5P interactive elaborates on the OER development model and presents two case studies of model integration into undergraduate and postgraduate studies.

An interactive H5P element has been excluded from this version of the text. You can view it online here:
https://oercollective.caul.edu.au/designing-learning-experiences/?p=56#h5p-2

By guiding the implementation of this model and ensuring compliance with open access and intellectual property policies, learning designers contribute to the broader goal of making educational resources freely accessible to a wider audience and extending the benefits of student work to several communal goals. Finally, it is important to note that this knowledge generation not only benefits the students themselves but also enhances the availability of quality educational materials for learners everywhere.

OER and open textbooks

Open education, encompassing content, practices, policy, and a global community, offers the unprecedented opportunity for universal access to cost-free, high-quality, open learning resources. This educational revolution is driven by OER, materials freely shared with legal permissions, empowering learners and educators worldwide.

According to Creative Commons (n.d.), OER have become important in learning and teaching due to several key factors.

- **Storage**: The digital nature of educational resources allows for easy storage, duplication, and distribution at minimal cost.
- **Access**: The public access of content and the widespread availability of the internet simplifies the process of sharing digital content with the public.
- **Licensing**: Legal sharing of content using Creative Commons licenses as they play a pivotal role by providing a straightforward and legal framework for individuals to both retain copyright and share educational resources openly with a global audience.
- **Adaptability and reusability:** OER's adaptablity nature enhances inclusivity in learning and teaching. The reusability of OER allows educators to tailor materials to accommodate the diverse needs of learners, including those with different learning styles, languages, or cultural backgrounds.

These combined elements have facilitated the emergence of OER in different learning environments.

Why OER?

Watch the following video and think about how Open Educational Resources align with your role as a learning designer and your commitment to enhancing student learning experiences.

> *One or more interactive elements has been excluded from this version of the text. You can view them online here:* https://oercollective.caul.edu.au/designing-learning-experiences/?p=56#oembed-2

Certainly, open textbooks are among the most prevalent and widely recognised forms of OER. Open textbooks are typically available in digital formats, making them easy to store, duplicate, and distribute at minimal cost. Importantly, traditional textbooks restrict pedagogical choices (Jhangiani et al., 2016), which results in constraining the learning experience for individuals with diverse learning preferences. However, through the creation and adoption of open textbooks, educators and learners gain the flexibility to customise the content to meet their specific needs and teaching priorities. For example, OpenStax is a non-profit organisation that offers a collection of free, peer-reviewed, openly licensed textbooks via their website. Academics can customise these resources to suit the diverse needs of their students, whether by translating content into different languages, adding supplementary materials, or structuring the material to accommodate various learning styles. This adaptability ensures that open textbooks can cater to a wide range of learners, promoting inclusivity and accessibility in education.

The adoption of open textbooks in learning and teaching has the potential to achieve two significant outcomes: it can significantly reduce the financial burden on students, particularly those from disadvantaged socio-economic backgrounds, and enhance their prospects for academic success. This transformative impact aligns with the concept of redistributive justice, one of the core principles of social justice within open education, as articulated by Lambert (2018).

In addition to redistributive justice, Lambert (2018) proposes that open education encompasses two other vital dimensions of social justice: recognitive justice and representational justice, both of which are emerging areas in the open education landscape. Recognitive justice focuses on the inclusion of diverse perspectives, images, and case studies within educational resources, fostering a broader and more inclusive educational experience. Representational justice, on the other hand, emphasises the amplification of voices from marginalised groups in textbooks and the open curriculum, ensuring that their narratives are both heard and respected (Lambert, 2018).

In their open textbook, Tualaulelei (2020) and her postgraduate students, present an example of utilising a renewable assessment approach. Importantly, this collaborative approach of generating open textbooks with students provides a practical example that reflects Lambert's (2018) framework of redistributive, recognitive and representational justice.

Renewable assignments show promise for perspective transformation as students will repurpose their assignment artefacts for a broader professional audience and step more fully into their future professional identities.

According to Tualaulelei and Green (2022), this approach helped 'to flatten out hierarchies within social structures such as the teaching profession' and engaged students in developing resources that address concerns related to reconciliation and intercultural education and continuing professional development or professional learning.

OER, open textbooks and learning designers

As learning designers, we recognise that OEP hold the promise of broadening access and championing inclusivity. It is imperative for us to comprehend the effective approaches for developing OER and open textbooks. Given our close partnerships with academics, it becomes essential to raise awareness among them about the available opportunities in the realm of OEP. As our understanding of the potential of OEP in enriching the learning experience deepens, we are committed to leveraging existing resources that align with our mission of fostering equitable, inclusive, and diverse education.

Approaches to open textbooks

development

I was interested in the different approaches for generating open textbooks and integration in learning and teaching. I reached out to a few people in my network and interviewed them about their techniques. I was keen to know about the motives behind the decision to create and publish an open textbook rather than using traditional publishing methods, finding content, support to get the book reviewed and published, timeframe from start to publish and the impact on student learning and engagement.

Read the blog and watch the three interviews.

The three examples above can be used as insights for us as learning designers on adopting OEP in our daily work. Importantly, we can consider several concrete actions to address the issues of inequitable access and exclusion of marginalised voices as highlighted in the following work by Andersen (2022).

Example of adapting open textbooks

Enhancing Inclusion, Diversity, Equity and Accessibility (IDEA) in Open Educational Resources (OER) was developed by Nikki Andersen, Open Education Librarian at the University of Southern Queensland, to provide the Australian OER content developers with practical strategies for producing diverse, inclusive and accessible OER and open textbooks. The work is an adaptation of Improving Representation and Diversity in OER Materials by OpenStax. The work has also received the 2022 Australian Award University Teaching Citation for Outstanding Contributions to Student Learning and OEGlobal award for Diversity, Equity & Inclusion 2023.

According to Andersen (2022): Content advertised as 'open access' and 'freely accessible' may give the impression that OER are universally accessible, but many users still face inequitable barriers to access. Additionally, access doesn't equal inclusion. Textbooks often express sexist and racist content and exclude marginalised voices. We need to consider how to contribute to a transformation and expand open access to resources to truly address diversity, equity, and inclusion."

Learning design, copyright and Creative Commons

As learning designers, we are required to pay attention to using and reusing materials to create new content in the learning management system or any instructional resources. However, often we question whether the content we use is covered by copyright. The copyright area is broad, and it is not the intention of this section to delve into legalese, but rather to highlight the aspects of copyright that are important to learning designers working in the Australian higher education sector.

Copyright is the automatic legal protection given to all original work that we create in a materialistic format. Copyright applies as soon as a work has been put into a material form such as being written down or recorded in some way, which applies to both print and digital material. However, copyright is for protection given to the expression of an idea and not the ideas themselves.

The concept of copyright originated in 1709, making it a long-standing idea. The main reasons for the need of copyright law were to protect the publishing and printing industries and to promote the advancement of knowledge. Its main mission was to protect authors' ideas and advance knowledge. Copyright law has two main reasons behind it, though the reasons may differ in different legal systems.

1. **Utilitarian:** To encourage authors by offering benefits of their work, such as commercial rewards and societal advantages.
2. **Author's rights:** To recognise and safeguard the bond between authors and their creative work. It is based on moral rights, which ensures authors receive credit for their

work and protect the integrity of their creations.

The utilitarian rationale is more commonly found in common law systems, while the author's rights rationale has historical connections to civil law systems.

Copyright covers various works, such as art, literature, recordings, and broadcasts. However, ideas, concepts, methods, styles, facts, names, and titles are not copyrighted; they may be protected under different laws like patents or trademarks. When using indigenous cultural and intellectual property, it is essential to respect relevant protocols and ethical guidelines.

It is important to note that copyright law might differ from country to country. So here in Australia, we do not need to register work in some way or have the copyright symbol on it to be protected. Therefore, images, text, and videos that you may find on the Internet are not free to use if they do not have a copyright notice! Copyright also lasts for a very long time, generally for 70 years after the creators' death. After the copyright has expired, the work then enters into the public domain, which means you can reuse it however you like.

The copyright owner holds exclusive economic rights, including publishing, communicating to the public, copying, reproducing, performing, and adapting the work. Additionally, moral rights safeguard the creator's personal rights, such as the right to attribution and protection of the work's integrity.

Copyright questions I heard from learning designers

Copyright laws in Australia protect the intellectual property of learning designers and creators. Copyright automatically applies to original works once they are created, and it grants the creator exclusive rights to use and distribute their work. This means that learning designers have certain rights and protections for their educational materials and content. However, this may change if you belong to a higher educational institution in Australia. When it comes to learning designers working in Australian higher educational institutions, copyright, is still, of utmost importance. We are usually responsible for creating and designing educational materials, online subjects, and other content used in teaching and learning. In most Australian higher education institutions, we often collaborate with educators and subject matter experts to develop educational materials, instructional resources, and interactive content. This content can include lecture notes, presentations, multimedia, assessments, and more.

As my experience primarily resides in the learning design sphere, I often encounter intriguing questions from colleagues regarding copyright and Creative Commons. While I am not an expert in copyright, I respond to all questions from my perspective and recommend that they reach out to the university library's copyright officer for legal advice. In the following paragraphs, I have categorised each question and listed both the question and the corresponding response under each category.

 An interactive H5P element has been excluded from this version of the text. You can view it online here:
https://oercollective.caul.edu.au/designing-learning-experiences/?p=56#h5p-3

To ensure compliance with copyright laws and policies, as learning designers we should stay informed about copyright regulations, seek appropriate permissions when necessary, and work closely with our institution's legal and intellectual property experts.

Creative Commons essentials for learning designers

While there is a vast amount to discuss regarding Creative Commons, immersing oneself in the content of the Creative Commons Certificate open textbook can offer a thorough guide to effectively utilising Creative Commons licenses within educational environments.

Creative Commons story

The creators of Creative Commons acknowledged the disparity between the possibilities enabled by technology and the limitations imposed by copyright. They offered an alternative method for creators who wish to distribute their work. This approach is now embraced by countless creators worldwide. It all began with the case of *Eldred v. Ashcroft* (2003), which was argued in the Supreme Court of the United States by Lawrence Lessig, a Stanford law professor who would go on to found Creative Commons. For detailed background, listen to this podcast about the Creative Commons story

> One or more interactive elements has been excluded from this version of the text. You can view them online here: https://oercollective.caul.edu.au/designing-learning-experiences/?p=56#audio-56-1

Audio transcript

For learning designers, obtaining a fundamental grasp of Creative Commons licenses may appear adequate. Yet, as you delve deeper into working with OER and creating or publishing them, you'll discover certain complexities that demand a thorough understanding of the nuances and legal terms within the licenses.

Creative Commons explainer: NonCommercial and ShareAlike

Among the different types of Creative Commons

licenses, the NonCommercial (NC) restriction and the ShareAlike (SA) condition often pose challenges for many, including novices and experienced users alike. The blog post titled 'Creative Commons Explained: NonCommercial and ShareAlike' offers an in-depth explanation of both types, illustrated with examples from academic contexts.

Hot topics in open learning design

Open education and decolonising the curriculum.

One of the key aspects of decolonising the curriculum is to incorporate diverse perspectives and voices from different cultures and regions. Academics can use OER that are freely available and accessible to all learners and adapt these resources to produce inclusive learning experiences. By curating OER from various sources, including non-Western authors, Indigenous knowledges, and marginalised communities, academics can create a more inclusive curriculum that challenges Eurocentric perspectives.

"Decolonising is not about deleting knowledge or histories that have been developed in the West or colonial nations; rather it is to situate the histories and knowledges that do not originate from the West in the context of imperialism, colonialism and power and to consider why these have been marginalised and decentred." Rowena Arshad, University of Edinburgh (Arshad, 2021, para. 4).

Educational materials that utilise OEP and OER enable the integration of multiple voices and perspectives and produce student-centered content. Importantly, these practices aim to address social injustice in the classroom. In her article 'Decolonising the curriculum – how do I get started?', Rowena Arshad suggests that decolonising the curriculum has to be contextual to our discipline and subject areas. She proposes four guiding points that can be used in decolonising the curriculum approach. The following points integrate OER/OEP as the fifth guiding point to demonstrate their introduction in Arshad's guide and to reveal where to revise the curriculum, spotting chances for decolonisation.

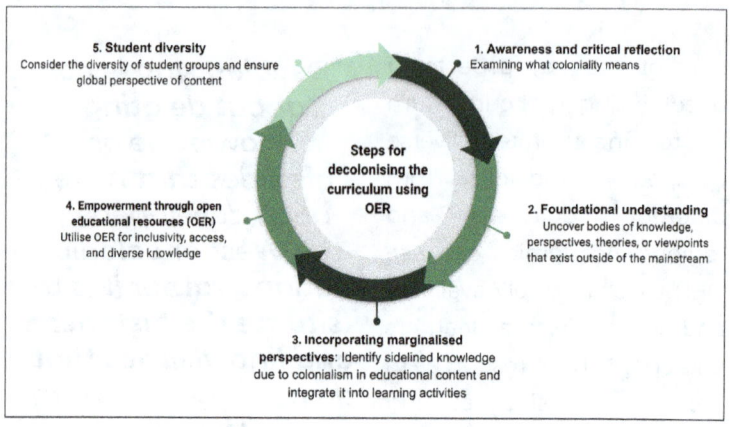

Adapted from Arshad, R. (2021). Decolonising the curriculum–how do I get started. Times Higher Education.
https://www.timeshighereducation.com/campus/decolonising-curriculum-how-do-i-get-started

Awareness and critical reflection: Start by examining what coloniality means and why decolonising the curriculum is important as part of our commitment to justice. Read Walter D. Mignolo's 2017 paper 'Coloniality is far from over, and so must be decoloniality'. This paper emphasises that the impact of colonialism persists in various aspects of modern society.

Foundational understanding: Review your subject materials to uncover bodies of knowledge, perspectives, theories, or viewpoints that exist outside of the mainstream or dominant narratives knowledge canons that may have been marginalised or disregarded due to colonial influences.

Determine if there are perspectives, theories, or contributions that have been overshadowed by colonialism and should now be integrated into the subject's discourse for meaningful discussion with students.

Incorporating marginalised perspectives: Identify side-lined knowledge due to colonialism in your educational content and integrate it into learning activities (e.g., ice-breaker, discussions boards, assessments, etc). Include various voices, re-imagine the learning content to encompass broader global and historical viewpoints.

Empowerment through Open Educational Resources (OER): Curate and identify OER to replace identified content. Ensure the chosen resources have open licenses for adaptability. A good start is in Indigenisation, Decolonisation and Cultural Inclusion. A common CC license used by an OER such as the Creative Commons Attribution-NonCommercial (CC BY-NC) license is a good option. This license allows others to reuse, remix, and redistribute the resource as long as they provide appropriate attribution to the original creators and do not use it for commercial purposes. Another CC license, that can also be used, is the Creative Commons Attribution (CC BY) license which allows even greater freedom for users, permitting both commercial and non-commercial use if attribution is given to the original authors.

Student diversity: Consider the diversity of your student groups and ensure that the learning content transcends Western perspectives, encompassing broader global frameworks.

Importantly, as learning designers it is crucial for us to continuously assess, gather feedback, and enhance content design to ensure its relevance to students' diverse backgrounds.

Openness: From social justice to liberation

This hot topic holds great personal significance for me as it resonates with my cultural identity, as a first generation Palestinian in the diaspora, and underscores the transformative potential of openness in advancing social justice to achieve liberation. As I compose this chapter, the atrocities of the Israeli army on civilians in the Gaza Strip persist. Regrettably, by the time of completion, additional tragic incidents are anticipated, including the loss of innocent lives, particularly children, as a result of Israeli military actions and rocket attacks on civilian spaces such as refugee camps, educational institutions and hospitals. This has also resulted in the loss of lives of academics, artists, journalists, scientists, and historians. Furthermore, the atrocities of the occupation have extended to archives, libraries, museums, and historical buildings.

> The educational system lies at the heart of this devastation, with the persistent war preventing approximately 608,000 students from exercising their fundamental right to school education, and interrupting the studies of over 90,000 university students. Moreover, the loss of 17 professors, 59 holders of Ph.D. degrees, and 18 individuals with master's degrees has dealt a severe blow to the intellectual foundation of Gaza's universities (Mediterranean Universities Union, n.d.).

Education serves as a moral compass for Palestinians as they strive for learning at all stages, making them the country with the lowest illiteracy rate in the world per capita. Palestinian universities stand as symbols of pride and resilience for the Palestinian people; however, due to the occupation, their participation in generating knowledge remains limited, encountering barriers imposed by the Israeli occupation (Alfoqahaa, 2015). Preserving lives is crucial, as is safeguarding human intellectual property. Through openness, Palestinians can find ways to preserve their knowledge and pave the way towards liberation.

Openness, as a transformative force for equity, goes beyond its role in facilitating learning and teaching through OER. It acts as a catalyst for liberation, providing a platform to disseminate narratives and facts that illuminate the persistent challenges endured by the indigenous people of Palestine. In doing so, it actively contributes to the discourse surrounding the 76 years of occupation, fostering awareness about injustice, correcting media misconceptions about the history of the land and emphasising the urgent need for global attention and support.

Yet, preserving knowledge amidst occupation poses significant challenges, often entailing serious risks. Under Israeli occupation, access to material goods and decent living standards are often considered privileges to Palestinians rather than basic human rights. Consequently, these factors deprive Palestinians of having a robust health system, an income to secure basic needs without having to resort to working in subhuman conditions, and proper education.

According to Itmazi (2020), in the Arab States, including Palestine, a notable concern arises from the insufficient availability of open digital content in the Arabic language. Currently, all Arabic content on the web constitutes less than 3% of global digital content. Furthermore, the absence of political strategies or action plans from Arab Ministries has been identified as a hindrance to the development and implementation of OER. It is critical to carry out awareness campaigns about the importance of creating, using, and sharing OER. Importantly, the available OER could be translated from other languages into Arabic and further recontextualised to meet the needs of Palestinian education.

Javiera Atenas writes on how her trip to Palestine changed her views on OEP, stating that 'Opening up means to me to share, to do things in a transparent way, to collaborate, to support and to provide the tools for educators and students to be critical thinkers, to challenge and to question, to become communities and not to follow a rule that tells you if you are open enough according to someone else's agenda, so just be open, under your own terms, share, distribute, communicate, participate, engage, thinking that before Open rules there are human rights, and that accessing quality education is one of these.'

As previously discussed in this chapter, open education centres on principles such as access, agency, ownership, participation, and experience. It holds the potential to emerge as a significant global equaliser, empowering individuals worldwide to exercise their basic human right to education (Blessinger & Bliss, 2016, p. 11).

Importantly, in the Palestinian context, the role of openness in education extends beyond ensuring proper education. It has the potential to preserve historical events, narrate stories, and document innovations within a self-sufficient society. This entails preserving cultural heritage, documenting the innovations of Palestinian scientists, safeguarding patents from destruction, and offering a global platform for Palestinian artists and poets to persist in their noble call for liberation and justice (Mahn et al., 2020).

As learning designers, understanding the perspectives and needs of learners can inform the design decisions, therefore adopting human-centred approaches is usually seen as a core commitment in designing for the better, both for people and the planet. It is our ethical duty and commitment to design for better futures, acknowledge ethical responsibilities and to speak out against injustices. We cannot be learning designers who stay disconnected from brutal war crimes while claiming to operate from a space of empathy when we design for spaces, technology, and interfaces. Empathy, as we understand it, is the ability to feel deeply and resonate with the human experience.

Practical steps to support liberation through OEP

There are many ways we can consider to pave the way to liberation through an open education lens:

- Cultivate empathy for the enduring struggle of Palestinians over the long term.
- Educate ourselves on the history of the occupation dating back to 1948.
- Curate OER tailored to address the specific needs and infrastructural challenges (See OERs for Gaza).
- Challenge and rectify misconceptions by decolonising available resources.

The principles of open education pave the way for individuals across various learning design roles to contribute to a more informed, empathetic, and socially responsible approach to addressing the challenges posed by conflicts and displacements. As learning designers, our contribution can be through global awareness and solidarity, documenting and preserving narratives, as well as cultural preservation and restoration, to name a few possibilities.

Generative AI and Open Educational Practices

Part of this section is adapted from Getting Started: OER Publishing at BCcampus by BCcampus Open Education Team, available from https://opentextbc.ca/gettingstarted/chapter/generative-artificial-intelligence/#decisiontree under a Creative Commons Attribution 4.0 International License,

The introduction of generative AI has brought a significant disruption in higher education, although it is worth noting that disruption is the norm in the higher education sector. Before exploring generative AI and OEP more extensively, it is crucial to recognise that, at the time of writing, higher education is primarily reacting to the emergence of generative AI. Numerous uncertainties surround the integration of these new technologies into learning and teaching. Consequently, this discussion will focus on examining potential applications of generative AI in the development of OER.

What is artificial intelligence (AI)?

> UNESCO World Commission on the Ethics of Scientific Knowledge and Technology, UNESCO (2019) defines Artificial Intelligence (AI) into two distinct aspects: theoretical or scientific AI and pragmatic or technological AI. The theoretical aspect explores AI concepts and models to answer questions about human beings and other living things, intersecting with disciplines like philosophy, logic, linguistics, psychology, and cognitive science. It addresses questions about intelligence, distinguishing natural from artificial intelligence, the role of symbolic language in thought processes, and the possibility of achieving "strong AI" comparable to human intelligence. On the other hand, pragmatic or technological AI is engineering-oriented, leveraging branches of AI such as natural language processing, knowledge representation, machine learning, deep learning, computer vision, and robotics. It aims to create machines or programs capable of independently performing tasks that typically require human intelligence. The success of pragmatic AI is evident in its integration with information and communications technology (ICT), leading to widespread applications in areas like transport, medicine, communication, education, finance, law, military, marketing, customer services, and entertainment (UNESCO, 2019).

As technology develops, so too do the ways we define it. There is no single or fixed definition of AI, but there is common agreement that machines based on AI "are potentially capable of imitating or even exceeding human cognitive capacities, including sensing, language interaction, reasoning and analysis, problem solving, and even creativity" (UNESCO, 2019).

Generative artificial intelligence (AI) is a type of artificial intelligence used to create images, text, audio, video, computer code and other types of content via text prompts from a user. Generative AI exists in the form of a standalone tool or can be incorporated or integrated into other content creation tools for example ChatGPT for text, Dall-e for images, or GitHub for computer code to name a few. In his short blog, David Wiley (2023) has attempted to respond to the question of what impact generative AI is going to have on education by starting with the assumption that 'Generative AI greatly reduces the degree to which access to expertise is an obstacle to education'. David's initial thought sparked more questions such as, how will generative AI tools impact the development of OER by learning designers, especially considering they may not always be subject matter experts?

Using generative AI in developing OER

Some ways in which generative AI could be used when creating or adapting OER are as follows:

- To create questions sets, case studies, and other types of instructional resources.
- To analyse a photo to create alt text for accessibility purposes.
- To create illustrations and photo-realistic images

> for both decorative and instructional purposes.
> - To generate scripts that can be used for videos and podcasts.
> - To create instructional videos.
> - To generate sentences, paragraphs, and chapters for a textbook.
> - To analyse and create summaries of longer sections of text.
> - To automate the creation of an audio version of text, usually for accessibility purposes.
> - To translate text to another language.

Nonetheless, ensuring the quality of OER will remain a challenge that learning designers need to address. Generative AI tools can handle routine and bulk tasks, accelerating the content development process and reducing the necessity for expertise in all aspects of content creation. These tools also aid in generating accessible content, such as alt text. However, human intuition and an expert's final touch are unlikely to become obsolete and remain a necessity to ensure the overall quality of content.

Intentional vs. unintentional use

With the proliferation of generative AI tools and the continual integration of these tools into other software packages, you may not know that a tool you are using to create learning materials is using generative AI. Therefore, these guidelines are intended to be interpreted with leniency and flexibility to allow for the possibility that generative AI use may not always be visible or apparent to the person who is using a tool. Here are guidelines to consider if you plan to use generative AI tools during the OER content creation process.

Considerations and risks

While these tools can be of great value, there are numerous ethical concerns and potential risks you should be aware of when you consider using generative AI tools to develop OER.

1. **Lack of transparency:** The source of the training data and the programming logic used by many generative AI tools is not always made available to the public. Indeed, even the companies that develop the tools may not be able to explain exactly how they work, or how they arrived at the outputs they did.
2. **Bias:** Because there is a lack of transparency in how the tools are constructed and what data is used to train them, this can lead to biases being present in the output.
3. **Accuracy:** Generative AI systems can sometimes produce inaccurate or made-up answers (also referred to as hallucinations).
4. **Intellectual property (IP) and copyright:** There are three areas where copyright and IP should be considered; the content that the AI tool has been trained with, the content that the AI tool generates, and using AI to generate summaries of copyrighted content.
    I. **Use of content to train AI models:** Many generative AI tools have been trained on copyrighted works often without the permission of copyright holders. While organizations such as Creative Commons argue that this use is considered fair use under current copyright legislation, there are a number of lawsuits where creators are arguing that AI tools are creating unauthorised derivatives. This also means that AI-generated content could be subject to copyright claims.
    II. **Applying copyright to generated output:** Legal decision and rulings around copyrighting AI

generated content has been very clear in the United States. AI generated content is not human made and therefore cannot be protected by copyright. In Canada there has not been as definitive legal rulings around this, although the emerging consensus in Canada is that Canadian copyright law will follow closely with the US when it comes to copyright and AI due to the shared international copyright and trades agreements the two countries have with each other. To date, there isn't a specific legal reference available for Australia's stance on copyrighting AI-generated content.

   III. **Using AI to generate summaries of copyrighted work:** It is unlikely that using generative AI to summarise copyrighted content is a violation of copyright as the AI generated summary is machine and not human generated.
5. **Sustainability:** Generative AI uses massive amounts of electricity to operate, which has led to examinations as to how environmentally sustainable generative AI is.

Is it safe to use ChatGPT?

Use the following flowchart to check if the content generated by GenAI is safe to use:

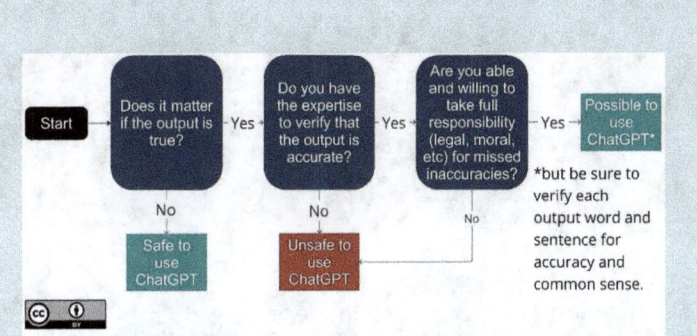

"When is it safe to use ChatGPT" flowchart by Aleksandr Tiulkanov, in ChatGPT and artificial intelligence in higher education: A quick start guide, by UNESCO. Used under a CC BY 4.0 licence. Flow chart recreated by BCcampus to improve readability.

Is it safe to use ChatGPT image description

1. Does it matter if the output is true?
    I. No. It is safe to use ChatGPT.
    II. Yes. Continue to next question.
2. Do you have expertise to verify that the output is accurate?
    I. No. It is unsafe to use ChatGPT.
    II. Yes. Continue to next question.
3. Are you able and willing to take full responsibility (legal, moral, etc.) for missed inaccuracies?
    I. No. It is unsafe to use ChatGPT.
    II. Yes. It is possible to use ChatGPT, but be sure to verify each output word and sentence for accuracy and common sense.

Key Takeaways

Guidelines and recommendations:

1. Be cautious with your use of AI generated content. While we do provide some guidelines and suggestions, AI generated content is an area that is in considerable flux right now and these guidelines and recommendations may change as the field evolves.
2. Manually review and assess all AI generated content for accuracy, appropriateness, and usefulness before including it in any OER. AI generated content should be reviewed by more than one subject matter expert to ensure the validity of the content. As an OER author, you are ultimately accountable for the content that you share in your OER, therefore you must manually verify the accuracy of the content.
3. Closely review any AI generated content for bias, including language or images that reinforce cultural or societal stereotypes around race, ethnicity, colour, ancestry, place of origin, political beliefs, religion, marital status, family status, ability, sex, gender identity and expression, sexual orientation, age, and class and/or socioeconomic status. Consider reviewing and assessing the outputs of AI generated content using the lenses

of equity, diversity and inclusion and ask whether the content aligns with these considerations.
4. Do not use generative AI to generate content for an area or subject where you do not have the appropriate level of knowledge or understanding to verify the accuracy of the content.
5. Be transparent about your use of generative AI. Just like attributing the reuse of open content, you should include statements within the OER that let others know that you have used generative AI in the creation of the OER. This should include:

    - what content was generated
    - what tools were used to generate the content, including links to the tool,
    - how you used that tool (i.e., what prompts was the tool given that generated the content?)
    - the date the content was generated
    - what steps were taken to review the content to ensure it was valid and correct.

6. As much of the legal consensus around AI generated content suggests AI created content is not copyrightable, you should not apply a Creative Commons license to AI generated content as Creative Commons licenses can only be applied to content that is copyrightable.
7. You should avoid generating content that may include content that is protected by a trademark or patent. For example, you should avoid creating an image using an AI image generator that

> includes a trademarked corporate logo unless you are doing so under the purposes of Fair Use.
> 8. If you use AI to create a summary of another work, you should ensure that you are familiar enough with the original work to determine whether or not the generated summary is an accurate representation of the original work before using the summary.

Evaluating OER

Publishing an OER is a valuable endeavour that requires careful planning, creation, and dissemination. The following sequence can be useful for learning designers to consider before publishing OER:

- **Quality of content and use of third-party content**
  When evaluating the quality of content for OER, several crucial considerations come into play. Firstly, it is imperative to review the content for accuracy, ensuring it is free from errors. Additionally, a critical aspect of quality control involves addressing biases and conflicting information to present an unbiased and cohesive resource. The content should align with the values of the institution where its developed and should not convey messages contradictory to these principles. Furthermore, adherence to accessibility guidelines is essential to guarantee that the content can be accessed and utilised by all learners. In the case of third-party content incorporation, it is crucial to verify licenses for compatibility with the broader OER and

ensure compliance with legal and ethical standards. This first step of the evaluation process is fundamental to maintaining high quality and the integrity of the OER.

Practical tool for OER development and evaluation in the Australian context

EmpoweredOER is a website and practical tool designed to guide the development and evaluation of inclusive OER. This platform provides simplified explanations and concrete examples of good practice. EmpoweredOER adapts the Equity Rubric for OER Evaluation developed by a non-profit organisation, Branch Alliance for Educator Diversity (BranchED) (Grunzke et al., 2021). Barber's work (2023) incorporated into EmpoweredOER provides valuable insights into good practices, featuring illustrations from an Australian context. These practices are intricately woven into three overarching themes: (1) accessibility, (2) the intersection of Universal Design for Learning (UDL) and inclusive open education, and (3) perspective and representation.

- **Publishing guidelines**
The process of license selection and definition is a crucial step in the creation and publication of OER. As you decide

on how the work will be disseminated, consider the following:

- Firstly, and foremost, it is essential to carefully choose an appropriate license that aligns with the intended use and sharing of the OER.
- Secondly, to ensure institutional alignment and compliance, obtaining approval from the relevant academic unit or faculty is imperative, as this step helps validate the chosen license and the decision to publish the OER.
- Finally, a copyright officer's advice should also be sought to address any potential copyright-related concerns and to maintain legal integrity. Copyright officers, who are most of the time embedded in university libraries, can identify and resolve any copyright issues that may arise during the development and sharing of the OER. This step in the evaluation process safeguards the proper dissemination of OER while upholding legal and institutional standards.

OER licensing tools

Open Attribution Builder

To simplify the process of licensing, an attribution builder tool developed by Open Washington OER Network (Washington State Board for Community and

Technical Colleges, n.d) can be utilised to generate the license, ensuring that it accurately reflects the desired permissions and restrictions.

This tool facilitates convenient citation of open materials by automatically generating attribution as you fill out a form. It is designed specifically for citing openly distributed work, including content licensed by Creative Commons or released into the public domain. Keep in mind that the tool offers a default attribution statement, which can be modified to better suit specific needs.

Open Education Licensing Toolkit

The OEL Toolkit is a web application designed to assist teaching staff in Australian higher education institutions. It is a decision tree system that provides easy access to relevant support resources regarding open educational resources. The tool was developed by a team from Swinburne University and the University of Tasmania and was supported by the Australian Government Office for Learning and Teaching.

- **Technological considerations**
  When it comes to hosting OER, several essential considerations need to be addressed. Firstly, it is crucial to determine the most suitable platform or location for hosting the OER content, ensuring it aligns with your goals and target audience. Once hosted, there should be a well-defined plan in place for the ongoing maintenance and preservation of the OER to ensure its long-term accessibility and relevance. Additionally, it is important to

review the terms and conditions of global OER repositories, such as OER Commons, to confirm that they align with your objectives and any licensing agreements you've chosen for your OER. These repositories can provide valuable platforms for sharing your educational resources.Recommendations for suitable OER repositories should be made considering the nature of your resource and its intended audience. For example, OER Commons is recommended as a publishing platform. It is essential to ensure that publishers, if involved, adhere to the original purpose of making the resource open and accessible.Lastly, the inclusion of sufficient meta-data attributes is crucial for effective discovery and categorisation of the OER. These attributes enhance the resource's visibility and usability, facilitating its access by educators and learners seeking relevant educational materials.

OER infrastructure

Open Educational Resources Search Index

OERSI, or the Open Educational Resources Search Index, is a search engine designed for open educational materials in higher education. Launched in 2021, it connects various OER repositories, including initiatives, university libraries, and subject-specific repositories. OERSI, developed as an open-source service, does not store content but centralises metadata for uniform searching. Users can integrate OERSI into other platforms and customise searches based on specific criteria. The project encourages open participation, allowing feedback, bug reporting, and feature requests through transparent processes on the GitLab platform.

OER Commons

Developed in 2007 by Institute for the Study of Knowledge Management in Education (ISKME), OER Commons provides a robust infrastructure for curriculum experts and instructors at all levels to discover high-quality OER that can be downloaded directly through the curated resources. Individual learning content developers can also share their own materials directly through this platform.

ISKME's technology platform, tools, and metadata enhancements in OER Commons emphasise fostering accessibility and inclusive design principles. By aggregating resources and standardising metadata from OER content providers, the site supports knowledge sharing and access to teaching and learning materials, strategies, and curricula online.

Conclusion

This chapter has presented practical approaches for the adoption of OEP in higher education, offering insights from Australia and other places around the world. The concept of openness holds immense potential to enrich higher education, particularly as it aligns with strategies commonly embraced by universities, emphasising principles of social justice. Key takeaways from this chapter can be summarised as follows:

- In our roles as learning designers, it is imperative that we intentionally approach open education with confidence and courage, recognising that our unique qualifications empower us to leverage the 5Rs (retain, revise, remix, reuse and redistribute) effectively in our learning design processes.
- As learning designers, a thorough understanding of the fundamentals of open education is indispensable for our daily interactions with academics. Utilising the insights of open pedagogy provides a common language that bridges the understanding gap between us and academics, making it essential to be cognisant of diverse teaching approaches grounded in open pedagogy.
- In our routine tasks, we often encounter inquiries about open textbooks or copyrights, typically better addressed by library copyright officers. However, it is crucial to share our insights with academics, guiding them in unpacking the benefits of open textbooks. This involves empowering them to infuse their perspectives into a curriculum that might be outdated and inherently biased.
- Lastly, delving deeper into the role of OEP beyond social justice becomes increasingly vital in the face of the disruptions we experience, whether due to political challenges or technological advancements. Open education holds the potential to decolonise and elevate the quality of education, enabling us to foster inclusivity for everyone in the learning journey.

I unequivocally concur with Ash Barber's (2023) assertion in her paper that '… the reality is OER alone cannot achieve this goal [inclusive, equitable and diverse education] because OER itself is not the goal. OER is the vehicle to the goal of dismantling the education exclusion zone'.

Similarly, the exclusion zone within the learning content we construct, the interactivity infused into resources, and the innovations embedded in our designs must be dismantled. This dismantling need is essential to amplify the voices of those at the margins and foster inclusivity for everyone within the learning environment.

References

Alfoqahaa, S. A. A. Q. (2015). Economics of higher education under occupation: The case of Palestine. *Journal of Arts and Humanities, 4*(10), 25-43.

Andersen, N. (2022). *Enhancing inclusion, diversity, equity and accessibility (IDEA) in open educational resources (OER)*. https://usq.pressbooks.pub/diversityandinclusionforoer/

Arshad, R. (2021). Decolonising the curriculum – how do I get started? *Times Higher Education*. https://www.timeshighereducation.com/campus/decolonising-curriculum-how-do-i-get-started

Atenas, J. (2017). Open education in Palestine: A tool for liberation. In M. Bali, C. Cronin, L. Czerniewicz, R. DeRosa, & R. Jhangiani (Eds.), *Open at the margins: Critical perspectives on open education* (ch. 8). Pressbooks. https://press.rebus.community/openatthemargins/chapter/open-education-in-palestine-a-tool-for-liberation/

Atenas, J., Havemann, L., Cronin, C., Rodés, V., Lesko, I., Stacey, P., ... & Villar, D. (2022). Defining and developing 'enabling' open education policies in higher education. In *UNESCO*

World Higher Education Conference, 18-22 May 2022. Barcelona, Spain. https://oars.uos.ac.uk/2481/

Barber, A. (2023). Dismantling the education exclusion zone: Empowering OER authors towards inclusive design. In T. Cochrane, V. Narayan, C. Brown, K. MacCallum, E. Bone, C. Deneen, R. Vanderburg, & B. Hurren (Eds.), *People, partnerships and pedagogies* (pp. 281–285). Proceedings ASCILITE 2023. Christchurch, N.Z. https://publications.ascilite.org/index.php/APUB/article/view/560/597

Blessinger, P., & Bliss, T. J. (Eds.). (2018). *Open education: International perspectives in higher education*. Open Book Publisher.

Bossu, C. (2016), Open educational practices in Australia. In F. Miao, S., Mishra, & R. McGreal (Eds.), *Open educational resources: Policy, costs and transformation*. UNESCO and Commonwealth of Learning. http://oasis.col.org/handle/11599/2306

Creative Commons. (n.d.). Unit 5: CC for educators. *Creative commons certificate for educators, academic librarians and GLAM*. https://certificates.creativecommons.org/cccertedu/

Cronin, C. (2017). Openness and praxis: Exploring the use of open educational practices in higher education. *International Review of Research in Open and Distributed Learning, 18*(5), 15-34. https://doi.org/10.19173/irrodl.v18i5.3096

DeRosa, R., & Jhangiani, R. (2017). Open pedagogy. In E. Mays, R. DeRosa, R. Jhangiani, T. Robbins, D. Squires, J. Ward, A. Andrzejewski, S. Burns, & M. Moore (Eds.), *A guide to making open textbooks with students*. Rebus Community. https://openlibrary-repo.ecampusontario.ca/jspui/bitstream/

123456789/334/4/A-Guide-to-Making-Open-Textbooks-with-Students.pdf

DeRosa, R., & Robison, S. (2017). From OER to open pedagogy: Harnessing the power of open. In R. S. Jhangiari & R. Biwas-Diener (Eds.), *Open: The philosophy and practices that are revolutionizing education and science* (pp. 115-124). https://uilis.usk.ac.id/oer/files/original/0a7d9404b1852e09ccb43fabfab74aad.pdf#page=124

DiBiase, D. (2011). GIS&T in the open educational resources movement. In D. J. Unwin, K. E. Foote, N. J. Tate, & D. DiBiase (Eds.), *Teaching geographic information science and technology in higher education* (pp. 421-437). John Wiley & Sons.

Elliott, J. (1973). Is instruction outmoded? *Cambridge Journal of Education, 3*(3), 169-181. doi: 10.1080/0305764730030305

Falconer, I., McGill, L., Littlejohn, A., & Boursinou, E. (2013). *Overview and analysis of practices with open educational resources in adult education in Europe*. Brussels. https://oro.open.ac.uk/50933/1/JRC-Adult%20Learning%20Report%202013.pdf

Fatayer, M. M. (2016). Towards a sustainable open educational resources development model: Tapping into the cognitive surplus of student-generated content (Unpublished doctoral dissertation, Western Sydney University).

Fatayer, M., & Tualaulelei, E. (2023). Making the most of cognitive surplus: Descriptive case studies of student-generated open educational resources. *Education Sciences, 13*(10), 1011.

Grunzke, R. Z., Jiles, T. Mayo, S., Grotewold, K., & Ianniello, P. (2021). *Equity rubric for OER evaluation*. Branch Alliance for

Educator Diversity. https://oercommons.org/courseware/lesson/82102/overview

Itmazi, J. (2020). Open educational resources in Palestine: High hopes promising solutions. In Huang, R., Liu, D., Tlili, A., Gao, Y., & Koper, R. (Eds.), *Current state of open educational resources in the 'belt and road' countries* (pp. 135-149). Springer, Singapore.

Jacobi, R., Jelgerhuis, H., & Van Der Woert, N. (Eds.). (2013). *Trend report: Open educational resources 2013*. OER Knowledge Cloud. https://www.oerknowledgecloud.org/record542

Jhangiani, R. S., Green, A. G., & Belshaw, J. D. (2016). Three approaches to open textbook development. In P. Blessinger & T. J. Bliss (Eds.), *Open education: International perspectives in higher education* (pp. 179-198). Open Book Publishers.

Lambert, S. R. (2018). Changing our (dis)course: A distinctive social justice aligned definition of open education. *Journal of Learning for Development, 5*(3), 225–244. https://jl4d.org/index.php/ejl4d/article/view/290

Mahn, C., Malik, S., Pierse, M., & Rogaly, B. (2020). Radical openness in a hostile world. In S. Malik, C. Mahn, B. Rogaly, & M. Pierse, *Creativity and resistance in a hostile world* (pp. 19-40). Manchester University Press.

Mai, R. P. (1978). Open education: From ideology to orthodoxy. *Peabody Journal of Education, 55*(3), 231-237. doi: 10.1080/01619567809538192

Mediterranean Universities Union. (n.d.). *Supporting Gaza's students and universities, the TESI Initiative: How could you contribute?* https://www.uni-med.net/news/supporting-gazas-students-and-universities-the-tesi-initiative-how-could-you-contribute/

Morgan, T. (2019). Instructional designers and open education practices: Negotiating the gap between intentional and operational agency. *Open Praxis, 11*(4), 369-380.

Neary, M. (2010). Student as producer: a pedagogy for the avant-garde? *Learning Exchange, 1*(1). https://bpb-eu-w2.wpmucdn.com/blogs.lincoln.ac.uk/dist/e/185/files/2014/03/15-72-1-pb-1.pdf

Open Education Resource University. (n.d.). *About OERu*. Retrieved November 18, 2023, from https://oeru.org/about-oeru/

Open Educational Quality Initiative. (2011). *Beyond OER: Shifting the focus to open educational practices. The 2011 OPAL Report*. http://duepublico.uni-duisburg-essen.de/servlets/DerivateServlet/Derivate-25907/OPALReport2011_Beyond_OER.pdf

Open University. (2010, July 17). *Brief history of the OU*. The Open University. Archived from the original on November 17, 2023. https://web.archive.org/web/20100717081233/http://www.open.ac.uk/about/ou/p3.shtml

Paskevicius, M., & Irvine, V. (2019). Open education and learning design: Open pedagogy in praxis. *Journal of Interactive Media in Education, 2019*(1), Article 10. https://doi.org/10.5334/jime.512

Pérez-Mateo, M., Maina, M. F., Guitert, M., & Romero, M. (2011). Learner generated content: Quality criteria in online collaborative learning. *European Journal of Open, Distance and E-Learning, 14*(2). https://openaccess.uoc.edu/handle/10609/124786

Rennie, F., & Morrison, T. (2013). *E-learning and social networking handbook: Resources for higher education*. Routledge.

Roberts, V., Havemann, L., & DeWaard, H. (2022). Open learning designers on the margins. In T. Jaffer, S. Govender, & L. Czerniewicz (Eds.), *Learning design voices*. Advance preprint. https://doi.org/10.25375/uct.21355089

Rogers, E. M. (2003). *Diffusion of innovations* (3rd ed.). Simon and Schuster.

Sener, J. (2007). In search of student-generated content in online education. *e-mentor, 4*(21), 90-94. https://citeseerx.ist.psu.edu/document?repid=rep1&type=pdf&doi=588afa505e531019a819058657d3174d85ad56f6#page=90

Shirky, C. (2010). *Cognitive surplus: Creativity and generosity in a connected age*. Penguin UK.

Tietjen, P., & Asino, T. I. (2021). What Is open pedagogy? Identifying commonalities. *The International Review of Research in Open and Distributed Learning, 22*(2), 185–204. https://doi.org/10.19173/irrodl.v22i2.5161

Tualaulelei, E. (2020). The benefits of creating open educational resources as assessment in an online education course. *ASCILITE 2020 Conference Proceedings* (pp. 282-288). ASCILITE Publications. https://publications.ascilite.org/index.php/APUB/article/view/439

Tualaulelei, E., & Green, N. C. (2022). Supporting educators' professional learning for equity pedagogy: The promise of open educational practices. *Journal for Multicultural Education, 16*(5), 430-442. https://www.emerald.com/insight/content/doi/10.1108/JME-12-2021-0225/full/html

UNESCO. (2002). *Forum on the Impact of open courseware for higher education in developing countries: Final report*.

UNESCO. http://unesdoc.unesco.org/images/0012/001285/128515e.pdf

UNESCO. (2019). *World Commission on the Ethics of Scientific Knowledge and Technology. Preliminary study on the ethics of artificial intelligence*. https://unesdoc.unesco.org/ark:/48223/pf0000367823

Weller, M. (2014). *The battle for open*. Ubiquity Press. https://www.ubiquitypress.com/site/books/m/10.5334/bam/

Wiley, D. (2013). *What is open pedagogy?* https://edtechbooks.s3.us-west-2.amazonaws.com/pdfs/341/5314.pdf

Wiley, D. (2023, December 20). The near-term impact of generative AI on education, in one sentence. *Open Content Blog*. https://opencontent.org/blog/archives/7350

Wiley, D. (n.d.). *Defining the 'open' in open content and open educational resources*. http://opencontent.org/definition/

Wiley, D., & Hilton III, J. L. (2018). Defining OER-enabled pedagogy. *The International Review of Research in Open and Distributed Learning, 19*(4). https://doi.org/10.19173/irrodl.v19i4.3601

Media Attributions

- Screenshot 2024-04-20 at 4.32.22 pm
- When-is-it-safe-to-use-ChatGPT

About the author

Dr Mais Fatayer
UNIVERSITY OF TECHNOLOGY SYDNEY
https://www.uts.edu.au

Mais Fatayer is an educational technology specialist, learning designer with extensive experience in higher education and open education advocate. As of the publication of this book, she was the Learner Experience Design Manager at the University of Technology Sydney (UTS). Mais specialises in creating engaging learning materials and leading transformative projects and initiative in learning design and open education. She has received the 2023 UTS Vice Chancellor's Professional Staff Excellence Award and the 2018 Blackboard Catalyst Award for Student Success. Her PhD research focused on developing a sustainable open educational resources development model.

4. Negotiating the assumptions and identity tensions surrounding third space academics/professionals

PUVANESWARI P ARUMUGAM

Introduction: What is the fuss about third space practitioners?

One or more interactive elements has been excluded from this version of the text. You can view them online here: https://oercollective.caul.edu.au/designing-learning-experiences/?p=65

Video transcript

Hi, I am Puva P Arumugam, and I am a third space academic – I am a Lecturer, Learning Futures in an Australian university and I belong to a very prominent workforce in the higher education sector known as third space practitioners. As an academic, I am very interested in the research involving third space practitioners. Recently, colleagues asked me what the fuss was about third space practitioners in the higher education landscape and why third space practitioners warrant any research interest. My answer is that third space practitioners will always be an ever-developing important aspect of the higher education workforce, and there is no better time than now to be involved in this research.

Among the many hats that I wear in my role, I am an academic lead of teaching and learning course and unit development projects and I enjoy my work because I get to work with a variety of discipline-based academics and projects, and I can indulge in lifelong learning in my role. As a third space academic, I am also constantly working to make an impact with the work that I do and to bring about awareness of my hybrid identity in the higher education teaching and learning space.

As this textbook is aimed at providing an inclusive and diverse learning experience for learning designers who also come under the umbrella of third space practitioners (either as third space professionals or third space academics), it is right to point out that their roles have at times been

> perceived as an appendix to the discipline-based academics and/or higher education professional workforce. This perception causes assumptions, and these assumptions cause blurred boundaries in terms of professional identity and having a sense of belonging in the higher education landscape. As such, third space practitioners do often find that they have to navigate a fair bit of tension and challenges before completely understanding this space in which they operate.
>
> I hope to unpack a few of the tensions and challenges and show what the fuss is about third space practitioners as I narrate through my own reflections of being a third space academic and by drawing references from literature and research that has been done in this space.

Who are these third space practitioners?

Third space practitioners, who are often referred to as third space professionals and third space academics, have been in the higher education landscape for quite some time now. A fair amount of research has been done across the globe regarding the work of third space practitioners, the liminal space they occupy and their identity in the higher education landscape. The work and presence of third space professionals has become more prominent through the work of Celia Whitchurch. Whitchurch (2008) highlights the mixed background and portfolios that third space professionals come from and how their appointments span across the domains of both academics and professionals. She highlights that because third space professionals are likely to have work experiences in settings external to higher education, third space professionals may feel a sense of outsider status. During the recent global COVID-19 pandemic, third space practitioner roles such as learning designers, educational technologists, educational developers, academic developers and instructional designers, to name a few, become increasingly necessary as higher education institutions moved to a more integrated learning environment and the roles gained popularity as a career choice (Heggart & Dickson-Deane, 2022). This chapter discusses details surrounding the professional identity of and the assumptions about the role of third space practitioners. It highlights the tensions and challenges faced by third space professionals and third space academics within the liminal space (Manathunga, 2007) they occupy within the higher education landscape and provides an 'industry' (i.e., working in the higher education space) perspective. This chapter also describes the difference between third space professional and third space academic roles and the way learning designers are perceived by traditional teaching staff, and how this perception affects the way they function in both roles. Using the lens of Homi Bhabha's concept of ambivalence and liminal space (Bhabha, 1994), this chapter highlights certain tensions and challenges faced by third space practitioners in higher education as they navigate expectations and assumptions held by traditional institutional and discipline academics.

Your task

Let's take a moment to reflect on your own practice and your experience of either being a third space practitioner or having worked with third space practitioners.

Using the Padlet activity 'Navigating the tensions and challenges as Third Space Practitioners', share your thoughts about the following questions:

What has been your experience of working with third space practitioners? Please feel free to share your own experience of being a third space practitioner within the higher education context.

Teaching and learning staff members in higher education

One or more interactive elements has been excluded from this version of the text. You can view them online here: https://oercollective.caul.edu.au/designing-learning-experiences/?p=65

Video transcript

I didn't really think I would end up being a third space academic. I actually stumbled into this role by chance. I worked as a casual academic for four years while completing my PhD. I truly enjoyed my role as an academic and just before my graduation I was acting as the unit chair for several units that were related to my area of expertise. After my PhD, owing to personal circumstances, I had to leave academia and I took a job in the corporate world. I brought to my corporate roles many transferable skills from my experience as a casual academic. I knew how to work technology, manage people, meet deadlines, prepare and deliver presentations and train and mentor people on the job.

The pay and work in the corporate sector were good, but deep down inside I knew that I wanted to work in academia as I didn't want to 'waste' my PhD. Wanting to go back into academia is also a cultural thing for me. I come from Southeast Asia, and I grew up in a multicultural environment. And we are measured by our achievements. Having a PhD and being an academic do rank quite high in terms of personal achievement. I personally pursued a PhD because I wanted to be an academic. But with a niche discipline background like Cultural Studies and Performing Arts, it was hard to get back into that discipline. So, after 11 years of not being in academia, I returned to working in the university and took on a third space professional role as a Senior Educational Designer. Within a year, I applied

> for a third space academic role within a faculty in the university, and I became a Lecturer, Learning Futures.
>
> I was very happy that I got an academic role, but there was also this sense of curiosity about what exactly I would be doing in this role.

Discipline-based academics

In many universities, the discipline-based academics (Manathunga, 2007), also known as traditional academics, experience a clear sense of belonging, because there is clear alignment between their professional identity, the job they do and the relationship these have to their discipline. Usually, discipline-based academics do not hold any teaching qualifications and they teach content based on their knowledge of the subject matter as it relates to the field, and they are usually trained in their area of expertise by way of working or research. Their role is to teach in the discipline they belong to with a minimum of contact time with students, and they must prepare, curate or develop the teaching materials and manage the administrative and content development related tasks that are attached to this role. These may include curriculum development, writing of assessments and rubrics, developing teaching plans and learning content, lecture and seminar teaching, as well as developing learning materials, marking, grading, producing final reports, sitting on academic committees, contributing to scholarship of teaching, presenting at conferences and collaborating with other institutions and getting grants from industry partners. This ties in very much with Boyer's scholarship model, where 'the priorities of the academic encompassed four main themes, namely: teaching and learning, integration, application, and discovery' (Boyer, 1990, p. 2). Discipline-based academics are paid according to academic pay scales that recognise seniority. Of course, this is a general description, and the role of a discipline-based academic is by no means confined to these elements. However, it is important to note that many discipline academics love being academics. They are usually in ongoing roles and because they fit in this space very easily, they are happy to move from one higher education institution to another to continue to grow their career.

Casual Academics/session tutors

Another group of academics that are part of the higher education teaching staff are casual academics. This group is made up of aspiring academics who are doing their PhD or have just completed their PhD. They are generally seeking to become academics after completing study or working in the industry of their expertise. Casual academics often take on several roles in the university including those of tutors, seminar leaders, acting lecturers and acting unit chairs, depending on the need for teaching staff within their school and faculty. They engage in teaching and developing content as needed. They usually work on short-term contracts, and they do not enjoy the full remuneration benefits of paid leave in many institutions. They do not have to do the administrative work, but some might get paid to do it. They do engage in research and are eligible for awards and grants, depending on the particular higher education institution, but often this research is either in their own time or limited.

Professional staff

The next important group of teaching and learning staff would be the professional staff members who support administrative functions in the universities. These professional staff would be stationed in areas such as Finance, Student Enrolment, Human Resources, Timetabling, Library, Information Technology, Unit Site Development, Assessment Submission and Office Procurement. There is no research load for professional staff, and they can attend conferences and other professional learning opportunities to enhance their understanding of the higher education space without having to publish or engage in research. In Australia, professional staff do not have to work beyond agreed hours and they have flexibility to go full or part time. They, too, often consider the higher education landscape to be their home and place where they belong.

Third space practitioners

While professional staff in the past have provided support for administrative tasks, some of them have also, for the past two decades or so, crossed into the realm of preparing teaching and learning materials and co-designing teaching and learning with academics, hence navigating a space in between teaching and administration. They have become known as third space professionals (Whitchurch, 2008). Figure 1 shows the liminal space that is occupied by third space practitioners, who are often in both academic and professional roles. This pool of staff, owing to the hybrid space they occupy, have often struggled to find their place in the university and hence are often 'homeless' when it comes to finding their place in the university setting (Manathunga, 2007). Unlike the other categories discussed above, they often only have a very vague sense of belonging within the higher education landscape.

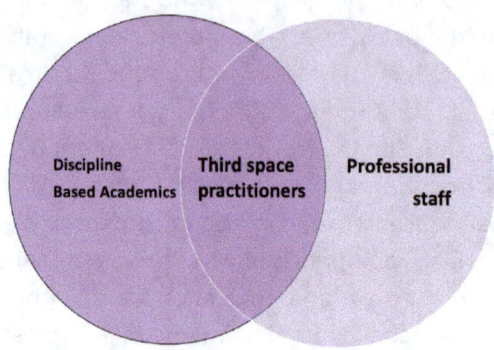

Figure 1: Space occupied by third space practitioners in higher education institutions.

Third space professionals

Third space professionals are non-academic staff who come under the umbrella of third space practitioners. They might be educational technologists, or librarians, or school administrative staff who create or assist with the creation of teaching and learning materials to support teaching staff. These are often professional roles such as Educational Developer, Learning Designer, Instructional Designer, Educational Technologist, among others. Third space professionals have a varied educational background; many do have postgraduate qualifications, sometimes related to the discipline they work in. These roles are often categorised by Higher Education Worker (HEW) levels in Australia. They are non-teaching roles. They do provide capacity building or professional learning to teaching staff members, but not because they have a teaching component attached to their roles.

Third space academics

> *One or more interactive elements has been excluded from this version of the text. You can view them online here: https://oercollective.caul.edu.au/designing-learning-experiences/?p=65*

Video transcript

> I recall an incident when an academic whom I had not worked with in the faculty met me as I was making my cup of tea in the shared kitchen. She asked: 'What is it you do?' I replied happily: 'Oh, I help support academics in the faculty with their teaching and learning practices and material, I co-design their teaching and learning cloud site and I also help to review their assessment and rubrics, and I build academics' capacity to transition smoothly into the blended teaching space.' Her response shocked me: 'Oh, I see … I am a real academic, unlike you. I teach students in class, we have to teach several units, and we have a research load that we have to do. It's hard work. Very busy.'

> I stood there looking at her blankly. I sort of missed most of the words after she said 'real academic'. My thoughts were along the lines of: How am I not a real academic? Why am I not a real academic? I have a PhD. I teach. I work on several units. I write learning objectives, I care about students and their learning experience. I care about all the things she cares about. I have a research load and I am so busy too! How am I not a real academic?
>
> Her reaction and response never left me and won't leave me as long as I am in this role.

According to Smith et al. (2021), third space academic is a term used to describe roles that are held by non-discipline academics who are not necessarily subject matter experts although they support a wide variety of teaching academics from all disciplines with curriculum development, assessment and rubric design, learning design, content management, project management, and people and time management, and they have a research component as part of their workload allocation model. These academics have migrated from other disciplines (Manathunga, 2007), transferring their prior identities and knowledge from their home discipline into teaching. Karen Dowd and David Kaplan have categorised academics into several groups; two that relate to third space practitioners would be Mavericks and Connectors, as they are both listed as being boundaryless (Dowd & Kaplan, 2005). Dowd and Kaplan describe Mavericks as academics who are independent and seemingly unconstrained by the structural limitations of the tenure-track nature of academia; and Connectors are academics who perceive their roles to go beyond the traditional boundaries of teacher and researcher. Within this conceptualisation, third space academics would sit in between the parameters of being Maverick and Connector in terms of academic career types. Their career trajectories in terms of what they teach and learn are boundaryless, but they are bound by academic requirements to publish. Academics in these roles also have postgraduate qualifications including PhDs that might or might not be related to the discipline in which they work. In some universities they are described as Academic Developers, Senior Educational Developers, Learning Design Developers, among others, and they have teaching, service and research components attached to their roles. Their pay is classified according to academic pay scales and they follow academic promotion pathways. Given that discipline-based academics view them as not being 'real academics' owing to the lack of industry knowledge about what exactly they do, third space academics often find it hard to have a sense of belonging to their professional identity and to the higher education landscape.

Polymathic nature of the third space practitioners' role

One or more interactive elements has been excluded from this version of the text. You can view them online here: https://oercollective.caul.edu.au/designing-learning-experiences/?p=65

Video transcript

> When I became a Lecturer, Learning Futures seven years ago, I struggled for the first four years when people asked me what my job was about. I would tell them that I am an academic in the faculty, but I don't lecture in any of the units and I work with academics more than students. They would give me a puzzled look. I would quickly add that I am in an academic role, and I have a PhD in another discipline although I help to support teaching and learning in a completely different discipline. Usually I would have lost them at 'I work with academics'. It was just too hard. No one understood the entirety of my role. So, I started to tell them I am a third space academic. Believe me, I didn't do any research about this term when I first started using it – it just seemed apt for my role because I knew that if I called myself a third space professional, then discipline-based academics and those who aren't familiar with that term would not take me seriously. But even now, people don't get what exactly I do. What in the world does third space academic mean to the lay person? You are either an academic or you're not! What is this blurred space that is attached to the role and identity?

Polymathic nature of the role

Similar to third space academics, the work that third space practitioners do can be categorised as unbounded. This distinguishes them from other professional staff (Whitchurch, 2008). Aranee Manoharan (2020) states that third space professionals are *polymathic* in their expertise. She argues that third space professionals are able to navigate multiple lifeworlds and disciplinary areas within a university. As such, they understand different professional motivations and are able to connect with a range of occupational dispositions. Polymathic (Manoharan, 2020) means to go beyond a singular specialisation and to function with multiple expertise. It is not a 'jack of all trades and master of none' proposition. On the contrary, third space practitioners, owing to the broad areas of teaching and learning projects that they work on, can have in-depth knowledge of more than one area of specialisation.

Table 1 shows the similarities and differences in role titles held by third space professionals and third space academics. However, there will be differences in work experience, understanding of position descriptions and expectations of the output for third space professionals and third space academics. Even within the same university, the roles of third space professionals and third space academics are not defined by a standard set of position descriptions and they often play a variety of roles within their capacity of supporting educational development. Hence, they are often expected to have a variety of skills, knowledge and practice about educational development, learning design, curriculum development and assessment and rubrics design. In the current higher education landscape, the lack of role clarity regarding the differences in expectations and functions may cause third space practitioners to become more liminal in terms of their understanding of their roles and their own professional identity.

Text-based version of Table 1

Table 1 titled Examples of different titles and roles held by third space practitioners. The table has three columns and nine rows

Table 1: Examples of different titles and roles held by third space practitioners.

Types of roles	Third space professionals	Third space academics
Learning Designer	Yes	Yes
Librarian	Yes	No
Educational Technologist	Yes	No
Instructional Designer	Yes	No
Academic Developer	Yes	Yes
Senior Educational Designer	Yes	Yes
Educational Consultant	Yes	Yes
Lecturer, Central Teaching Team	No	Yes

including the header row. Header row has 'types of roles', 'Third Space professionals' and 'Third Space Academics'. The first row contains the learning designer.

What are the skill sets necessary to become a third space practitioner?

 One or more interactive elements has been excluded from this version of the text. You can view them online here: https://oercollective.caul.edu.au/designing-learning-experiences/?p=65

Video transcript

> I was never trained to the job I am doing now. I picked up all the skills, all the good stuff about teaching and learning practices, over the last ten years as I worked my way across the realm of being a third space practitioner.
>
> In my current role, I am very much involved in the designing, developing and deciding side of teaching and learning practices. When I first started as an academic developer, I had no clue what an LMS was, what terms like pedagogy and andragogy meant; for that matter, I had no idea what a flipped classroom was. But I have been exposed to all of them as an academic. I just didn't know that what I was doing had names and theories attached to it.
>
> Now, I am a fully-fledged higher education academic strategist – well, here's an additional term to describe third space academics/practitioners like me, and I do call myself that in my LinkedIn profile description.

Heggart & Dickson-Deane (2022) present several skills for learning designers that are applicable to third space professionals. These skills include 'prioritisation of communication and collaboration skills; we need to be able to make adaptive decisions, we need to be able to work in teams'. Very often, third space practitioners are involved in projects which are of differing scales. They can be short-term or one-off projects such as learning transformation or implementing a new learning management system (LMS), or they can be ongoing projects within a faculty or school such as subject development and/or professional development. Given the various projects that third space practitioners manage, they also need to know project management. They need to know how to manage their workload ebbs and flows. These are skills that are not picked up in courses but are only developed during work placements. These are the skills that discipline academics might not necessarily have in their skill set, depending on their discipline, and that is what makes third space academics less 'academic' in their view.

Your task

If you identify as a third-space practitioner, reflect on a situation where you had to explain your role and consider whether the reaction aligned with your expectations. Visit the 'Navigating the tensions and challenges as Third-Space Practitioners' Padlet activity to share your thoughts.

Navigating the liminal space

Source: Photo by Kristjan Kotar on Unsplash

> *One or more interactive elements has been excluded from this version of the text. You can view them online here: https://oercollective.caul.edu.au/designing-learning-experiences/?p=65*

Video transcript

> I am not sure if you have noticed that for those of us who have been to interviews for any third space roles, one of the questions will focus on how well we can deal with difficult academics. Here they are referring to discipline-based academics. I can't see you, but I know that a few of you will be nodding. They have asked this question in all the interviews that I went for. And initially, I went home wondering, why are they asking about difficult academics? I am an academic and I don't think I would be difficult. But when I took my first few roles, and started working with discipline academics, difficult academics made up a good proportion of the people I have worked with. These academics are not difficult people, but because they don't understand my role, and they don't understand how as a non-subject matter expert I can help them, they simply become difficult because they don't want someone like me telling them how to teach their units.

Third space practitioners have been described as being in a liminal space within the higher education landscape as they work together with academics and professionals (Veles et al., 2019). Their roles are described as 'liminal, binary/overlap or borderless' (Veles et al., 2019, p. 77). Although Bhabha (1994) uses the term 'liminal space' to describe the feeling of dislocation experienced by both slave and master – the coloured and the white – purely in the context of post-colonial national identity, this idea of being in a dislocated space applies quite well to the liminal space occupied by third space practitioners in the higher education landscape.

According to Bhabha (1994), a liminal space is the space occupied in the stairways where it is neither at the top nor at the bottom. Third space practitioners are entrapped by their liminal space of not being a discipline-based expert when they work across various faculties and schools. They are often perceived to be 'lesser' than discipline-based academics, and university professional staff members and fail to see the value of their expertise in the area of teaching and learning. This is because they do not get the validation they deserve when they engage in their area of expertise. It can also be argued that discipline-based academics and professional staff members feel a sense of surprise, and discomfort at times, to find that their expertise and knowledge of subject matter content can be further enhanced when they are supported by third space practitioners to provide better teaching and learning experiences for both academics and students. Hence, these three sectors that currently exist in the higher education workforce often find that it is never easy to work cohesively. These different spheres 'then behave in accordance with a neurotic orientation creating the challenges and tensions in the way they work together' (Bhabha, 1984).

> *Your task*
>
> Using the Padlet activity 'Navigating the tensions and challenges as Third Space Practitioners', share some of your thoughts and experiences of the challenges you have faced as a third space practitioner.

Expectations and assumptions

> *One or more interactive elements has been excluded from this version of the text. You can view them online here: https://oercollective.caul.edu.au/designing-learning-experiences/?p=65*

Video transcript

> Just before the 2020 pandemic, two of my third space practitioner colleagues and I started autoethnographic research about assumptions pertaining to the role that we held and how that had an impact on the work that we did in the third

space. This research has been accepted for print in the form of a journal article and we are working on the paper now. What brought about this research was the fact that we realised we are not always talking about the same thing when we talk about templates, or unit build, or terms like chunking or curriculum development. One of my colleagues came from a teaching background and the other came from an information systems background, and I am from a cultural studies and theatre studies background. Our exposure to learning design work has been varied.

I have worked on several learning management systems, but it is not my forte. I like working on curriculum development and that too from a holistic point of view. I love conducting high-level mapping meetings and doing audits to facilitate whole-of-course approaches. My colleagues in the research team like to work on assessment design and improving the learning design on the learning management system. And we realised that we all thought of different things during team meetings even as we nodded away to indicate our understanding of who was going to do what and so on. All of us had the assumption that we were working from the same page at the same level. But when we came together, we were unpleasantly surprised to discover that we had misunderstood our understanding of common terms such as templates, or unit content, or constructive

> alignment for that matter. We started to see that we had gaps in our understanding of what we were meant to do owing to this assumption that we all did the same thing in a very similar manner. That led to us having frank conversations about what we actually thought we knew about each other's work and what we thought discipline academics thought of our work. This started a great research project which is hopefully going to come to fruition very soon.

Much of the tensions and challenges experienced by third space practitioners occur because of the boundless nature of their roles. The fact that they do not sit within an easily recognised function in the higher education landscape creates a lack of a sense of belonging. This lack of a sense of belonging and displaced boundaries cause constant challenges to navigate in terms of understanding who they are in the workplace, the impact of their role and the work they do, thereby affecting their professional identity.

There are two sides to this notion of assumptions causing the lack of a sense of belonging and adding to the tensions and challenges of being a third space practitioner. One is the assumptions that other colleagues, both discipline-based academics and professional staff, make about the roles of third space practitioners. For example, we have established that discipline-based academics are not always receptive to ideas about teaching and learning advice or support given by third space practitioners. This could be due to a lack of knowledge about the roles third space practitioners perform and/or just an aversion to ideas suggested by people outside the sphere of their professional/industry knowledge. Their expectation of third space practitioners is someone who is technologically savvy; someone who will upload their teaching content into the learning management system and set up their assessment submission pages and discussion areas. This is the type of administrative support teaching academics need to make their work easier. They do not perceive third space practitioners to be a support to aspects relating to teaching and learning pedagogies, strategies and frameworks.

The other assumption that causes tensions and challenges is the perception held by third space practitioners about other third space practitioners' skills and knowledge. As stated by Manathunga (2007) and Manoharan (2020), we come from different roles outside the discipline we work in, and we are not all trained in the same way. However, owing to similar titles and roles, it is easy for third space practitioners to assume that there will be similarities in work style, management of time, meeting delivery timelines and so on. However, in many cases, there will be instances where learning designers join a team of third space practitioners with varied skill sets and experiences but are expected to work like the rest of the team. These unspoken expectations and assumptions can be the cause of much tension and misunderstanding among third space practitioners themselves, and also strengthen misconceptions held by discipline-based staff members about the work third space practitioners do.

Assumptions of third space practitioners regarding their role is a great contributing factor to internal tension and confusion. Many a time, for the third space practitioner, be they learning designers or educational developers or third space academics, it is imperative that their voice is heard during learning design or the scoping of teaching and learning projects. They assume that their voice will be taken seriously. However, in many real-life scenarios, this assumption is not met by people they work with. Discipline-based academics can hold preconceived ideas about how they will be working on a project. They often want their voice to be registered as a teaching and learning specialist or expert. For example, they may know ways to enhance engagement of students and motivate self-regulated learning.

Case study

Andrew is a subject matter expert in the School of Business. He attends the first scoping meeting with the learning design team in his faculty. At the meeting, Sarah, who is a learning designer, asks him about the support that he needs from the learning design team. Andrew replies that he wants Sarah to make the PowerPoint slides look nicer. Sarah asks him what he means by 'nicer'. Andrew replies that he inherited his teaching slides and that they are just too fancy, there are bits about the way the content appears that he doesn't understand, and that he wants them to look less boring. Sarah takes notes that he wants transitions removed, information on slide to be updated and icons and graphics to be reviewed. Sarah asks if he has had time to review the content within the slides and if he wants to move some of the content in his deck of 71 slides per week to the LMS, for example. Andrew stares blankly and states that he has not been given time to

> review the slides or the content. All he wants are presentable teaching materials.
>
> As a learning designer, what sort of support and advice can Sarah provide to Andrew? Use the Padlet activity 'Navigating the tensions and challenges as Third Space Practitioners', to share your thoughts.

Role clarity of third space practitioners

Many institutions are still not clear about the role third space practitioners play. For example, many third space practitioners will have similar job titles across the university but do very different work depending on a few factors such as:

- who they work with
- which faculty they work with
- their existing workload
- the team they are part of, whether they are with a central team or within a faculty, and last but not least
- which project they are part of.

It can be really frustrating to see this sort of disparity and to be able to do nothing about it as some of these factors are beyond the control of the third space practitioners.

For some third space practitioners, the lack of role clarity can cause tensions. There will be this constant battle about how much of the work they must do and where they draw a line before they have stepped into the work area of either a professional or an academic. For example, academics may only expect learning designers to add a few visual elements to their teaching content without having to go into detail about the purpose of adding the elements. They may not have considered the cognitive load or universal learning design aspects of being inclusive and presenting accessible materials. And there will be a few academics who are not keen to involve third space practitioners in the design or development of assessment, simply because they do not view them as being subject matter experts. These barriers cause tensions in the work third space practitioners do. One way to navigate this sense of frustration is to understand what is causing some of these tensions.

The third space professional and third space academic divide

> One or more interactive elements has been excluded from this version of the text. You can view them online here: https://oercollective.caul.edu.au/designing-learning-experiences/?p=65

Video transcript

> I recall an instance where I was working in a team of four third space practitioners: two third space academics and two third space professionals. We had had several discussions among ourselves about

our roles. Apart from the contribution made by third space academics to research, there were no clear indicators as to what distinguished the role of the third space academics from that of the professionals. As a third space academic, I often lead in unit redevelopment projects and take on the role of academic lead. The expectation is that I manage the project in terms of timelines, academic correspondence, meetings, content delivery, liaising with a third party for multimedia creation and delivery, and overall quality assurance of the project. However, in my absence, the third space professionals who do the learning design part of the work in the project can also do all these functions.

Given that we worked on several projects at a time, we sometimes crossed over into the territory of one another, and sometimes I had to work on developing content into the learning management system as well. So, the boundaries were blurred. And that led to many frank conversations as to what the value-add of our presence would be for each project. I looked across other faculties and central teams within the university for some form of role clarity regarding third space academics and I realised that the role can never be the same for all. The way we work on projects really depends on the project, the discipline, the timing, and the intended outcome of the project. Not one learning and teaching team functioned the same way across the university. And this lack of clarity in the role can cause a lot of

> internal and external tensions for all third space practitioners involved. I have at many times wondered why my colleagues in other faculties had more academic freedom or why they had more university-wide exposure to projects. I haven't found the answers.

The role clarity and the recognition of third space practitioners must come from the institution for a start. When the higher education institution makes the objectives and role clarity associated with third space practitioners clear to the university, for both academic and professional roles, it becomes easier to navigate the tensions and challenges that exist in these roles. In certain universities, teaching teams comprise discipline-based academics and third space practitioners. In that case, it is clear who does what and who oversees what and they work towards a common goal of delivering purposeful teaching and learning practices.

Conclusion

> *One or more interactive elements has been excluded from this version of the text. You can view them online here: https://oercollective.caul.edu.au/designing-learning-experiences/?p=65*

Video transcript

> I have often been asked if I would move out of being a third space academic. I am not sure, to be frank. There are always times that make me want to leave this role and go to a more research-focused role. In that way, I can get papers published and at least see a promotion in my lifetime as an academic. However, the team in which I work is really good. I have developed lots of good relationships in the faculties that I have worked in, and I can learn constantly in this role. There is always something I pick up in terms of tech expertise, or teaching and learning practice, or a current innovative assessment project and so on. And I have learnt to navigate my tensions and challenges. I am still navigating them, but I think I have learnt to accept my role's limitations and growth. So the short answer to the question is that I really don't know.

The aim of this chapter was to highlight that the role of third space practitioners – both academics and professionals – is not an easy ride, just like other roles in the higher education landscape. There are many factors contributing to the displacement that practitioners in the third space might experience and endure. However, not all is gloom and doom. Understanding that this role is in a liminal space, and that it will take time for perceptions, assumptions and role clarities to be worked out, will make working in this role a very rewarding experience and possibly create a much-needed sense of belonging.

Takeaway activity

Position description for Learning Designer in higher education

About the role

Join our Teaching and Learning Innovation team to transform education through digital assessment innovation! Shape modern pedagogy and assessments across the University. Leverage your pedagogical insights and learning design background to lead the transformation of assessment practices. Be a driving force in shaping the future of learning!

Your responsibilities will include:

– providing expertise on assessment improvements. Collaborating with staff to create evidence-based, engaging assessments that enhance student learning.

– advising on assessment design process, including iterative templates and learning modules.

– collaborating with the digital exams team, advising on assessment and exam design with teaching staff.

– creating and maintaining support resources, workshops, and training for implementing assessment solutions. Developing digital assessment expertise University wide.

Who we are looking for:

Seeking an organised, detail-focused learning designer with a strong work ethic, openness to innovation, and adept problem-solving in tight schedules. Utilise exceptional stakeholder management and interpersonal skills to collaborate with diverse stakeholders for successful outcomes. Flourish in team settings, offering guidance amidst dynamic priorities.

You will also have:

Postgraduate qualification with relevant experience or an equivalent combination of relevant experience and/or education/training.

Proven expertise in applying education theories, design principles, and modern assessment techniques to create exceptional learning experiences and activities.

Skilled in translating stakeholder needs into educational resources using enterprise technologies like LMS, ensuring an optimal student experience, seamless journey, and accessibility considerations.

Proven track record in creating online or in-person professional development, guiding the use of digital technologies, assessments, and learning design within subjects.

Example of a job advertisement that was once advertised on Seek.com in 2023

Position description for a Lecturer role in

Teaching and Learning

Support and provide advice to academic staff on teaching and learning matters across the University by applying an evidence-based approach. Contribute to enhancing the quality of student learning experiences and outcomes. Provide specialist hands-on support for curriculum and learning design, produce teaching and learning resources, and work with teaching teams to improve teaching practice. Contribute to the planning, development, implementation and evaluation of programs and initiatives enabling innovation and excellence in educational practices.

Responsibilities

Education and employability

- Provide advice, support, academic leadership, and capability building in all aspects of teaching and learning in higher education, particularly in learning design and assessment.
- Apply an evidence-based approach to support and advise academics to enhance the quality of student learning experiences and outcomes.
- Work positively and effectively with Faculty colleagues and Deakin Learning Futures team members to support unit and course enhancement across the University.
- Develop and maintain an in-depth understanding

of educational issues, educational methodologies and technology issues facing higher education and work with Faculty staff to develop tailored educational design solutions accordingly.
- Research, publish and present individually, or in collaboration with peers at conferences and through scholarly publication.

Selection

Qualifications and experience

- PhD in a relevant discipline and/or other relevant qualifications and experience
- Evidence of excellence in contribution to innovative teaching at undergraduate and/or postgraduate levels, in online, campus based and blended learning environments.
- Emerging reputation in research and scholarship through publications and/or exhibitions and/or success in obtaining external research funding.
- Evidence of experience in providing effective and practical support and advice to academics in relation to matters pertaining to enhancing learning, teaching and assessment.
- Evidence of ability to establish and maintain effective and collaborative working relationships with students and colleagues.
- Excellent interpersonal skills and a proven ability to undertake capability building in a collaborative and consultative manner.

Example of a Lecturer, Learning Futures Position Description – Deakin University, 2021

Your task

The first sample is a job advertisement for a third space professional. The second sample is a position description for a third space academic. Identify the areas in which these jobs in the higher education landscape intersect in terms of similar responsibilities. What are the key differences? Use the Padlet activity 'Navigating the tensions and challenges as Third Space Practitioners', to share your thoughts.

References

Bhabha, H. (1984). Of mimicry and man: The ambivalence of colonial discourse. *October*, *28*, 125-133. https://doi.org/10.2307/778467

Bhabha, H. K. (1994). *The location of culture*. Routledge.

Boyer, E. L. (1990). *Scholarship reconsidered: Priorities of the professoriate* (ED326149). ERIC. https://eric.ed.gov/?id=ed326149

Dowd, K. O., & Kaplan, D. M. (2005). The career life of academics: Boundaried or boundaryless? *Human Relations*, *58*(6), 699.

Heggart, K., & Dickson-Deane, C. (2022). What should learning designers learn? *Journal of Computing in Higher Education*, *34*(2), 281-296. https://doi.org/https://doi.org/10.1007/s12528-021-09286-y

Manathunga, C. (2007). "Unhomely" academic developer identities: More post-colonial explorations. *International Journal for Academic Development*, *12*(1), 25-34. https//doi:10.1080/13601440701217287

Manoharan, A. (2020). Creating connections: Polymathy and the value of third space professionals in higher education. *Perspectives: Policy and Practice in Higher Education*, *24*(2), 56-59. https://doi.org/10.1080/13603108.2019.1698475

Smith, C., Holden, M., Yu, E., & Hanlon, P. (2021). 'So what do you do?': Third space professionals navigating a Canadian university context. *Journal of Higher Education Policy & Management*, *43*(5), 505-519. https://doi.org/10.1080/1360080X.2021.1884513

Veles, N., Carter, M.-A., & Boon, H. (2019). Complex collaboration champions: University third space professionals working together across borders. *Perspectives: Policy and Practice in Higher Education*, *23*(2-3), 75-85. https://doi.org/10.1080/13603108.2018.1428694

Whitchurch, C. (2008). Shifting identities and blurring boundaries: The emergence of third space professionals in UK higher education. *Higher Education Quarterly*, *62*(4), 377-396. https://doi.org/10.1111/j.1468-2273.2008.00387.x

About the author

Dr Puvaneswari P Arumugam
DEAKIN UNIVERSITY
https://www.deakin.edu.au/

Puvaneswari P Arumugam (Puva) is a Lecturer in Learning Futures at Deakin University's Faculty of Business and Law. Her research focuses on third space academics and digital literacy. A Senior Fellow of the Higher Education Academy, Puva leads the academic development of programmatic course redevelopment and contributes to several university-wide projects. She has been a mentor at ASCILITE and serves on the HERDSA Victoria Branch Executive Committee. Puva co-published a book on the cultural identity of an Indian minority group in Singapore and has presented and published extensively, including in ASCILITE's Horizon Report 2022.

5. Indigenous-led learning design: Reimagining the teaching team

KATRINA THORPE; SHAUN BELL; AND SUSAN PAGE

Introduction

University graduates' capacity to work effectively with Indigenous Australians to enhance equity has been a growing concern for more than two decades. In that time, a variety of reports have argued that university graduates can contribute to improved outcomes for Indigenous Australians but that requires the development of specific skills and knowledges to enable them to work effectively with Indigenous Australians (Behrendt et al., 2012; Bradley et al., 2008; Indigenous Higher Education Advisory Council, 2006; Universities Australia, 2011). There are similarities with universities in other colonised nations – for example, Canada (Battiste & Findlay, 2002), New Zealand (Jones, 2009) and Bolivia (Drange, 2011) – where inequity remains of concern. Concurrently, there has also been a growing need for staff to engage with Indigenous Knowledges and to develop cultural capability (Universities Australia, 2017). However, few universities in Australia have ready-made professional development resources to ensure that academic staff are prepared to teach, supervise Indigenous research or develop relevant curriculum.

In the absence of such professional development resources, in

2019, a team of scholars from the Centre for the Advancement of Indigenous Knowledges (CAIK) at the University of Technology (UTS), set out to develop a suite of microcredentials to address this significant gap. The suite of microcredentials consisted of three, 3 credit point online courses. Recognising that the learner group would be scholars from our own and other Australian universities, the CAIK team aimed to develop innovative offerings that allowed learners to progress independently and at their own pace. In this chapter we outline our approach to developing the first microcredential, *Supervising Indigenous Higher Degree Research*, through an innovative collaboration between a group of discipline experts working with a group of learning designers and media specialists.

The CAIK is an Aboriginal-led centre focused on teaching and research in Indigenous Studies. The curriculum development project reflected the motivations of the CAIK scholars, including the need to grow Indigenous student participation in higher degree research (Moreton-Robinson et al., 2020). The project was also supported through an institutional Postgraduate Strategic Funding Program grant, reflecting the university's commitment to a national policy focused on technological advancement through retraining and upskilling of the workforce (Productivity Commission, 2017) and a global pressure to digitise teaching (Weitze, 2015). *Supervising Indigenous Higher Degree Research* curates a program that is relevant to the academic workforce, draws on the CAIK staff research strengths and contributes to social change through supporting excellence in Indigenous education.

The grant provided a modest amount of funding which facilitated the employment of an Indigenous project manager, but critically, provided access to a team of learning designers to work with the CAIK scholars on the design and development of the course. Vital to the successful development of *Supervising*

Indigenous Higher Degree Research, was the collaborative effort of the CAIK's discipline experts and the instructional design team. The learning design team supported the innovation the CAIK staff were so keen to embrace, by ensuring that the 'content' knowledge was presented in interesting and engaging ways, and the design of the online learning was conducive to student learning.

Through a reflective process, we found the success of our collaboration hinged on three key factors: trust, iterative discussion, and the combined skills of scholars and learning designers. Through this collaborative process we have reimagined the composition of a teaching team, beyond the traditional academic model. In the next section we provide a brief contextual background to Indigenous research supervision and showcase examples from the microcredential to illustrate the vital roles of each team member, illuminating the creative synergy which propelled the teaching development and inspired learning well beyond the curriculum content.

Context

Indigenous research supervision context: Supporting Indigenous higher degree research

In Australia, Indigenous research has rapidly grown into a prominently scholarly field (Moreton-Robinson, 2013; Nakata, 2007; Rigney, 1999) and internationally (Brayboy & Chin, 2018; Smith, 2012) and includes methodological, methods and ethical dimensions. There is also a growing literature related to the supervision of Indigenous research and Indigenous higher degree research (HDR) students (Barney, 2013; Moodie et al., 2018; Trudgett et al., 2016). Growing from concerns about the exploitation of Indigenous peoples and communities in research (Smith, 2012), along with sector wide concern about the intertwined problem of needing to grow the Indigenous researcher population and the lack of Indigenous supervisors or non-Indigenous supervisors of Indigenous HDR students, with the capability to supervise or undertake ethical Indigenous research (Hutchings et al., 2019), there have been increasing calls for professional development for staff (Australian Council of Learned Academies [ACOLA], 2016; Behrendt, 2012; Trudgett, 2014). Many scholars in Australian universities have limited knowledge of Indigenous research, having not engaged with Indigenous Studies as part of their own disciplinary education. Other scholars have come to Australia more recently from overseas and do not have the disciplinary, cultural or social knowledge to work effectively and ethically in this field. Developing the professional capability of non-Indigenous students and supervisors of higher degree research to 'work with and for Indigenous peoples' was therefore a significant ethical driver for curriculum development in this area.

The CAIK team previously delivered workshops on supervising Indigenous HDR candidates for university staff. The workshops included content such as Indigenous research methodologies and ethics, as well as best practice in supervising Indigenous graduate students and Indigenous research. We began the development of the subject imagining that we would develop our existing materials into a more efficient and potentially widely available offering.

The microcredential: Supervising Indigenous Higher Degree Research

Supervising Indigenous Higher Degree Research is a fully online asynchronous subject that runs over six weeks. It was first offered in December 2020 and in 2023 was in its sixth offering. To date, it has attracted 230 learners from 18 universities across Australia. In the first cohort, learners were primarily academics working in the humanities, social sciences and health sciences with a few from the information technology disciplines. Since this time, we have been pleased to witness academics enrolled from the full diversity of disciplines represented in Australian universities. It has been exciting to see writers, plant scientists, mechatronics engineers, architects, musicologists, astrophysicists and a gastronomy historian (to name a few) share knowledge and experience throughout the course. A number of learners recently moved to Australia for research and teaching positions and were interested in engaging with Indigenous communities but felt that Indigenous peoples and research were invisible within their workplaces. The wide interest has been particularly encouraging at a time when university funds were generally limited at the end of a few challenging years due to the COVID-19 pandemic.

We sought feedback early, frequently and often from our learners during the initial development of the microcredential, and continued this practice through subsequent course offerings, making adjustments in areas such as assessment based on learner feedback. What is most heartening is the way in which our learners have come to embrace the approaches described and modelled in the subject.

Dr Elizabeth Humphrys, one of our early learners who was

interested in both supervising and Indigenous teaching and learning, shared the following:

We have growing numbers of Indigenous students at my university and in my School, so I completed the course to be better prepared if I was asked to contribute to the supervision panel of an Indigenous student in the future. The course was incredibly useful in terms of the content, and one of the best organised and designed training courses I've done. Despite having done methods subjects at postgraduate level, many of the ideas in the course – in particular around quantitative Indigenous methodologies – were new to me. The most significant outcomes to date have been on my undergraduate teaching and in assisting a non-Indigenous HDR student.

The course also inspired Elizabeth's own practice:

The section of the course on Indigenous quantitative methodologies led me to enhance the 'data lab' weeks in our subject Global Economies, where we introduce students to the basics of locating, using and analysing statistics. Last year I developed an extra topic for students on responsible use of data using some of the ideas from the microcredential (with acknowledgment to CAIK), and Maggie Walter and Michele Suina's 2019 paper 'Indigenous data, indigenous methodologies and indigenous data sovereignty'. Students also read about 5D data and the CARE Principles for Indigenous Data Governance. This year I introduced an additional tutorial case study on Indigenous employment, where students use a 5D lens to explore data gathering possibility and policy options.

Elizabeth further explains how her learning impacted on her supervisory practice:

> *The course was also useful in assisting one of my HDR students to plan their research methodology and apply*

for ethics approval. Their study on climate justice movements in part involves interviews with Indigenous activists. While this student's co-supervisor works in Jumbunna, as a wholly non-Indigenous team I felt the course provided a better framework than I'd had previously for this supervision. The course assisted me in advising him on research design, the CARE principles, and needing to work with relevant Indigenous people during the design of the methodology and prior to submitting the ethics application.

Overall, the course was really thought provoking, and I have returned to my notes from it several times over the last couple of years.

Dr Elizabeth Humphrys, Social and Political Sciences, School of Communication, University of Technology Sydney.

The curriculum and learning design team

The course design team included the Director at that time, CAIK academic staff, a learning designer, other learning design professional staff, their senior supervisor, and was further supported by educational media technologists and producers. We also had significant contributions from many of the CAIK doctoral students. What is potentially unusual or unique about this project was how the combined academic subject matter expert team and core members of the learning design team met frequently at regular intervals over the course of more than 12 months, and how we created a relationship and workflow that generated a high degree of mutual understanding and collegial respect.

The three discipline experts and the project officer working on the project were all Aboriginal. All had expertise and experience in Indigenous Studies and Indigenous research. The Aboriginal members of the team had been working together for some time and were familiar with one another's strengths and approaches to disciplinary theory. There were three staff members on the learning design team: a Senior Learning Designer, a Learning Designer and a Learning Technologist, all of whom were non-Indigenous. While the learning design team were experts in learning design, they had less experience in Indigenous education. The authors of this chapter include two of the academic collaborators (Thorpe and Page) and the Learning Designer (Bell) who worked most closely on the curriculum design project. As the project developed, it became clear that for both the academics and learning designers this was 'uncharted ground'. This was the first time the academic staff had experienced such intensive learning design support in the development of teaching materials. The academics had no idea of the learner engagement that was possible in the online learning environment and the potential for this mode of delivery in developing a community of learners. The learning design collaborators had varied experience in Indigenous education and the Indigenous protocols that the academics almost reflexively brought to the project.

While the academic team had experience writing content for subjects using the Canvas Learning Management System (LMS), this was mainly for 'flipped classroom' learning where students engage in preparatory activities such as watching a pre-recorded lecture or engaging in set readings ready to come to class to participate in deeper discussion and structured in-class activities to enhance and consolidate learning. In designing for this microcredential, we were working towards an exciting and engaging, asynchronous, fully online learning experience, with optional 'live and online' Zoom seminars to supplement the learning in Canvas. The examples shared below show how the team approach led to far more ambitious outcomes.

We (the authors) analysed the conversational modes, communicative practices, and analogue and digital workflows that constituted the main forms of our team's engagement over the course of the subject co-design in the context of scholarship of theories and practices that support quality online learning design. At the time of our co-design engagement, our learning designers were supported by research-based practices and guidelines through the UTS Model of Learning (University of Technology Sydney, 2019) that worked to maximise the presence of learning experiences that are authentic, aligned, active and social. These guidelines provided a strong foundation; however, anyone working with Indigenous Cultural and Intellectual Property (Janke, 2021) acknowledges that there are significant complexities in the design of quality online learning (Phren et al., 2020) in relation to Aboriginal and Torres Strait Islander cultures, peoples, knowledges and histories. Some of our team of designers had prior experience in this domain at other institutions and had some understanding and training of practices and approaches that can better support such projects. As our further discussion highlights, such understanding or adherence to available protocol guidelines does not replicate authentic, consistent and sustained collaboration between diverse members (or stakeholders) of the academic and professional staff on the project, or the specific experience and knowledge of an Indigenous-led unit. Our reflection identified a number of practices we undertook that we argue contributed significantly to our success, including a 'flat' team structure, common team understandings and understanding of wider university structures. A 'structural' or organisational approach within the co-design team meetings that was arguably 'flat', enabled the sharing by multiple voices and experiences.

Flattening the hierarchy

This lack of hierarchy within the group led to sustained synchronous and asynchronous feedback discussions relating to learner experience, content design and presentation, as well as issues surrounding 'modality', tone and voice. These collaborative discussions were enabled by strong rapport with honest, deliberate, and kind interactions between team members. In addition, all the people who worked on the project felt a strong sense of personal and professional learning through this multiskilled and multidisciplinary engagement and academic and professional staff collaboration (Cheek, 2021; Osguthorpe, 2007). While our course design team were not aware of this at the time, the work by scholars like Osguthorpe and colleagues (2018) articulates an ethical or moral imperative in learning design, with models that enable transformative learning at all levels.

Seeking permissions and protocols

A 'common point of understanding' among core team members were the additional requirements around seeking permission for materials used in the module, respecting cultural and intellectual authority and ownership (Janke, 2021). Some non-Indigenous team members had some specific training and experience and understood concepts like Indigenous Cultural and Intellectual Property rights, and they worked with their non-Indigenous colleagues to understand the 'stakes' by exploring resources available through reputable protocol documents, (Australia Council for the Arts, 2019), but they could not rely on this knowledge in place of deliberate discussion with co-design partners. This checking by the non-Indigenous team members even where they had existing knowledge is a practical demonstration of cultural humility (Burgess et al., 2022; Cox & Simpson, 2020) that aims to 'develop and maintain respectful processes and relationships based on mutual trust' (p. 2). Non-Indigenous people acting like experts in Indigenous matters can often be abrasive for Indigenous colleagues, so 'checking in' is one of the elements contributing to the development of trust.

Rapport and reciprocity

It is well recognised in the literature that relationship building, rapport and reciprocity are important when working and researching with Aboriginal communities and this can take time (Australian Institute of Aboriginal and Torres Strait Islander Studies, 2020; NSW Department of Community Services, 2009). Indeed, taking time and providing the appropriate resources are essential to ensuring successful outcomes; however, one of the common criticisms is that universities do not adequately accommodate this vital work (Smith et al., 2017). The broader university environment recognised our project's unique status as an Indigenous-led project with a goal to exemplify best practice in respectful use of Indigenous cultural and intellectual property. There was a clear recognition that this approach necessitated different and specific ways of working, including a higher degree of consultation and collaboration with stakeholders including students, artists, external academics and other experts. Supportive management within faculty and the learning design unit, including learning design supervisors who were across issues related to ownership, copyright and permissions, provided support within the project to allow for practical issues like long lead-times to commence discussions with experts and figures external to the university. As we discuss below, we had support to engage media producers and design experts who actively changed their processes to ensure our efforts to enhance the presentation of content and create interactive multimedia were respectful of issues related to cultural sensitivity and appropriateness.

Enacting the curriculum development collaboration

We have discussed the way in which our team structure and institutional context might have contributed to, or enabled, a co-design partnership that has produced a quality online learning experience with an enduring impact on learners. What enabled this in practice was how institutional supports, moral/ethical investment in the work, specific experience and expertise, and interpersonal and individual capacity building all came together in the specific design of explicit 'learning moments' or objects within the Canvas LMS (see Figures 1 and 2 below). Our workflow built on existing co-design models and learning approaches within UTS and more broadly, and capitalised on a shared understanding of other common academic production workflows, but was most significantly enhanced by a 'dialogic model' exemplified by the CAIK academic team – a kind of open, collaborative, deliberative conscious discussion – as well as specific design knowledges of core team members. In practice, this often meant an 'all in' approach to the collaborative authoring and design of pages, as we've outlined.

The examples below are from one of the pages within Module 2 (related to Indigenous research ethics) of the Canvas LMS subject that helps highlight three important things we learnt during this project, which are: (1) the importance of trust; (2) the value of conversation and iteration; and (3) the strength of a multidisciplinary team.

The importance of trust

The two figures below show how one page developed over time. In Canvas, you can create pages through a combination of rich-text and HTML formatting. The intuitive nature of the platform meant that the learning design team invited our academic partners to draft directly on the Canvas page, fostering opportunities for the academic staff to learn and develop digital skills in a supported environment (Huizinga et al., 2014). Through this process, the team built the trust that became a critical feature of the course development and which is so important for success in collaborative relationships (Bond-Barnard et al., 2018; Buanduchi, 2013). One of the useful features of Canvas is that it is very hard to 'break' something, and it has robust versioning abilities which means it is also hard to lose your work. The CAIK team took to Canvas with gusto, but that does not mean it was always easy-going. Figure 1 shows where we started in July of 2020, while Figure 2 shows a 'final version' of the page finalised in November. We authored this page through 20 iterations of distinct edits, involving in-page design, and many hours of online video discussion between learning designers and academics as changes were made to this single page.

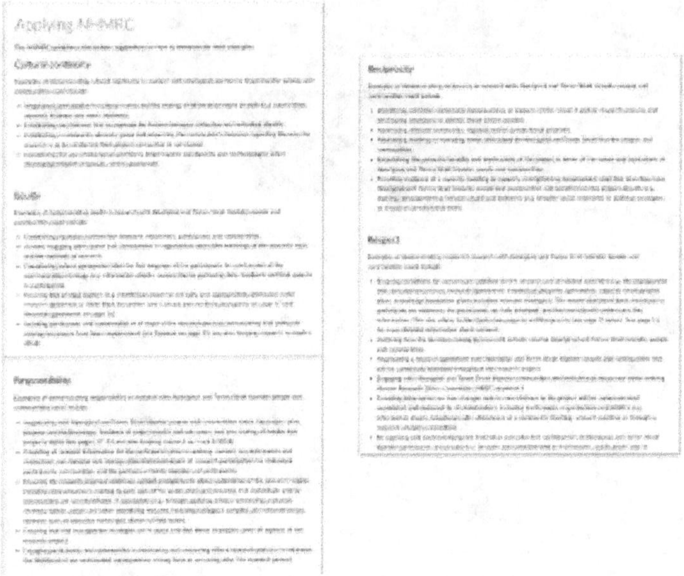
Applying NHMRC

Figure 1. 'NHMRC page: Before'. Source: National Health and Medical Research Council (representing the Commonwealth of Australia). Used with permission. All rights reserved by NHMRC.

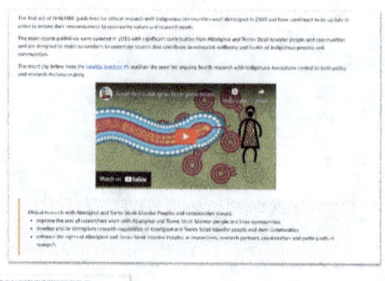
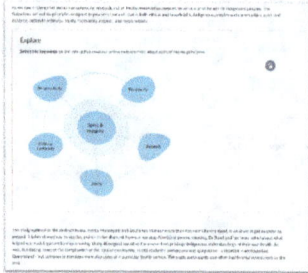
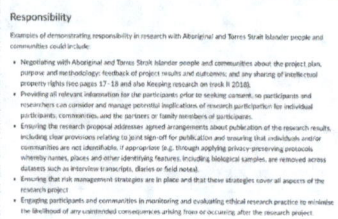

Figure 2. 'NHMRC page: After'. Based on material provided by the National Health and Medical Research Council (representing the Commonwealth of Australia). Used with permission. All rights reserved by NHMRC.

We include this example for several reasons. Firstly, because the text from the *NHMRC Ethical conduct in research with Aboriginal and Torres Strait Islander Peoples and communities: Guidelines for researchers and stakeholders* covers fundamental knowledge for researchers and research supervisors working in health-related disciplines, and outlines ways of thinking about ethical research guidelines more broadly. Secondly, because we collectively found the development of this page content challenging as the material covered is important, but also somewhat 'dry' and policy-driven. The desire to move beyond the presentation of content to learner engagement led to the pedagogical choice to use a variety of media. The 'After' page includes a short video, interactive elements and a reflective task, as well as a link to the original document to ensure learners could locate the document for future reference. There is ample evidence to support the improvements in student efficacy through providing opportunities for learning across multiple media modalities (Wayan, 2020), and providing learning that includes a degree of meaningful interactivity, choice, and agency (Dailey-Herbert, 2018). Those engaged in design work can easily find helpful checklists and protocols to unpack the selection of meaningful technology-enhanced interactivity.

Every learning design project has its challenges. Occasionally, these arise from a disconnect between the academic and the learning designer and team because they may have a different vision for a specific resource, a page or whole subject! We found that the only way around this was to 'talk it out', and a strong working relationship might be one of the 'hidden ingredients' in a successful course design build (Mason & Lefrere, 2003).

The value of conversation and iteration

This leads, to the second point, which is the value of iteration through ongoing conversation. This 'teacher talk' has been identified as important to successful design collaborations (McKenney et al., 2016). In our case, this was via weekly meetings and an agreed mode of communication in the form of colour coded notes in the pages themselves – a bit like when you collaborate on a document. This workflow was arguably also very 'flat' in structure: no single team member's comments had any more or less prominence, and all comments were visible to the whole team. Everyone worked together on the pages, which resulted in a very clean and polished final presentation, but it also meant a sometimes-messy process of drafting.

We were able to work through the challenges related to the NHMRC and other pages as we'd already developed a strong and collaborative basis of trust because of our collective response to design challenge we faced earlier in the project.

Early in our design journey we found ourselves needing to down tools and talk through one such issue. Our team of multidisciplinary designers had collaborated on an interactive resource introducing learners to concepts of a 'Welcome' and 'Acknowledgment of Country', which we made using a common rich media authoring tool, using a standard production workflow. The design concept for the artefact was simple, comprising an engaging visual background with a clickable object that revealed text content set against an illustrated background depicting Australian flora – too easy, right?

We were relatively early in the co-design of this subject, and relationships between the CAIK team and the learning design team were still forming. To say our team of designers were keen to impress is an understatement – internally, we knew this project had the potential to garner attention from senior figures in other parts of our university, and our designers working across early phases of the project also had a degree of personal investment. We'd already had several conversations and had some material in draft form, but we'd yet to 'crack' the overarching shape of the microcredential subject.

This is fairly common when designing a new learning experience with a new group of co-designers, and as part of our design process, we aim to rapidly design, prototype and implement educational resources to 'get us into the drafting', with the goal of creating familiarity and comfort with the authoring tools and process, and then iterating and refining the materials once deployed. This workflow can sometimes be at odds with the 'durations' and timelines of the other kinds of work that make up the workloads of our main co-design partners, working academics: teaching and publishing.

In this example, the result of our different approaches led to the selection of a visual element – a design featuring a flower, the Gymea lily – that was not just inappropriate, but held important cultural meanings that the learning designers were unaware of – In this instance, we did not take the time to talk through the design, and we rushed into production, hoping to spur our new co-design partners into activity, without being conscious of how our design choice was playing out in discussions within the subject matter expert team.

What did this experience teach us?

- It is vital that learning designers work with their expert co-designers to understand the appropriateness of their learning design approach, especially when working with cultural content that carries a specific, sacred, or sensitive meaning.
- There is a wealth of protocol and guideline documents to support designers who are unsure of issues of process, or procedure. These resources will help, but trust and courtesy are arguably more important because protocols or guidelines cannot possibly provide the means to understand all situations, and should not be used in place of honest and direct conversation with co-designers. You cannot replace or replicate knowledge and mutual respect.
- It was not all bad news: this experience provided our academic co-designers their first real sense of the power of design and the 'wow' factor and wonder that well-designed interactive learning can create.

The value of the multidisciplinary team

including learning designers, teachers and academics

The importance of conversation leads to the third point: a strong multi-disciplinary team can make all the difference in the process of designing a good learning sequence. There is now a growing body of research that highlights how differing team structures and compositions can enable design through 'ill-structured' or poorly understood design problems and contexts (Ertmer, 2008; Pan & Thompson, 2009; White et al., 2021). There is also a growing interest in the affordances provided by 'third space' education professional staff who bring their own expertise, and share common understandings or motivations around work culture and goals with academic staff (White et al., 2021).

Our project had the typical issues of overworked dedicated academic staff managing multiple competing imperatives, on top of commencing right at the start of the COVID-19 pandemic and our university's rapid transition to fully online learning. We often met online over Zoom in between many other Zoom meetings. There was also a degree of experimentation and uncertainty around the scope and ambition for the subject. We worked online, at first on documents, and then in our LMS. Most importantly, though, we engaged in a kind of relationship of mutual teaching and learning. While our learning designers had some awareness of some of the issues and concepts our microcredential subject engages with, our academic co-design partners did need to spend time to educate our learning design team so they could understand enough to be able to effectively support our goal. At the same time, our academic team were relatively unfamiliar with the affordance, possibilities and limitations of the online learning environment. Our learning design team spent time engaging in forms of design thinking, prototyping and troubleshooting to create activities, design resources and engaging presentation of knowledge, as well as developing systems to enable the smooth delivery of the completed learning experience.

This dynamic resulted in meetings focused on content creation, alongside discussions on the best ways to present and deliver this content through digital and online learning techniques. The academic team would engage in theoretical discussions in an inclusive manner with the designers, inviting us into the discussion and even considering some of the points we raised deriving from our experience as learners of this knowledge. There are ample accounts of negative dynamics between academics and learning designers, often centred around authority, positionality and our different roles and drivers related to the creation of a learning experience or product (Tay et al., 2023). It is common for learning designers in Australian higher educational settings to be employed as professional staff, although many also have teaching or academic experience, or hold relevant qualifications.

In some instances, the specific experience of our learning designers is that they often must take on the unpleasant role of managing deadlines or chasing academic co-designers for their contributions – the worst outcome being when a co-design partnership is undermined or forestalled by disengaged or oppositional team members, potentially using their authority and position in a way that invalidates more junior and precarious team members (Tay et al., 2023).This was not the case in this project where mutual respect for different competencies, skills and knowledges created a collaborative and iterative workflow that enabled the production of highly engaging and well- authored learning sequences.

We can see this successful co-authoring in the final version of the NHMRC page introduced earlier. There are some good learning design elements on the page. For example, we present a 'choice' for learners by providing optional links to more information (e.g., to the NHMRC website); we also 'chunked' information in different formats like videos, and through the 'explore' interactive, which was made using a tool called genial.ly. There is also a 'scaffolding' activity that progressively moves students to a stronger understanding of the material through the 'read, consider, compare' activity using HTML layout, an H5P document tool and a Canvas social poll.

A specific example can be seen in Figure 3 below, also from the NHMRC page in Module 2. The creation of this image involved the whole team discussing issues related to content organisation, authenticity of imagery and design, and ease of access and Web Content Accessibility Guidelines (WCAG) standards. Everyone on the team brought a perspective, and the result is an inviting presentation of the content.

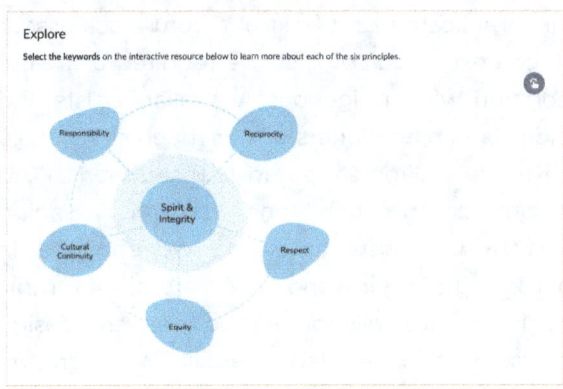

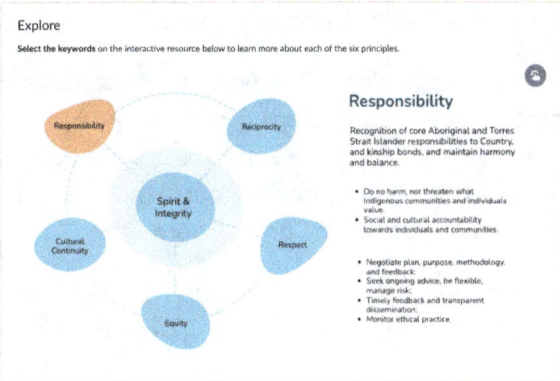

Figure 3. 'NHMRC interactive made using genial.ly'. *Based on material provided by the National Health and Medical Research Council (representing the Commonwealth of Australia). Used with permission. All rights reserved by NHMRC.*

In designing the interactive, our interactives expert found that the key was chunking the sections and deciding what knowledge was at the core of all the information in what is a very lengthy document. As for the visuals, we discussed how we already had a style guide for this specific suite of courses developed over many months, and it was important to use this consistently to keep the course site clean and matching the existing style. In our context at UTS, these style guides are typically 'uncomplicated' and built out from stock assets. In the specific context of our project, we required a greater deal of collaboration with Indigenous Australian artists and knowledge holders and practitioners, and as much as we could we engaged external collaborators and licensed works. This was not without complication, and required ongoing conversations with the artists to ensure we engaged in respectful repurposing of their work. In terms of the example in Figure 3, this interactive collaboration between the design team and the discipline experts led to excellent design and content – which learners found deeply engaging. Dr Natalie Morrison from Western Sydney University noted:

'This course has been exceptional. The flow, the materials and all the presentation aspects are second to none. I will have to rethink everything I do in my teaching practices – both to reflect what I am learning here by intent (course materials) but also that which is unintentional (the delivery format).'

Dr Natalie Morrison, Senior Lecturer, School of Medicine and the Translational Health Research Institute, Western Sydney University.

Conclusion

While there has been much discussion of the digital revolution, the scramble to switch to largely online learning in Australian schools and universities at the beginning of the COVID-19 pandemic would suggest, at the level of the classroom at least, that there has been less a revolution and more an intermittent evolution. The need for skills development is clear (Sousa & Rocha, 2019), but that development will require trust, ongoing dialogue and, vitally, access to multidisciplinary teams. Skills development for academic staff is important; however, there are specialist skills that for the sake of efficiency and effectiveness require learning designers to be integral parts of a teaching team. There is ample opportunity to increase efficiency and effectiveness through the exploration of different design models and team structures. As our experience has shown, combining academic and professional staff members, and encouraging the co-design of subjects and enabling their co-development with support through funding models, staffing resources and time, not only enabled the creation of a unique, highly regarded and successful fully online learning experience, it also generated significant capacity for individuals and institutions who are further supporting specifically Indigenous ways of learning and teaching across the sector. Such is the strength of this collaboration that we authors have come together to document the journey and outcome of this Aboriginal-led co-design process. Alongside this, we've seen substantial capacity and knowledge growth of online learning approaches and methodologies in our academic and professional staff, as well as the learners who have undertaken the subject.

Acknowledgements:

As authors we would like to acknowledge the contributions of the team, whose collaborative efforts brought the microcredential to fruition.

Professor Gawaian Bodkin-Andrews played a significant role in the development of curriculum content, Dr Danièle Hromek (Project Officer) contributed to the literature review, content and early design work. PhD scholars (and now) Dr Ros Sawtell and Dr Rhonda Povey shared their experiences of navigating their PhD candidature and Artist Nathan Peckham's artwork is featured throughout the course (with formal agreement). UTS Designers Jessy Mai, Learning Designer Eleanor Rowan, Senior Learning Designer John Vulic, Post Graduate Learning

Designer (PGLD) Media Manager Anthony Bourke and PGLD Media Producer Matilda Fay enhanced the visual presentation of our ideas and transformed the academic content into interactive and engaging activities. UTS FASS Short Forms of Learning Director Sita Chopra and Short Forms of Learning Coordinator Ines Soares provided strategic advice on microcredential development, industry engagement and impact. The project was funded through the UTS Postgraduate Strategic Funding Program.

References

Australia Council for the Arts. (2019). *Protocols for using First Nations cultural and intellectual property in the Arts*. https://australiacouncil.gov.au/wp-content/uploads/2021/07/protocols-for-using-first-nati-5f72716d09f01.pdf

Australian Council of Learned Academies. (2016). *Review of Australia's research training system: Final report.* ACOLA. https://acola.org/research-training-system-review-saf13/

Australian Institute of Aboriginal and Torres Strait Islander Studies. (2020). *AIATSIS code of ethics for Aboriginal and Torres Strait Islander research*. https://aiatsis.gov.au/sites/default/files/2020-10/aiatsis-code-ethics.pdf

Barney, K. (2013). 'Taking your mob with you': Giving voice to the experiences of Indigenous Australian postgraduate students. *Higher Education Research & Development, 32*(4), 515–528.

Battiste, M., Bell, L., & Findlay, L. M. (2002). Decolonizing education in Canadian universities: An interdisciplinary, international, indigenous research project. *Canadian Journal of Native Education, 26*(2), 82–95.

Behrendt, L. Y., Larkin, S., Griew, R., & Kelly, P. (2012). *Review of higher education access and outcomes for Aboriginal and Torres Strait Islander people*. Department of Industry, Innovation, Science, Research and Tertiary Education. https://www.education.gov.au/download/2658/review-higher-education-access-and-outcomes-aboriginal-and-torres-strait-islander-people/3703/document/pdf

Bond-Barnard, T. J., Fletcher, L., & Steyn, H. (2018). Linking trust and collaboration in project teams to project management success. *International Journal of Managing Projects in Business, 11*(2), 432–457.

Bradley, D., Noonan, P., Nugent, H., & Scales, B. (2008). *Review of Australian higher education: Final report*. https://vital.voced.edu.au/vital/access/services/Download/ngv:32134/SOURCE2

Brayboy, B. M. J., & Chin, J. (2018) A match made in heaven: Tribal critical race theory and critical indigenous research methodologies. In J. T. De Cuir-Gunby, T. K. Chapman, & P. A. Schutz (Eds.), *Understanding critical race research methods and methodologies: Lessons from the field* (pp. 51–63). Taylor & Francis.

Bunduchi, R. (2013). Trust, partner selection and innovation outcome in collaborative new product development. *Production Planning & Control, 24*(2–3), 145–157.

Burgess, C., Thorpe, K., Egan, S., & Harwood, V. (2022). Towards a conceptual framework for Country-centred teaching and learning. *Teachers and Teaching, 28*(8), 925–942.

Cheek, D. (2021). Analogies, metaphors, proverbs, and similes for learning. In B. Hokanson, M. sExter, A. Grincewicz, M. Schmidt, & A. A. Tawfik (Eds.), *Learning: Design, engagement and definition: Interdisciplinarity and learning* (pp. 87–97).

Springer International Publishing. https://doi.org/10.1007/978-3-030-85078-4_7

Cox, J. L., & Simpson, M. D. (2020). Cultural humility: A proposed model for a continuing professional development program. *Pharmacy*, *8*(4), 214–223.

Dailey-Hebert, A. (2018). Maximizing interactivity in online learning: Moving beyond discussion boards. *Journal of Educators Online*, *15*(3), 1–26.

Drange, D. L. (2011). Intercultural education in the multicultural and multilingual Bolivian context. *Intercultural Education*, *22*(1), 29–42.

Ertmer, P. A., Stepich, D. A., York, C. S., Stickman, A., Wu, X., Zurek, S., & Goktas, Y. (2008). How instructional design experts use knowledge and experience to solve ill-structured problems. *Performance Improvement Quarterly*, *21*(1), 17-42

Huizinga, T., Handelzalts, A., Nieveen, N., & Voogt, J. M. (2014). Teacher involvement in curriculum design: Need for support to enhance teachers' design expertise. *Journal of Curriculum Studies*, *46*(1), 33–57.

Hutchings, K., Bainbridge, R., Bodle, K., & Miller, A. (2019). Determinants of attraction, retention and completion for Aboriginal and Torres Strait Islander higher degree research students: A systematic review to inform future research directions. *Research in Higher Education*, *60*, 245–272.

Indigenous Higher Education Advisory Council. (2006). *Partnerships, pathways and policies: Improving Indigenous education outcomes.* Conference report of the Second Annual Indigenous Higher Education Conference. Commonwealth of Australia. https://vital.voced.edu.au/vital/access/services/Download/ngv:17061/SOURCE2

Janke, T. (2021). *True tracks: Respecting Indigenous knowledge and culture*. UNSW Press.

Jones, C. (2009). Indigenous legal issues, Indigenous perspectives and Indigenous law in the New Zealand LLB curriculum. *Legal Education Review*, *19*(1/2), 257–270.

Mason, J., & Lefrere, P. (2003). Trust, collaboration, e-learning and organisational transformation. *International Journal of Training and Development*, *7*(4), 259–270.

McKenney, S., Boschman, F., Pieters, J., & Voogt, J. (2016). Collaborative design of technology-enhanced learning: What can we learn from teacher talk? *TechTrends*, *60*(4), 385–391.

Moodie, N., Ewen, S., McLeod, J., & Platania-Phung, C. (2018). Indigenous graduate research students in Australia: A critical review of the research. *Higher Education Research & Development*, *37*(4), 805–820.

Moreton-Robinson, A. (2013). Towards an Australian Indigenous women's standpoint theory: A methodological tool. *Australian Feminist Studies*, *28*(78), 331–347.

Moreton-Robinson, A., Anderson, P., Blue, L., Nguyen, L., & Pham, T. (2020). *Report on indigenous success in higher degree by research: Prepared for the Australian Government Department of Education and Training*. Indigenous Research and Engagement Unit, Queensland University of Technology. https://eprints.qut.edu.au/199805/1/49092585.pdf

Nakata, M. (2007). The cultural interface. *The Australian Journal of Indigenous Education*, *36*(S1), 7–14.

NSW Department of Community Services. (2009). *Working with Aboriginal people and communities: A practice resource*. https://www.facs.nsw.gov.au/__data/assets/pdf_file/0003/322248/working_with_aboriginal_people.pdf

Osguthorpe, R. T. (2007). Instructional design in a flat world. *Educational Technology*, *47*(2), 48–50.

Osguthorpe, R. T., Osguthorpe, R., Jacob, W. J., & Davies, R. S. (2018). The moral dimensions of instructional design. In R. E. West (Ed.), *Foundations of learning and instructional design technology*. EdTech Books. https://edtechbooks.org/lidtfoundations/instructional_design_moral_dimensions

Pan, C., & Thompson, K., (2009). Exploring dynamics between instructional designers and higher education faculty: An ethnographic case study. *Journal of Educational Technology Development and Exchange*, *2*(1), 33–52.

Prehn, J., Peacock, H., Guerzoni, M. A., & Walter, M. (2020). Virtual tours of Country: Creating and embedding resource-appropriate Aboriginal pedagogy at Australian universities. *Journal of Applied Learning and Teaching*, *3*(Sp. Iss. 1), 12–20.

Productivity Commission. (2017). *Upskilling and retraining, shifting the dial: 5 year productivity review: Supporting paper no. 8*. Productivity Commission. https://www.pc.gov.au/inquiries/completed/productivity-review/report/productivity-review-supporting8.pdf

Rigney, L. I. (1999). Internationalization of an Indigenous anticolonial cultural critique of research methodologies: A guide to Indigenist research methodology and its principles. *Wicazo Sa Review*, *14*(2), 109–121.

Smith, J. A., Larkin, S., Yibarbuk, D., & Guenther, J. (2017). What do we know about community engagement in Indigenous education contexts and how might this impact on pathways into higher education? In J. Frawley, S. Larkin, & J. A. Smith (Eds.), *Indigenous pathways, transitions and participation in higher education: From policy to practice* (pp. 31–44). Springer. https://doi.org/10.1007/978-981-10-4062-7_3

Smith, L. T. (2012). *Decolonizing methodologies: Research and indigenous peoples* (2nd ed.). Zed Books.

Sousa, M. J., & Rocha, Á. (2019). Digital learning: Developing skills for digital transformation of organizations. *Future Generation Computer Systems*, *91*, 327–334.

Tay, A., Huijser, H., Dart, S., & Cathcart, A. (2023). Learning technology as contested terrain: Insights from teaching academics and learning designers in Australian higher education. *Australasian Journal of Educational Technology*, *39*(1), 56–70. https://doi.org/10.14742/ajet.8179

Trudgett, M. (2014). Supervision provided to Indigenous Australian doctoral students: A black and white issue. *Higher Education Research & Development*, *33*(5), 1035–1048.

Trudgett, M., Page, S., & Harrison, N. (2016). Brilliant minds: A snapshot of successful Indigenous Australian doctoral students. *Australian Journal of Indigenous Education*, *45*(1), 70–79.

Universities Australia. (2011). National best practice framework for Indigenous cultural competency in Australian universities. Universities Australia. https://universitiesaustralia.edu.au/wp-content/uploads/2019/06/National-Best-Practice-Framework-for-Indigenous-Cultural-Competency-in-Australian-Universities.pdf

Universities Australia. (2017). *Indigenous Strategy 2017–2020*. Universities Australia. https://universitiesaustralia.edu.au/wp-content/uploads/2019/06/Indigenous-Strategy-2019.pdf

University of Technology Sydney. (n.d.). *What students learn: The UTS model of learning*, https://www.uts.edu.au/research-and-teaching/learning-and-teaching/uts-model-learning/what-students-learn

Wayan K. Y. (2020). Multimedia learning theory. In J. Egbert & M. Roe (Eds.), *Theoretical models for teaching and research*. PressBooks. https://opentext.wsu.edu/theoreticalmodelsforteachingandresearch/chapter/multimedia-learning-theory/

Weitze, C. L. (2015). Pedagogical innovation in teacher teams: An organisational learning design model for continuous competence development. In A. Jefferies & M. Cubric (Eds.), *Proceedings of the 14th European Conference on e-Learning ECEL-2015* (pp. 629–638). Academic Conferences and Publishing International.

White, S., White, S., & Borthwick, K. (2021). Blended professionals, technology and online learning: Identifying a socio-technical third space in higher education. *Higher Education Quarterly*, 75(1), 161–174.

Media Attributions

- NHMRC page – Before
- After
- genially interactive element
- genially interactive element – Responsibility

About the authors

Associate Professor Katrina Thorpe
UNIVERSITY OF NEW SOUTH WALES
https://unsw.edu.au

Katrina Thorpe (Worimi) is the Academic Lead at Nura Gili: Centre for Indigenous Programs at the University of New South Wales (UNSW). Previously a Senior Lecturer at the University of Technology Sydney (UTS), she has over two decades of experience teaching Indigenous Studies in various fields. Her work focuses on culturally responsive pedagogies that connect students with Aboriginal communities and Country. Katrina has received numerous teaching awards, including the Faculty of Education and Social Work's Teaching Excellence Award at the University of Sydney. Her co-authored paper on Aboriginal curriculum narratives won the 2023 Colin Marsh Award from the Australian Curriculum Studies Association.

Dr Shaun Bell
UNIVERSITY OF TECHNOLOGY SYDNEY
https://www.uts.edu.au

Shaun Bell is a learning designer at the University of Technology Sydney (UTS) Education Portfolio, partnering with experts to co-design innovative digital learning. They hold a PhD in Literature from UNSW and have published award-winning essays and reviews on literary culture and English teaching. Shaun has taught in the English Program at the University of New South Wales (UNSW) and has extensive experience designing eLearning and distance education materials.

Professor Susan Page
WESTERN SYDNEY UNIVERSITY
https://www.westernsydney.edu.au

Susan Page is the Director of Indigenous Learning and Teaching at Western Sydney University and a national teaching award-winning Aboriginal educator. Specialising in Indigenous higher education, her research focuses on Indigenous Australian experiences in academia and student learning in Indigenous Studies. Susan has held several leadership roles, including Associate Dean and Centre Director, and serves as an Indigenous representative for the Universities Australia Deputy Vice-Chancellor (Academic) Committee.

6. Designing for equity in learning

JOHN VULIC

Understanding your learners

> When I was in kindergarten I noticed that when the teacher would ask a question, children with their hands up wouldn't get asked to respond. The teacher had a tendency to pick children who didn't have their hands up to attempt the question. As a five-year-old, I figured out how to avoid embarrassment by raising my hand for every question, 'gaming the system' in a way. On the rare chance that I was picked to answer, I had a back-up plan. I would say 'I forgot' and escape through the laughter of the class. Reflecting on my schooling, Maths was always a subject where I gamed. With teacher-centred instructional approaches consistently used, the combination of possibly missing a key step, not understanding a procedure, not wanting to hold up the class, and not wanting to show that I didn't know something, meant I needed to game to get through each class. This was by pretending I was following along, nodding with agreement, and creative doodling penmanship.

> However, it didn't necessarily have to be this way. Reflecting on my schooling I'm left wondering whether some of my teachers knew this about me and what they could have possibly done to help me see myself differently in order to get the best out of my schooling.

At the core of effective learning design is a deep understanding of students. It is crucial to recognise and address the unique experiences, needs, and identities of all students to foster their well-being and sense of belonging (OECD, 2023, p. 29). Embracing diversity is essential for creating an inclusive educational environment where every student feels recognised and valued. Learning designers and educators must acknowledge the significant impact of culture on learning and adapt their teaching methods to align with the sociocultural contexts and perspectives of ethnically diverse students (Gay, 2018, p. 52). By understanding these backgrounds, learning designers and educators can devise materials and methods that resonate with students, effectively bridging cultural and socio-economic divides. This approach aims to help students see themselves in what they learn, enhancing their sense of belonging.

In this chapter I'll introduce you to some inspirational educators based in the United States that I have had the pleasure of working with through a 21st Century Partnership for STEM Education project titled Mathematical Thinkers Like Me. The strategies and advice from these educators can be used by both learning designers and educators in the design of their learning. My first interview with Annie Fetter introduces you to a simple yet powerful technique to start understanding your students – Notice and Wonder (Ray, 2013, pp. 42-55).

Interview with Annie Fetter

Annie Fetter is a Mathematics and Education specialist in the Philadelphia area. Annie has been a key figure in formalising the Notice and Wonder routine. This routine asks students what they notice about something and what they wonder about it. Student insights can be leveraged by the teacher to guide the discussion towards critical thinking and deeper understanding of the subject matter. This approach fosters a student-centred learning environment, where curiosity and inquiry drive the learning process. The routine is inclusive, allowing all students, regardless of their skill level, to participate and contribute. It also values all student observations and questions, which can boost confidence and encourage participation from students who might be hesitant to engage. The routine also provides teachers with insights into students' thinking processes, helping them to identify potential misconceptions and knowledge gaps, and ultimately, help them to understand students.

Designing Notice and Wonder

In 2011 at a National Council of Teachers of Mathematics (NCTM) Ignite Talk, Annie shared an anecdote to illustrate the Notice and Wonder routine. In the clip Annie describes an experience of sitting on an aeroplane next to a child and their father. Annie noticed the child continuously asking his father questions about what he saw out of the plane window, to which the father would reply directly. Annie intervened at one point while the father was distracted by encouraging the child to think and express his thoughts on what he saw. This led to more original and personal insights from the child, and the child's father ultimately realising the impact of this approach. Annie recalls the father saying that the Notice and Wonder routine 'really made my son think'. When applied to teaching subjects such as maths, the technique demonstrates that even students who supposedly 'cannot do maths' can come up with insightful mathematical observations when encouraged to explore and think critically. Annie advocates for teachers to broadly adopt this technique, emphasising its ability to leverage what students notice and wonder, ultimately enhancing their learning and understanding.

> One or more interactive elements has been excluded from this version of the text. You can view them online here: https://oercollective.caul.edu.au/designing-learning-experiences/?p=97#oembed-1

What issue does noticing and wondering address?

> Annie: So school in general is not very great at nurturing and valuing students' ideas. And math is like the worst, right? It's like, you have to be able to replicate this set of things that somebody, white and male, figured out a while ago. And that's not entirely

> true, but I think that's people's impression of it. And so what do we do to flip math around? How can you change math?
>
> Imagine in English class, even if you don't like it, occasionally you're asked to write about something that comes from you, from within you. Like tell a story of what you did over summer. You're bringing 'you' to that classroom, and that matters, what you have to say matters. And in math class, that doesn't always happen. So the idea of starting off, particularly any scale of things, a unit, a lesson, a moment, by asking kids what they notice about something and what they wonder about it, that can really change how kids look forward to participating in that learning community.

What does Notice and Wonder look like in the classroom?

> Annie: Let's assume that I'm going to ask kids to notice and wonder on paper for a few minutes because they're old enough to write things down, pick an age, say sixth grade. And then I might ask them to talk at their table and share what are three things you all noticed and three things you all

wondered that you would like to share with the group.

And then when they share those, I'm just gonna go around and ask every table, okay, table one, what's one thing you noticed? And I'm gonna write it on the board. Table two, what's one thing? So I'm assuming every table has things to share. Everyone has something to say, and I'm gonna go around once or twice, depending on the thing, and then say like, okay, does anyone have anything that we don't have up here that you think we should have.

But I'm also not reacting to any of their ideas, because I don't want to judge them. I don't want to be like, oh, Marissa, you're really awesome. And then go like, John, what have you got? And John's sitting there going like, I don't have anything awesome. I'm not going to say anything. So you just want to go like, oh, thank you. Inside you're going like, that is awesome, or that is not as much as I hoped for, but you don't, it's all like, take it in. And write down exactly what they said, because another thing we do in math is we the grownups, tend to reword things to make them mathier or more concise or more something, because we think that's important. And all that's telling the kid is that their ideas aren't good enough, and that I have to fix them so that we can move on. So don't do that. Write down exactly what they said, don't judge what they said.

If they say too much, you don't want to write it down, you say to them, could you say that shorter so

> I can write it down? Put the onus on them to change their ideas. And then things that they wonder are really things that they wonder. But it's the same thing. Don't judge, write them down.
>
> If kids say a wrong thing, you just write it down. It's not big, you know, everyone's worried that, oh, there's a wrong answer on the board. First off, there's research that shows it's not that important. And secondly, it'll probably police itself out by the end. Like someone will go like, well, I noticed this but I also noticed that that doesn't agree with the other thing that someone else noticed. Or someone will say, Oh, those two things don't agree. Or some kid will go like, can I change mine?

How does Notice and Wonder change teaching practice?

> Annie: I'm working with a high school teacher this year. And then she watched that video of the kid on the plane. She says a thousand times, but I think she was exaggerating. And then she tried to notice and wonder with her kids. And what happened was her kids were amazing and it could have ended there, but what happened was it made her much more open to notice and wonder, as a teacher who used

> to tell kids what to do and expect them to do it. And I suspect she was probably pretty decent at that, like a very traditional teacher model.
>
> She became much more open to their ideas and ended up doing much more facilitating than telling, because she's like, the kids can do the work. And so she describes herself as now a completely different teacher. Just trying noticing and wondering was like the catalyst that moved her from here to there. You know, it's not the only thing, it's not the only change she made, but she made that change and then things snowballed from there. And she's like, I'm a completely different teacher. And she was, I don't know, a 10, 15 year teacher at that point. So that's a big shift for someone to make.
>
> And I think just for kids to feel that they have ideas that someone's listening to, and for the teachers to elicit their ideas and start listening to them, and then getting better at hearing them, and valuing them, and then actually using them, that's a big change in a classroom. And I know a lot of people who say that it changed their careers. Like it saved their careers because of that shift in their room.

Thoughts on Notice and Wonder

Implementing the Notice and Wonder routine as a learning designer or educator involves several key steps that are straightforward to implement. First, identify the learning objectives you aim to achieve through this approach. Next, select relevant content or topics and design observation prompts to stimulate students' curiosity and observation skills. Ensure your design of facilitated observation sessions also prompts students to articulate their questions and curiosities based on their observations, engage in discussions to explore connections and deepen understanding. The design of facilitated sessions should also provide guidance and feedback throughout the process, and include follow-up activities to extend learning. Building in reflective prompts for students to reflect on the effectiveness of the routine and encouragement for students to transfer their skills to other contexts may also be beneficial.

Some key benefits stood out from my chat with Annie on the Notice and Wonder routine. In particular, the routine serves as a pivotal tool in promoting engagement, critical thinking and deeper understanding in students. As Ray (2013, p. 55) notes, 'Learning depends on mulling, connecting, wondering, and repeatedly thinking about, and noticing and wondering enables this to take hold and blossom'. Consequently, I see potential for the broader application of the routine across domains outside of mathematics teaching. For designers and educators, this method also promotes inclusivity, as it allows for participation and contribution from all students. Each student's contributions can build towards a complete understanding of the problem (Ray, 2013, p. 55). Furthermore, this routine also helps to shift the role of educators from merely delivering information to actively promoting students' engagement with ideas (Ritchhart et al., 2011, p. 26), something learning designers also need to keep in the forefront of their practice. Thus, this technique is not just a teaching strategy for designers and educators to utilise, but a facilitator of a more engaging, thoughtful, and inclusive learning environment.

Being culturally responsive

Cultural responsiveness in education can be defined as the practice of 'using the cultural knowledge, prior experiences, frames of reference, and performance styles of ethnically diverse students to make learning encounters more relevant and effective to them' (Gay, 2018, p. 36). When reflecting on my schooling, there were what I would term tokenistic gestures to promote cultural responsiveness. Examples include celebrating annual events, such as International Day, where students could bring in and share food from a different culture. However, beyond these isolated events, school really did nothing to integrate cultural awareness into the everyday curriculum and address the deeper issues of inclusion, equity and respect for diverse cultures. The history, literature and perspectives taught in the classroom remained predominantly centred on the dominant culture, with little to no exploration of other worldviews, histories, or contributions of students from diverse cultural backgrounds. Growing up as a child of post-war migrants, I often felt out of place at school, feeling that I didn't truly belong there. This was true for me in maths, a subject commonly seen as culturally impartial and objective, which leads to questions about how teachers could broadly integrate culturally relevant teaching methods (Matthews, 2018).

In multicultural societies, classrooms can be seen as melting pots of diverse cultures, languages and experiences. This diversity isn't just a demographic fact; it's a valuable resource that can enrich learning for everyone. The cornerstone of capitalising on this diversity is cultural responsiveness, being able to design for learning experiences that 'teach to and through' the strengths of these students (Gay, 2018, p. 36). Instead of seeing cultural diversity as a hurdle, it's viewed as an asset that enriches education. This is crucial because students may face negative learning consequences if they feel compelled to hide or downplay their identity, culture or language (Nieto & Bode, 2018, p. 135). This mindset shift has far-reaching effects on how teaching and learning take place. For learning designers and educators, this extends beyond merely recognising different cultures to actively integrating them into the curriculum, design of resources, activities, teaching methods and classroom practices.

The impact of this approach can be significant. Students who see their cultures and backgrounds represented in learning materials may experience a greater sense of belonging and validation. This can positively influence their engagement, participation and academic performance. However, achieving genuine cultural responsiveness involves more than surface-level changes. It requires ongoing self-reflection, professional development and collaboration with students and communities. As Hollie (2018, p. 18) emphasises, cultural responsiveness 'begins with you and where you are in your heart and mind'. It involves questioning existing norms and being open to deep, transformative change within educational institutions. Additionally, it needs to acknowledge the inherent complexity of diverse learning environments, such as concepts like hybridity, recognising that students may identify with multiple identities beyond race and ethnicity (Nieto & Bode, 2018, p. 139), and Intersectionality, a way of understanding how different aspects of a person's identity, such as race, gender and class, combine to create unique experiences of oppression and privilege (Zack, 2024). In essence, cultural responsiveness is not just a technique; it's a philosophy. It embodies a steadfast belief in the value of each student's cultural heritage, coupled with a commitment to ensuring that this value is acknowledged, celebrated and woven into the fabric of education.

My interview with Melynee Naegele introduces you to some innovative and practical approaches that help learning designers and educators to provide a rich understanding of students, their culture and lives.

Interview with Melynee Naegele

Melynee Neagele is an accomplished middle-school maths teacher in Oklahoma. Melynee stands out for her dedication and inspirational teaching methods. Renowned for her commitment to education, Melynee utilises an extensive array of pedagogical tools to effectively engage and educate her students. Her approach to teaching is characterised by innovation and adaptability, allowing her to meet the diverse learning needs of her students. Melynee's passion for teaching and her ability to inspire young minds make her a remarkable educator, widely respected in her field for her contributions and the positive impact she has on her students. This part of the chapter unpacks just a few of Melynee's tools.

 One or more interactive elements has been excluded from this version of the text. You can view them online here: https://oercollective.caul.edu.au/designing-learning-experiences/?p=97#oembed-2

Designing 4Hs of Belonging Centred Math Instruction

One tool that Melynee has in her pedagogical toolbox is the 4Hs of Belonging Centred Math Instruction: Home, Hobbies, Hopes and Heritage (4Hs), a heuristic and partner activity for students (Matthews, 2018). The heuristic presents four key areas where students can find meaningful connections. This is delivered via an interest interview questionnaire. These questions encompass: 'Home', covering regular activities and the characteristics of their home environment, like cooking or family interactions; 'Hobbies', including personal activities done weekly, such as playing sports or using smartphone apps; 'Hopes', related to individual aspirations, interests, or goals, like career ambitions or financial management; and finally, 'Heritage', which connects students to their cultural traditions or communities, aimed to instill a sense of pride through elements like local heroes or historical figures in their community. The questionnaire is followed by a partner activity interest interview, which serves as a complementary tool to the 4H framework. These interviews utilise the collective 4H-related knowledge and experiences of the students in a class, guiding the development of lessons that are deeply connected to these 4H elements. Matthews (2018) also highlights establishing trust and showing a real interest in the students' lives as key factors that enhance the effectiveness and genuineness of 4Hs, and essential for integrating students' cultural perspectives into educational planning. With 4Hs, students are encouraged to express their views on their culture and interests from their own perspective, rather than relying on assumptions that might perpetuate stereotypes.

How do you introduce the 4Hs?

> Melynee: During the meet-the-teacher night, I distributed the 4Hs questionnaire to parents,

though not every family returned it. I explained to parents that understanding their child's interests and experiences through the questionnaire would enable me to personalise and humanise the learning experience.

In class, I dedicate time to discussing the 4Hs with students, emphasising the relevance of math to their lives. We explore various methods for completing the questionnaire, including Google Slides, paper, or voice recordings.

After collecting their responses, I compile them into a list and align them with curriculum standards. This snapshot of my class's interests allows me to integrate relevant examples into my lesson planning, ensuring that math concepts resonate with students.

For instance, students interested in music can explore mathematical concepts like ratios and rates through musical notation. When planning lessons, I refer to this list to ensure that I incorporate students' interests into the curriculum.

During class discussions, I reference the information gathered from the 4Hs questionnaire to reinforce students' connections to the material. This intentional approach helps students see themselves in the math curriculum, fostering engagement and understanding.

Thoughts on the 4Hs of Belonging Centred Math Instruction

The 4Hs of Belonging Centred Math Instruction presents a valuable technique for both students and learning designers and educators, to enhance the educational experience through personal relevance and cultural integration. For students, this method offers a platform to express their individuality and connect their learning to personal aspects of their lives – Home, Hobbies, Hopes and Heritage. This connection not only makes learning more engaging but also aims to foster a deeper understanding and retention of mathematical concepts by relating them to familiar contexts. It empowers students by valuing their backgrounds and aspirations, which can be crucial for supporting self-esteem and motivation.

For learning designers and educators, the 4Hs technique provides invaluable insights into students' lives, facilitating the creation of more tailored and effective lesson plans. Dr Jamaal Matthews in his 2018 working paper, 'on mindset and practices for re-integrating "belonging" into mathematics instruction' (pp. 12-17), provides a clear and comprehensive justification and methodology for implementing the 4Hs. By understanding students' environments, interests, goals and cultural backgrounds, learning designers and educators can design and deliver lessons that are not only educational but also empathetic and inclusive. This approach aligns with culturally responsive pedagogy, grounded in four core pillars of practice – "teacher attitudes and expectations, cultural communication in the classroom, culturally diverse content in the curriculum and culturally congruent instructional strategies" (Gay, 2018, p. 53). Furthermore, the emphasis on building trust and genuine interest in students' lives strengthens the teacher-student relationship, creating a more positive and conducive learning environment. This technique, therefore, not only enhances academic achievement but also contributes to a more inclusive, respectful and supportive classroom culture.

Ingenious Influencers

Melynee also promotes the concept of Ingenious Influencers in her classes. This involves introducing her students to famous, inspirational or influential individuals each day and a quote by that person. Promoting Ingenious Influencers in schools can offer significant educational and cultural benefits, contributing to a more inclusive and representative learning environment. This approach aligns with the broader objectives of multicultural education, as outlined by scholars like James A. Banks (2015), emphasising the importance of incorporating diverse cultural perspectives into the curriculum.

Can you walk us through your daily routine with your students?

> Melynee: Absolutely. Every day, I start by introducing my students to inspirational figures such as Katherine Johnson and Ellen Ochoa, or individuals who resemble them and come from similar backgrounds. I find Dolly Parton to be particularly impactful. We discuss these role models and reflect on quotes that resonate with their dreams and aspirations.

What happens next?

> Melynee: After our discussions, the students take the inspiration from these sessions and create vision boards. These boards serve as visual representations of their goals. They also write letters to themselves detailing how they plan to achieve these goals, which I then attach to the back of their boards. These letters are personal and confidential, serving as a commitment to their aspirations. At the midpoint of the year, we revisit their goals and progress. We discuss any obstacles they may have encountered and evaluate their achievements. I also check in on their well-being by revisiting what I call the 4Hs—asking if they have any additional questions or concerns.

What happens at the end of the year?

> Melynee: Towards the end of the school year, we revisit their vision boards. They have the opportunity to update them based on their growth and experiences throughout the year. It's a cyclical process that fosters continuous reflection and growth.

It sounds like a comprehensive approach. How do you view the significance of each component?

> Melynee: Each piece, from the introductions to the vision boards and goal-setting exercises, plays a crucial role in empowering my students and nurturing their aspiration.

How do you use Ingenious Influencers?

> Melynee: In my classroom, I have a dedicated space called 'Ingenious Influencers Like Me', where I feature a daily quote alongside an influential figure. For example, today's quote is 'Don't tell me the sky's the limit when there's footprints on the moon', paired with Ellen Ochoa. I make sure to highlight her achievements, such as being one of the first Hispanic women in space and her induction into the Astronaut Hall of Fame.
>
> After presenting the quote and the featured individual, I engage the students by asking them what they notice and wonder about our Ingenious Influencer and the accompanying mindset lesson. I encourage them to reflect on how these stories and

individuals can aid them in their goal-setting endeavours. This approach serves as a coaching tool, guiding them towards developing a growth mindset.

Similarly, during math class, I incorporate a daily quote and an Ingenious Influencer as part of our warm-up routine. I then facilitate discussions on how these individuals' accomplishments can inspire and assist the students in achieving their own goals.

By consistently incorporating these elements into our daily routine, I aim to instill a mindset of growth and possibility in my students. The expansive nature of my approach, which includes both daily quotes and overarching life principles, ensures that students are exposed to a variety of inspirational messages and themes. Following each presentation, I prompt students to reflect on whether the featured individual serves as a window or a mirror into their own lives, encouraging them to connect with those who resonate with their aspirations and values.

How do students relate to Ingenious Influencers?

Melynee: What I've observed is that when students hear the stories of these influential figures, it often

> prompts them to share their own experiences. They'll say things like, 'Oh yeah, she did this and that, which reminds me of something similar I've gone through'. I make a conscious effort to select figures who have relatable backgrounds or experiences to my students, which encourages them to engage with one another and recognise commonalities.
>
> I tailor the selection of these Ingenious Influencers based on the 4Hs, their Home, Hobbies, Hopes and Heritage. As the school year progresses, each student is likely to find connections with the individuals highlighted each day. This ongoing process fosters a sense of connection and community within the classroom as students recognise aspects of themselves in the stories of these remarkable individuals.

Thoughts on Ingenous Influencers

For learning designers and educators, designing experiences that expose students to a diverse range of cultures and perspectives in the educational setting is crucial for fostering cultural competence among all students. A key obstacle to culturally responsive teaching is 'mainstream ethnocentrism and hegemony' (Gay, 2018, p. 282), a tool that Ingenious Influences directly challenges. Beyond merely being an educational strategy, the promotion of Ingenious Influencers and diverse cultural representatives in educational settings plays a pivotal role in advancing social equity and encouraging cultural pluralism. It helps in dismantling stereotypes, broadening students' understanding and appreciation for different cultures, and preparing them to participate in a multicultural society with respect and empathy. This approach also aligns with educational goals of inclusivity, ensuring that students from various backgrounds see their cultures and histories reflected and valued in their learning environment. By integrating a wide array of cultural perspectives into curricula, educational environments not only enrich the learning experience but also contribute to a more equitable and culturally diverse society.

Designing collaborative maths

Reflecting on my experiences in mathematics classes, the concept of collaboration is notably absent. Typically, these classes were structured around individual tasks, with a strong emphasis on personal understanding and performance. For me, maths instruction often followed a traditional teacher-centred instructional approach, where students listened to explanations, took notes, and then worked through problems independently. This format left little room for collaborative learning, where students could actively engage with each other to solve problems, share diverse perspectives, or develop collective strategies. The focus was primarily on individual comprehension and skill mastery, assessed through solo homework assignments and tests. While this approach can aid in developing personal responsibility and individual problem-solving skills, it misses the opportunity to harness the benefits of peer-to-peer learning and the rich, diverse insights that collaborative discussions of different ways of seeing problems can bring to mathematical understanding (Boaler, 2016, p. 59). The lack of collaboration in these settings didn't just limit the social aspect of learning; it also potentially narrowed the scope of understanding, as it restricted the flow of ideas to a single source, typically the teacher or the textbook, rather than allowing for a more dynamic, interactive and multifaceted exploration of mathematical concepts. This can potentially prevent the establishment of a learning space where every student, irrespective of their background, has the opportunity to engage and contribute on an equal footing. While the lack of collaborative learning strategies may enhance educational disparities, Cohen & Lotan (2014, p. 23) note that if students are properly prepared, heterogeneous groups can allow students to use each other as resources, enabling exposure to challenging material and developing basic skills with peer support despite temporary skill gaps.

Virtual Math Teams (VMT)

Virtual Math Teams (VMT) is an online platform that represents a progressive approach in mathematics education, leveraging the power of digital technology to facilitate online collaborative problem solving and interactive learning experiences. Developed as part of a broader research initiative on technology-enhanced learning environments, VMT offers a platform where students engage in mathematical problem-solving and discourse in a virtual setting (Stahl, 2009). The platform enables the use of activities made with Desmos and Geogebra as its underlying workspace. A distinctive feature of the platform is an inherent focus on turn taking. This is promoted through a feature that allows only one participant to be in control of the workspace at a time, to perform actions such as manipulating interactives, or advancing and rewinding screens. Anonymisation is a configurable feature for designers and teachers within the platform. When activated, it allows students to work together anonymously, fostering an environment where they might be more inclined to take risks and experiment with their problem-solving approaches. VMT allows students from diverse locations to collaborate via text chat or voice to text, bringing together varied perspectives and problem-solving strategies, thus enriching the learning process (Roschelle & Teasley, 1995). Turn taking in the platform is promoted by students taking or requesting control in the shared space. Designers, teachers and students also have the ability to replay VMT sessions to learn from student interaction and chat conversations in each session. The Mathematical thinkers like me (MLM) with Desmos Activities on Virtual Math Teams video introduces students experiences with the VMT platform.

> *One or more interactive elements has been excluded from this version of the text. You can view them online here: https://oercollective.caul.edu.au/designing-learning-experiences/?p=97#oembed-3*

Interview with Richard Tchen

Richard Tchen is an Educational Program Developer based in Philadelphia. Richard has extensive experience co-designing with teachers in VMT and analysing student interactions within the platform. Both Richard and Annie Fetter make a point of trying to meet with students where possible to get their views on the platform and their input for improvements. They have also been active in collecting rich asynchronous exchanges and feedback from students via online Jamboards.

The importance of participation

> Richard: One major takeaway from my perspective [is] the sense that participation is important. When it doesn't happen, it's painful and it makes the experience a struggle. The depth of that feeling was particularly impactful on me, really impressed me. And ironically, having interviewed easily between the two of us, Annie and I, having interviewed at least half of, I guess, half of the eighth grade there, everyone was convinced that, oh, we are participating fully.
>
> Annie: It was also interesting that more of them, they were like, I think it's great, except when you're in the room with people who don't do anything. And it reminded me of these surveys, where they survey people of like, who's cheating on their spouse and who thinks their spouse is cheating and those numbers don't match up at all. It really seemed like they wanted to do math, they wanted to learn math, they wanted to have math conversations, they liked the environment, and they didn't want people to be lame. Worse off, they didn't want people to be jerks. So that was like when they spam the chat and all that. But I think there were two levels of you're a jerk, that's really not appropriate. And then you don't do anything. And it kind of almost made them sad, like, but wait, we're missing out on ideas and we want everyone to throw their ideas in so that we can think about stuff.

As a designer, what do you look for when replaying student VMT sessions?

Richard: There's such a rich range of activities and experiences. I guess it's affirming that there is no such thing as a typical chat or a typical replay experience, a typical kind of VMT experience. I will say when I go through them, I do rely a fair amount on chat and on the system messages about control, I like being able to see it in the context of what's happening in the interactive space.

So, you know, you can get a quick sort of overview about participation (in the VMT replayer). But I like to try to hear as much through the chat as I can about collaboration, about problem solving, and then texture that with observations from the VMT system messages about who's in control, how long they've been in control, how long it took for control to change when someone explicitly requested control or just made a suggestion, the unfulfilled proposition or something like that, you know, someone suggests an idea to the person who's in control and it never gets discussed and it never gets implemented.

So I try to look through and see who participated, when they were participating, how much they participated. And even before that, I actually make a point of looking at the roster list that the teacher has assigned for the specific room and reconcile that against who actually entered the room.

> Because, as we know, the pandemic and the reality of many public school students' lives in the United States, especially at these Title 1 schools, it doesn't guarantee attendance, you know, and their teachers have to account for that. So I focus a lot on just basic attendance and speech and actions. And I will add that, or complicate the analysis by pointing out that some of my favourite moments have been entirely wordless. They may have not really materialised in chat, but they have consisted of students almost silently, it's like the educational collaborative equivalent of Adam Smith's hand in capitalism, where there was an idea that got passed from one person to another, but each person took a different interpretation on it or had a different insight into. And yet very few words were spoken in the chat, but control passed from one person to the next. And at the end of it, the chat became one of, okay, so which one are we going to go with? And the whole sequence was beautiful.

What advice would you share with learning designers?

> Richard: I mean it's really humility. The more you design, the more you engineer, the more you're

> serving the software as opposed to the opportunities for learning. There is, I mean, with executive functioning, there's a tremendous amount of educational benefit to inhibiting some of the affordances that you know you could bake into [the platform]. Sometimes less is so much more, especially when the more we want is more learning. Like there is a certain amount of lifting and pivoting and change that we want to elicit from students that too much technology will do for them. So it's about humility of what you can bring as a designer and humility about what you should assume about your students. And of course, humility about what brilliance they will have.

Thoughts on Virtual Math Teams (VMT)

VMT exemplifies a progressive educational platform where students engage in real-time collaboration to solve mathematical problems. This approach not only fosters learning through diverse group interactions, enhancing empathy and appreciation for different perspectives, but also aligns with the needs of a globally interconnected world (Johnson & Johnson, 2009). For me, a critical aspect of collaborative tools like VMT is the design of pedagogical sequencing and related considerations, both inside and outside the platform, to help promote inclusive and equitable learning. For example, working with students to develop collaborative norms may help ensure that every student has an equal voice. As a learning designer or educator, one great feature of Virtual Math Teams is its support of existing Desmos and Geogebra activities. These may require some tweaking to ensure they work within the collaborative context of the VMT environment. For example, instructional prompts may need updating to promote discussion via the chat functionality.

Ensuring equitable access and engagement for all students is a consideration in the design of activities and resources before, during and after interaction with the platform. As a teacher, understanding when to intervene during online sessions is also vital, ensuring that guidance is provided while maintaining the collaborative integrity of the learning process. A fascinating aspect of VMT is the ability to replay sessions, learn from student interaction in the sessions, and iteratively improve their lessons. Such approaches in platforms like VMT not only enhance mathematical understanding but also ensure that all students, regardless of their background, have access to a rich, collaborative and equitable learning experience.

Final thoughts

This chapter introduces a few innovative pedagogical strategies: Notice and Wonder, 4Hs of Belonging Centred Math Instruction, Ingenious Influencers, and the collaborative online platform Virtual Math Teams (VMT). Collectively, these strategies and tools represent practical ways for learning designers and educators to help create inclusive and engaging educational environments. Notice and Wonder stands out as a versatile tool that encourages students to actively engage with their learning material, fostering critical thinking and curiosity. It shifts the focus from mere absorption of facts to a more interactive and reflective learning process. The 4Hs of

Belonging Centred Math Instruction, on the other hand, brings a personalised touch to learning by connecting class content to students' homes, hobbies, hopes and heritage, thus making learning more relevant, personal and engaging. Ingenious Influencers, by introducing students to diverse role models and thought-provoking quotes, not only broadens their horizons but also instills inspiration and relatability, contributing to a more culturally rich and motivating learning atmosphere. Lastly, VMT, as a platform for collaborative problem-solving, leverages digital technology to enhance mathematical understanding through interactive and cooperative learning experiences. Together, these approaches embody a holistic and progressive educational philosophy that not only enriches the student experience but also nurtures a more equitable, thoughtful and inclusive learning community.

References

Banks, J. A. (2015). *Cultural diversity and education: Foundations, curriculum, and teaching*. Routledge.

Boaler, J. (2016). *Mathematical mindsets: Unleashing students' potential through creative math, inspiring messages and innovative teaching*. Jossey-Bass.

Cohen, E. G., & Lotan, R. A. (2014). *Designing groupwork: Strategies for the heterogeneous classroom*. Teachers College Press.

Gay, G. (2018). *Culturally responsive teaching: Theory, research, and practice* (3rd ed.). Teachers College Press.

Hollie, S. (2018). *Culturally and linguistically responsive teaching and learning: Classroom practices for student success* (2nd ed.). Shell Education.

Johnson, D. W., & Johnson, R. T. (2009). An educational psychology success story: Social interdependence theory and cooperative learning. *Educational Researcher, 38*(5), 365-379.

Matthews, J. S. (2018). *On mindset and practices for re-integrating "belonging" into mathematics instruction.* TeachingWorks.

Nieto, S., & Bode, P. (2018). *Affirming diversity: The sociopolitical context of multicultural education* (7th ed.). Pearson.

OECD. (2023). *Equity and inclusion in education: Finding strength through diversity.* OECD. https://doi.org/10.1787/e9072e21-en

Ray, M. (2013). *Powerful problem solving: Activities for sense making with the mathematical practices.* Heinemann.

Ritchhart, R., Church, M., & Morrison, K. (2011). *Making thinking visible: How to promote engagement, understanding, and independence for all learners.* Jossey-Bass.

Roschelle, J., & Teasley, S. D. (1995). The construction of shared knowledge in collaborative problem solving. In C. O'Malley (Ed.), *Computer-supported collaborative learning* (pp. 69-97). Springer-Verlag. https://doi.org/10.1007/978-3-642-85098-1_5

Stahl, G. (2009). *Studying virtual math teams.* Springer. https://doi.org/10.1007/978-1-4419-0228-3

Zack, N. (2024). *Intersectionality: A philosophical framework.* Oxford University Press. https://doi.org/10.1093/oso/9780197693070.001.0001

About the author

Dr John Vulic
UNIVERSITY OF TECHNOLOGY SYDNEY
https://www.uts.edu.au

John Vulic is an academic for the Graduate Certificate in Learning Design at the University of Technology Sydney (UTS), with over 25 years of experience in education, teaching, and training across various sectors. Previously a Senior Learning Designer at UTS, he managed a team that developed online and blended learning products. John co-received the AECT Learner Engagement Division's 2022 Excellence in Innovation Award. His PhD research focused on learning designs that promote learning transfer. John has also contributed to the international "Mathematical Thinkers Like Me" project, supporting diverse students in developing their mathematical identities.

7. Designing for cultural responsiveness

NHUNG NGUYEN

Introduction and chapter objectives

Culture shapes our thoughts, perceptions, actions, and communication styles. It plays a pivotal role in mediating our learning experiences. Consequently, even in a learning environment where teaching methods, resources, curriculum, and relationships remain consistent, students may have diverse experiences. This variance arises because learning and experiences are processed through the lens of cultural viewpoints, prior knowledge and experiences.

This chapter explores the importance of acknowledging and celebrating cultural differences, and creating learning experiences that are relevant to diverse learners. It provides practical advice for learning designers to design learning experiences that are culturally responsive. The chapter will:

- unpack the notion of design for cultural responsiveness,
- discuss why we should design for cultural responsiveness,
- provide strategies and examples on how we can design for cultural responsiveness, and
- explore some challenges that we may encounter in the journey of designing for cultural responsiveness.

Culturally responsive design

In today's globally connected era, learning designers are tasked with the vital responsibility of shaping curricula and pedagogical approaches that resonate with the diverse cultural tapestries of learners' cultural backgrounds. This evolving landscape emphasises the criticality of designing learning environments that recognise, honour and actively harness the rich cultural assets each learner contributes. Within this section, we will explore the intricate dimensions of designing for cultural responsiveness. To set a firm foundation for this exploration, we will commence by clarifying the core definition of culture.

Culture

Culture represents a multifaceted phenomenon that encompasses evolving worldviews, traditions, beliefs, knowledge and relationships that underpin a group's actions and perspectives (Hargraves, 2022). While culture can be seen in tangible elements like cuisine or attire, it delves deeper and manifests in implicit behaviours associated with values, beliefs, social roles and communication. Culture can be collectively nurtured and shared among groups that are unified by history, geography, linguistics, religious beliefs or socio-economic status. However, culture remains fluid and multifaceted. Individuals can have different experiences and perspectives even within the same culture. This leads to nuanced variations even among individuals within the same cultural group.

Design for cultural responsiveness

Culturally responsive design embraces, deeply values and celebrates the diverse cultural heritage, knowledge, skills and dispositions that students bring into a learning environment. The design prioritises creating a learning environment that draws on students' inherent cultural backgrounds and experiences as a resource (Taylor & Sobel, 2011). Leaners in this environment are provided with opportunities to interact and collaborate with one another to learn from one another and develop multiple perspectives and ways of knowing. This means the foundation of learning and educational design becomes intertwined with students' unique cultural perspectives, frames of reference, language and communication styles (Wages, 2015). Culturally responsive design not only champions academic growth, it also fosters strong interpersonal relationships.

It is important to highlight that culturally responsive design is distinct from concepts such as diversity and inclusion initiatives. While diversity and inclusion initiatives try to increase the representation of minority groups in a learning environment, they may not necessarily address the inadvertent cultural biases or stereotypes within the curriculum. Culturally responsive design goes beyond mere representation. It actively weaves cultural backgrounds and experiences into the very fabric of the design.

Learners actively construct knowledge within a social context, based on their prior knowledge, cultural background, and experience (Kyei-Blankson et al., 2019). Their understandings continually evolve through interactions with their environment, peers and broader societal influences. Learning is not a mere passive absorption of information. It is a dynamic process shaped by interpersonal exchanges and cultural scaffolding.

Learners bring their unique and personalised knowledge, skills, and dispositions into a learning environment. Each learning experience is encompassed by the environment or context with which the learner engages (Boettcher & Conrad, 2016). Their understandings are shaped by their unique cultural and diverse backgrounds. Therefore, it is vital to value and weave diverse cultural experiences into educational design.

Culturally responsive design weaves learners' cultural backgrounds and life stories into course design, and harnesses the cultural insights, prior experiences and perspectives from diverse learners to make learning more personalised, relational and effective for them. Designing for cultural responsiveness draws on a wealth of diverse cultural insights, knowledge, skills and attitudes that varied learner groups contribute to educational settings. The design appreciates the distinct attributes of majority and minority students. Its objective is to equip learners to live in an increasingly multicultural world.

Educational theories underpinning designing for cultural responsiveness

Designing for cultural responsiveness is underpinned by three pivotal theories: Constructivist Learning Theory, Sociocultural Theory, and Culturally Relevant Pedagogy. In this section, we will outline the origins and core tenets of these theories, and their relationships to cultural responsiveness.

Constructivist Learning Theory

The origin of the Constructivist Learning Theory can be traced back to Jean Piaget's work on cognitive structures and developmental stages (Zajda, 2021). His research unveiled that children actively construct their understanding of the world by interacting with their environment. This perspective was expanded upon by Lev Vygotsky, who introduced the notion of socio-cultural influences on cognitive development (Daniels et al., 2007).

From a constructivist perspective, learning is a process where individuals construct new knowledge based on their prior knowledge and experiences (Biggs & Tang, 2011). This implies that learning is not passive but active, emphasising exploration, interaction, and reflection.

Within the constructivist paradigm, learners' cultural and experiential background is very important to their learning. They construct new knowledge based on and through the lens of their cultural knowledge and experiences. By integrating these into the curriculum, learning designers can make learning more meaningful and relatable. Designing for cultural responsiveness can foster a deeper, more holistic understanding of subjects, promoting both cognitive and emotional development.

Sociocultural Theory

Sociocultural Theory originates from Lev Vygotsky, who believed that individual cognitive development and societal influences are inextricably linked. Vygotsky argued that our cognitive development is heavily influenced by our sociocultural context. Tools from our culture – language, symbols, and societal norms – mediate our learning.

From a sociocultural perspective, learning is a social process, deeply intertwined with culture, interaction and the tools and artefacts of the society of which we are part (Nguyen & Williams, 2016). Individual cognitive processes are fundamentally rooted in social interactions and the context. Learners are not seen as isolated individuals in this perspective. Instead, they are viewed as part of social, cultural, historical and institutional networks. These networks influence their learning experiences, knowledge acquisition and cognitive development.

Vygotsky believed that cognitive development is mediated by cultural tools, like language, and by the interactions within one's community. These tools and interactions become the pathways through which knowledge is co-constructed. Culturally responsive design is about ensuring that these pathways are as diverse, inclusive and representative as possible. It recognises that for a learner from a different cultural background, a story, an example, or even a phrase might hold a completely different connotation.

Designing for cultural responsiveness is an embodiment of the principles of sociocultural theory. It recognises that every learner brings rich cultural backgrounds, languages, experiences, knowledge, and beliefs into the educational space. These are very important to who they are and how they learn. Culture, society, and interactions shape their learning experiences (Rogoff, 2003). Culturally responsive design in education aims to tailor learning resources, instructional strategies, assessment methods and the educational approach to resonate with the diverse cultural backgrounds of learners. This does not entail creating a different learning plan for each student; rather, it is about incorporating varied perspectives, narratives, histories, and values into the mainstream content (Gay, 2018). It is about ensuring that multiple voices are heard and represented, and that no single dominant culture overshadows the others.

Culturally relevant pedagogy

The term was introduced by Gloria Ladson-Billings in the 1990s (Ladson-Billings, 1995). It emerged as a reaction to educational environments that marginalised students of diverse cultural backgrounds.

Culturally Relevant Pedagogy is about creating a holistic learning environment where learners feel valued, are motivated to learn, and are equipped to bring about positive change in society. It has three components: student learning, cultural competence and sociopolitical/critical consciousness (Ladson-Billings, 2021).

- Student learning: At the forefront of Culturally Relevant Pedagogy is a commitment to ensuring learners achieve their full potential. It is important to promote intellectual growth without sidelining or undermining a learner's cultural identity.
- Cultural competence: This facet actively seeks to establish a symbiotic relationship between learners' home cultures and the educational environment. Rather than a scenario where learners' cultural identities are secondary or overlooked, Culturally Relevant Pedagogy advocates for these rich cultural narratives to be interwoven into the educational fabric. This not only contextualises learning but also empowers learners to recognise and value their culture in parallel with others, thus promoting a classroom culture of mutual respect and understanding.

- Sociopolitical consciousness: Beyond just acknowledging diversity, Culturally Relevant Pedagogy propels learners towards critical consciousness. It urges them to engage with, interrogate and challenge societal norms and structures that perpetuate inequalities. By doing so, learners are imbued with a sense of agency, transforming them from passive recipients of knowledge to active contributors working towards a more equitable society.

Culturally Relevant Pedagogy encourages learning designers to view diversity not as an obstacle but an asset. It is about infusing curricula with diverse cultural perspectives, thus making education more holistic and reflective of the world we inhabit. By adopting this pedagogical approach, designers ensure that learners do not feel compelled to choose between academic success and cultural identity – they can, and should, have both.

Constructivist Learning Theory, Sociocultural Theory and Culturally Relevant Pedagogy collectively champion the idea that culture, experiences and backgrounds of learners are central to the learning process. Constructivist Learning Theory emphasises that individuals actively shape their knowledge through experiences, highlighting the need to incorporate cultural understanding to foster the learning experience. Sociocultural Theory underscores the intricate nexus between individual cognition and the encompassing socio-cultural context. Culturally Relevant Pedagogy emphasises the triad of student learning, cultural competence, and sociopolitical consciousness. As we reflect upon these theories, it becomes patently clear that to design for cultural responsiveness is to recognise and celebrate the rich tapestry of diverse learner backgrounds. It means weaving an educational narrative where diverse cultural inputs are at the forefront, fostering a holistic and enriching learning experience.

Why should we design for cultural responsiveness?

In an era characterised by rapid globalisation and increasing intercultural interactions, the importance of designing for cultural responsiveness cannot be overstated. Designing for culturally responsiveness values and celebrates the cultural heritages of all learners. This section will unpack the answers to the question of why we should design for cultural responsiveness.

Learners' engagement and educational performance

> 'The diverse languages, literacies, and cultural ways of knowing and being of students of minority cultures are sometimes perceived as deficiencies that need to be overcome in order for students to learn the dominant language, literacies, and cultural ways of school. From this point of view, students are seen as culturally deprived because they do not have sufficient experiences of the knowledge and values of the dominant culture, and are subject to low expectations for achievement and family involvement. This can lead to a sense of disconnection from the school for many students and families.' (Hargraves, 2022, para. 6)

A culturally responsive approach can enhance learners' performance and engagement (Chuang, 2016). Conversely, lack of understanding for learners' cultures has been shown to be detrimental to their academic success (McGrady & Reynolds, 2013). Research has consistently shown that students learn best when the content is relatable, relevant and resonates with their experiences. By incorporating diverse cultural perspectives, educators can tap into students' prior knowledge and lived experiences, making the learning process more intuitive and engaging.

Language and communication style are closely intertwined with cultures and social class (Lareau, 2011). This can create challenges for certain minority learners to communicate, connect and engage with learning environments (e.g., classrooms, universities, online courses). Pressure to conform to the sociocultural and sociolinguistic norms of a dominant culture group may lead minority learners to feel alienated from a learning environment (White & Lowenthal, 2011).

A sense of belonging plays a pivotal role in determining a student's academic success and emotional well-being. When students see their cultures, languages, and experiences reflected in the curriculum and teaching methodologies, they feel valued and included. On the contrary, overlooking cultural diversity or perpetuating stereotypes can inadvertently alienate students, leading to feelings of isolation and disengagement. White and Lowenthal (2011) argue that perceived alienation may cause learners from minority groups to withdraw from their tertiary studies. Furthermore, studies have found that learners of colour frequently encounter microaggressions, both within the campus environment and during classroom interactions, and they feel that their perspectives are unheard in curriculum (Suarez et al., 2018).

Bishop and Berryman (2010) conducted a research project on culturally responsive professional development in New Zealand. The educational inequalities in New Zealand are prominently visible in schools between Māori students and their Pākehā (New Zealand European) counterparts. Within these mainstream educational settings, Māori students often exit the schooling system prematurely. They are more frequently subjected to school expulsions and suspensions than their Pākehā peers. This phenomenon is not unique to New Zealand. It is reflective of similar disparities faced by marginalised student populations in other nations such as the United States, Canada, Australia, and the United Kingdom. The research goal was to help educators to raise academic performance of New Zealand's indigenous Māori students. The research found that the culturally responsive approach not only narrows the gap between top-performing and struggling students but also elevates overall academic performance.

Taking a culturally responsive approach can potentially enhance educational achievement (Gay, 2002). Multiple scholars assert that a culturally responsive approach can be pivotal for the academic success of learners from a diverse range of cultural backgrounds (Green et al., 2017; Ware, 2006). It can contribute to learners feeling valued and connected to an online learning environment (Green et al., 2017). It enhances performance across all cultural groups and ensures that learners, irrespective of cultural background, can receive support and encouragement to fulfil their educational aspirations (Hindle et al., 2020).

Globalisation

Beyond academic outcomes, one of the primary objectives of education is to prepare students for life. In a world where intercultural interactions are commonplace, the ability to communicate, collaborate and empathise with individuals from different cultural backgrounds becomes crucial. Culturally responsive classrooms serve as training grounds for these vital life skills. By exposing students to diverse perspectives and promoting intercultural dialogues, educators foster critical thinking, open-mindedness, and a genuine appreciation for diversity.

Nowadays, learning environments (e.g., online courses, face-to-face classrooms, schools) have become more diverse due to migration, international collaborations, and technological advancements enabling online education. Learners are from various cultural backgrounds. Designing with cultural responsiveness in mind acknowledges the lived realities of our globalised world, where intercultural competencey is no longer a luxury but a necessity. By designing and fostering an environment that respects and integrates diverse cultural inputs, educators prepare students for an interconnected global future.

Decolonial movement

The decolonial movement aims to shape education systems to better represent the diverse cultures, histories, and experiences of learners and address the existing power imbalances in these systems (Kukulska-Hulme et al., 2023). In many countries, the mainstream educational systems and curricula have been predominantly shaped by colonial legacies, which often prioritise Western perspectives and marginalise indigenous/minority knowledge, practices and worldviews. This systemic bias has contributed to achievement gaps between different cultural and socio-economic groups. By intentionally designing for cultural responsiveness, educators can challenge these longstanding Eurocentric norms and give voice to the previously silenced narratives. This helps to ensure that all learners, irrespective of their backgrounds, have equitable access to quality education and opportunities to excel.

To wrap up the discussion on why we should design for cultural responsiveness, culturally responsive design does not solely benefit minority or marginalised learners. When curricula integrate diverse perspectives, they offer a richer, more nuanced view of topics, benefiting all learners. This encourages learners to step out of their comfort zones, challenge their preconceived notions, and gain a more holistic understanding of the world around them.

The process of incorporating cultural responsiveness also offers profound professional development opportunities for educators. It necessitates a continuous process of self-reflection, learning, and adaptation. As educators deepen their understanding of diverse cultures, they become better equipped to cater to varied student needs, enhancing their efficacy and adaptability.

How can we design for cultural responsiveness?

1. Laying the groundwork: Preliminary steps

1.1 Knowing yourself: Self-awareness and reflection

In the realm of educational design, it is important to understand and acknowledge our own beliefs and attitudes. These foundational beliefs directly influence the design of learning materials, interaction and overall educational experiences.

Every learning designer brings with them a tapestry of experiences, beliefs and values rooted in their own cultural upbringing. These beliefs are often shaped by personal experiences, societal narratives or established educational approaches. Recognising and understanding one's own cultural identity is essential, which entails delving into one's family history, traditions, values and even biases.

We usually operate within a framework of beliefs and assumptions. These impact the design decisions, from content selection to educational paradigms that underpin the design.

The ripple effect of the design decisions can have profound implications. For instance, learners perceive their capabilities and potential within the confines of the designed environment. A design infused with biases, even inadvertently, can alter a learner's self-efficacy and belief in their potential.

A significant component of self-awareness is challenging one's own assumptions about different cultural groups. Stereotypes can limit a designer's understanding of learners' potential, preferences, and challenges. Some common examples could be that all Asian learners excel in mathematics, and that students from lower socio-economic backgrounds lack ambition. Another common oversight in educational design is the inadvertent creation of content that caters predominantly to mainstream cultural norms, thereby sidelining learners from diverse backgrounds. To counteract this, designers can maintain a balanced expectation, ensuring that content, resources and tools are universally accessible and resonate across cultural divides. Elevating design expectations for inclusivity can bridge the gap between mainstream and diverse learning experiences.

Culturally responsive learning design entails continuous self-reflection. Designers should periodically evaluate their strategies and tools, biases, and cultural nuances. By recognising areas where existing beliefs might be limiting or even counterproductive, designers can pivot towards more inclusive and holistic strategies. A culturally responsive designer is more than just a content curator; they are advocates for an inclusive learning ethos. Such designers challenge mainstream narratives and methodologies, always searching for approaches that resonate with diverse learner profiles.

Self-awareness and reflection is an ongoing process. Feedback from students, peers, and community members can be invaluable in this reflective process. External perspectives can shed light on blind spots that one might have. Journalling, peer discussions or even structured professional development activities could also be very useful for reflective practice.

Prompting questions for self-awareness and reflection

- What personal beliefs and biases might I unknowingly bring into my designs?
- How can I mitigate the influence of my personal biases?
- How might my own cultural background and educational experiences shape the way I approach design?
- How can I broaden my perspective?
- Am I making assumptions about learners based on stereotypes, or am I truly understanding and addressing their unique needs and backgrounds?
- Do I ensure that the content I design is reflective of diverse cultural perspectives and not just predominant or familiar ones?
- Do I consistently challenge and update my design methodologies to ensure they are current, relevant, and cater to the evolving diverse needs of learners?
- Am I dedicating enough time and resources to continuous learning about cultures, experiences

> and histories different from my own to enrich my design practices?

Self-awareness and reflection are foundational for designing cultural responsiveness. Embarking on the journey of self-awareness and reflection might be uncomfortable at times. We might unearth deep-seated biases or realise past mistakes in our teaching practices. It is important to approach these realisations with a growth mindset. Every insight is an opportunity for growth, enabling us to create a more culturally responsive and effective learning environment.

1.2 Getting to know the learners

Knowing learner demographics and their respective needs is central to the design and implementation of a culturally responsive educational context. By understanding who the learners are, where they come from, and what unique requirements they might have, learning designers can shape instruction, content and assessment to be more relevant, inclusive and effective.

Before addressing the specific needs of learners, it is important to gather comprehensive data on the learner population. This encompasses not only age, gender and ethnicity but also languages spoken, socio-economic backgrounds, religious beliefs and other cultural identifiers. Such a nuanced demographic profile aids designers in predicting potential needs, challenges or preferences among learners.

Once demographics are mapped, the next step is to delve deeper into specific needs or challenges linked to these demographics. For instance, English as a Second Language (ESL) learners might need additional language support, while learners from certain religious backgrounds might have specific holiday observances. By identifying these needs, learning designers can better prepare and adjust the learning environment.

> ### Examples of methods to get to know the learners
>
> - Distributing surveys to learners can provide direct insights into their expectations, challenges or suggestions for the curriculum. These surveys should be anonymous to ensure honest feedback and can be tailored to gather information about both academic and non-academic needs.
> - Open dialogues or focus group discussions with learners can offer richer qualitative data on their needs. Such platforms encourage learners to voice concerns, share experiences and provide feedback, aiding designers in understanding and addressing specific needs.
> - Examining past data, such as performance metrics, drop-out rates or feedback forms, can help identify recurring challenges or needs tied to specific demographic groups. This historical perspective can inform current strategies and interventions.

- In many institutions and companies, there are specialised staff members – like counsellors, language specialists or special needs educators – who can offer insights into the specific needs of different learner groups. Collaborating with these professionals can provide learning designers with targeted strategies and resources.

Learner demographics and needs are not static; they evolve over time. To remain culturally responsive, designers should ensure that analysis of demographics and needs are regularly updated, allowing them to stay attuned to any shifts or emerging trends. Understanding learner demographics and their specific needs is foundational to culturally responsive education. By recognising, understanding, and addressing these needs, with ethical considerations in mind, learning designers can offer a learning environment that is culturally responsive for diverse learners.

1.3 Engaging with communities

When it is possible, learning designers should engage with the communities from which learners originate. Communities are reservoirs of cultural capital. They house traditions, languages, stories, and histories that can enrich the learning experience. By tapping into these resources, learning designers can create a curriculum that both mirrors learners' backgrounds and broadens their horizons. This not only validates the identities of learners but also fosters a sense of belonging and appreciation for diverse cultures. Incorporating community voices in curriculum design ensures that the content is both relevant and culturally sensitive.

Engaging with communities also equips designers with a nuanced understanding of cultural norms, values, and expectations. This knowledge can influence the design of the content and learning activities, communication strategies, and assessment methods. For instance, understanding the cultural significance of certain holidays or practices allows the scheduling of assessments or significant learning activities in ways that respect and accommodate learners' cultural engagements.

Examples of methods to engage with communities

- Conducting workshops, focus groups or community consultations can provide invaluable insights into what should be incorporated in the curriculum, how it should be presented, and which pedagogical methods might be most effective.
- Building partnerships with local community groups, cultural organisations and elders can help in offering authentic learning experiences. Guest speakers, field trips, or collaborative projects can provide learning designers with firsthand insights

- into various cultures. Additionally, these partnerships can support designers with supplemental resources and guidance in delivering culturally responsive instruction.
- Maintaining open communication between educational institutions and communities is vital. This could take the form of digital communication platforms, regular community meetings or feedback sessions. Such channels ensure that community members actively participate in the learning design process and can voice concerns, provide suggestions or share resources.
- Collaborating with community advocates or cultural ambassadors enhances community engagement efforts. These individuals, often esteemed within their communities, bridge the gap between institutions, companies and community members, facilitating a mutual flow of information and trust.

Engaging with communities is very beneficial for culturally responsive design. By establishing robust ties with communities, learning designers can curate a learning environment that celebrates diversity, recognises cultural richness and ensures every learner feels acknowledged, respected and valued.

2. Designing for cultural responsiveness

2.1 Empowerment through representation

For learners, seeing themselves reflected in the curriculum, resources, and instructional design is a potent indicator of belonging and validation (Green et al., 2017). Designing with cultural responsiveness through representation ensures that learners feel acknowledged, valued, and empowered. Here are examples of how to infuse representation in educational design.

> **Examples of empowerment through representation**
>
> - Use diverse resources: When choosing materials for inclusion in the curriculum, whether they are texts, multimedia resources, or case studies, learning designers should actively seek out sources from diverse authors, creators, perspectives, and historical accounts. Learners should encounter a multitude of voices and narratives, ensuring that no single story overshadows the rest. When learners encounter multiple viewpoints, they are more likely to see the richness and depth of a subject.
> - Employ a co-design approach: A co-design

approach involves actively engaging a range of stakeholders including teachers or academics, cultural experts, community members and people from indigenous cultures in the design process. By adopting this approach, learning designers can ensure that the learning experiences and materials are culturally responsive and relevant to learners' diverse backgrounds. This engagement allows for a more holistic and inclusive design process, where the voices and perspectives of those who are often marginalised or excluded from educational discourse are brought to the forefront.

- Utilise visual representation: Incorporate diverse images, symbols, and illustrations in learning materials. Visual cues are powerful mediums of communication, and culturally inclusive visuals can foster a sense of belonging for learners from various backgrounds.
- Highlight diverse role models: Feature achievements and contributions of individuals from various ethnic, racial, gender and socio-economic backgrounds. This provides learners with role models they can identify with, fostering motivation and aspirations.
- Encourage diverse voices: Create a learning environment in which learners from different cultural backgrounds feel safe and encouraged to share their experiences, insights and perspectives. This not only enhances representation but also enriches the learning experience for all.
- Incorporate culturally relevant scenarios: When

designing case studies, scenarios or examples, ensure they resonate with diverse cultural contexts. This allows learners to connect learning with their lived experiences, making the content more relatable and impactful.
- Invite experts: When designing courses and programs, experts can be invited and get involved in different stages of the learning design process. For example, Māori and Pacific/Indigenous experts are invited to work on the design and development of courses and programs of New Zealand institutions. These experts can work collaboratively with the team to brainstorm a course plan (an outline of the content, assessment and learning activities), writing some sections of a course, design some learning activities and assessment tasks, and/or review content and assessments. Inviting guest speakers from various cultural, professional or socio-economic backgrounds can introduce learners to a variety of lived experiences and expert knowledge. These engagements can also inspire learners by showcasing diverse role models and thought leaders in the field.
- Celebrate cultural events: Acknowledge and celebrate significant cultural, religious and ethnic events and festivals. This fosters a culture of respect and appreciation, underlining the importance of every culture in the educational community.
- Regularly review and update: The landscape of culture is dynamic and ever evolving. Regularly

> review and update learning materials to ensure they remain relevant and reflective of current cultural nuances and realities.

Empowerment through representation is an essential pillar of culturally responsive design. It transcends acknowledgement and moves towards holistic cultural responsiveness, where every learner feels seen and validated. When educational design mirrors the diverse tapestry of its learners, it sends a powerful message: every story matters, every perspective is valuable, and every learner is integral to the educational journey. Through culturally responsive design, educators have the profound opportunity to not just inform, but to empower and inspire, laying the groundwork for a more inclusive, understanding, and harmonious future.

2.2 Assessment and feedback

Within the realm of education, assessment and feedback are pivotal components. When the educational landscape is marked by a tapestry of diverse cultures and backgrounds, the design of assessments and the way feedback is given must be approached with cultural responsiveness. Below are some examples of how to ensure assessments and feedback are culturally sensitive and inclusive.

Examples of assessment and feedback

- Use diverse assessment methods: Different cultures may prioritise different modes of expression and understanding. Incorporating a mix of assessment styles – from written assignments and oral presentations to reflective journals, group projects and portfolios – ensures a more comprehensive evaluation of learners' grasp of content from various angles. Traditional tests may not capture the full range of a learner's understanding, especially if the learner comes from a background where different cognitive or communicative skills are emphasised. This variety acknowledges and respects the diverse ways in which learners from different cultures may best express their understanding.
- Provide choices in assessment: Rather than a rigid assessment structure, offering choices can be empowering. Some learners might excel in written tests, while others might shine in oral presentations or project-based assessments. Providing multiple avenues for learners to demonstrate their understanding acknowledges diverse skill sets and expressive styles.
- Provide flexible assessment timelines: Recognise that significant cultural, religious or familial events might clash with pre-set assessment

timelines. Providing flexibility or alternative assessment dates ensures equity for all learners.
- Incorporate self and peer assessments: Self-assessment encourages learners to reflect on their work from their cultural perspective, while peer assessments can foster cross-cultural understanding as learners engage with and evaluate the work of their peers from diverse backgrounds.
- Provide contexts in performance tasks: When designing performance-based tasks, ensure the contexts or scenarios provided are culturally neutral or offer multiple culturally relevant options. This approach ensures that learners can engage with tasks in a meaningful way, rooted in their own experiences or understanding.
- Design culturally relevant assessment content and tasks: Design assessments that are free from cultural bias. Questions and tasks that assume familiarity with specific cultural references or experiences can inadvertently disadvantage some learners. Instead, opt for universally understood contexts or provide a balanced range of culturally diverse examples.
- Provide feedback that respects cultural nuances: Language and tone in feedback should be constructive and compassionate. Avoid idiomatic phrases or culturally specific references that might not be universally understood. Acknowledge the diverse methodologies and thought processes that learners might employ, understanding that there are multiple ways to

> approach a problem or topic.
> - Pursue professional development: Continuous professional development can equip learning designers with the skills needed to design and implement culturally responsive assessments.

Assessments and feedback serve not only as tools for measuring understanding but also as reflective mirrors for learners. These indicate how the educational system perceives and values them. When designed with cultural responsiveness in mind, assessments and feedback can become powerful instruments of inclusivity, equity and mutual respect. It is essential that these tools, integral to the learning process, are wielded with an awareness of diverse cultural backgrounds to ensure learners feel seen, understood and valued.

2.3 Active engagement and participation

Achieving active engagement and participation is imperative for educational design work. In diverse classrooms, the challenge lies in ensuring that engagement and participation are culturally responsive. By acknowledging and addressing cultural nuances and variances, educational designs can offer experiences that resonate universally, yet remain deeply personal. Here are some examples of how to foster culturally responsive active engagement and participation.

Examples of active engagement and participation

- Design learning activities where learners can share their cultural heritage, knowledge, skills and dispositions. Examples are: (1) a discussion forum (an ice-breaker activity) at the beginning of a course where learners can introduce themselves, their cultural heritage, languages they can speak and their most important holidays in a year; and (2) oral presentations that allow for the sharing of cultural perspectives on a specific topic.
- Employ inclusive pedagogical approaches: Adopting pedagogies that honour different ways of knowing and learning is vital. For example, storytelling might resonate with some cultures more than analytical discussions. Similarly, collaborative activities might mirror community-oriented cultures, while individual projects might appeal to cultures that value autonomy.
- Encourage learner-led exploration: Learners can be instrumental in bringing diverse perspectives into the learning environment. Tasks that allow learners to delve into their cultural backgrounds or research global contexts can lead to enriching class discussions and knowledge exchange.
- Design contextualised content: Learners should

see their experiences reflected in the content. Case studies, examples and scenarios should pull from a variety of cultural backgrounds. This inclusivity validates diverse experiences and encourages active engagement from all learners.
- Use real-world tasks across cultures: Tasks that encourage learners to dive into cross-cultural scenarios or address global challenges compel them to view issues from various perspectives, fostering cultural responsiveness.
- Design inclusive collaborative spaces: Design platforms that celebrate diverse voices and experiences that enhance engagement. Encouraging discussions around cultural experiences, and comparing and contrasting them, can lead to rich, enlightening exchanges.
- Use reflection through cultural lenses: Providing learners opportunities to reflect on how a specific topic or lesson resonates with their cultural perspective encourages deeper connections and promotes understanding across different backgrounds.
- Provide feedback that honours diversity: Offering feedback should be done with cultural sensitivity in mind, acknowledging different perspectives and understanding that there is not always a 'one-size-fits-all' answer. Feedback should be constructive, validating diverse approaches to problem-solving.
- Support varied interaction styles: Some cultures value group discussions and collaborative learning, while others might emphasise

introspection and individual exploration. Flexible paths should accommodate these varied interaction styles, ensuring each learner finds a conducive environment to voice opinions, share insights or reflect.
- Use gamification with universal appeal: While gamifying learning experiences, choose elements like storylines, characters, names and challenges that are inclusive, ensuring they cater to a diverse audience and do not sideline any specific group. Some examples of names include: Marama – female character, Māori from New Zealand; John – male from England; Fhon – female from Thailand.
- Design for autonomy and cultural choice: Allowing learners to select culturally relevant resources or explore topics relevant to their backgrounds promotes autonomy and deepens engagement. By making cultural choices available, educational designers allow learners to carve out a personalised and relevant learning journey.
- Provide space for feedback: Open channels for feedback allow learners to share what perspectives they feel are missing or misrepresented. This continuous feedback loop ensures the content remains updated and reflective of diverse voices.

When striving for active engagement and participation, designing for cultural responsiveness is essential for today's diverse learning environments. Every learner deserves content and experiences that honour, respect, and reflect their cultural backgrounds. By integrating culturally responsive strategies into the design, designers can promote active participation and build bridges of understanding and respect across diverse learner groups. The goal is to create a learning environment where every voice is heard, every experience is validated, and every perspective is welcomed.

2.4. Multilingual approach

In the complex tapestry of today's globalised educational context, a significant number of learners come from multilingual backgrounds, bringing with them a rich linguistic repertoire. As we push towards more culturally responsive learning environments, employing a multilingual approach becomes more and more popular. This can cater to diverse learner profiles, enrich the learning experience and promote deeper understanding and wider engagement. By offering content in multiple languages or providing translation tools, learning designers validate these diverse linguistic assets, and help to remove the language barriers.

Examples of multilingual approach

- Use multilingual tools and resources: Integrating tools like auto-translation software, multilingual glossaries or subtitle options can bridge linguistic

gaps. Such tools empower learners to engage with content in their preferred or native language, promoting better understanding and reducing cognitive load.
- Integrate cultural and linguistic representations in content: By integrating diverse cultural narratives, idioms, examples and stories from various linguistic backgrounds, educators can make learning materials more relatable and engaging. Such representation reinforces the notion that every linguistic and cultural experience is valuable.
- Facilitate interactive multilingual forums: Facilitating spaces where learners can discuss, collaborate or ask questions in multiple languages fosters inclusivity. These forums can be supported by peer translations or educators proficient in various languages, making them accessible to all learners.
- Integrate language learning: In contexts where it is feasible, educational designers can integrate basic language learning modules. For instance, if a course has a significant number of Spanish-speaking learners, introducing basic Spanish terms or phrases related to the course content can foster cultural responsiveness and also enhance the learning experience for all participants. Embedding short courses from OpenLearn can be very useful.

Using a multilingual approach is a robust strategy to optimise learning outcomes. By acknowledging and catering to diverse communicative and linguistic needs, learning designers can create enriched learning landscapes where learners, irrespective of their linguistic background, find the tools and resources to thrive, engage deeply and achieve their full potential.

Challenges around design for cultural responsiveness

While design for cultural responsiveness is essential, achieving this is not without challenges. One of the primary challenges that educators face is the breadth and depth of cultural diversity. It is not just about culture, race or ethnicity but encompasses language, religion, socio-economic status, gender, sexual orientation, and more. Catering to such expansive diversity in a single learning environment (e.g., classroom or course) can be overwhelming. Striking a balance where multiple perspectives are included without diluting the core curriculum can be particularly daunting.

There is a thin line between understanding cultural tendencies and falling into the trap of stereotyping or overgeneralising. There is significant intra-cultural diversity, meaning members of the same cultural group can have varied experiences and beliefs. Designing educational content that respects this nuance without resorting to reductive stereotypes is a complex endeavour.

Many learning designers recognise the value of cultural responsiveness. However, they may feel ill-equipped to implement it due to a lack of resources or adequate training. Standardised curricula and educational materials are often in a dominant culture and sideline diverse perspectives and experiences. Designers wanting to incorporate varied cultural elements might struggle to find comprehensive, accurate, and accessible resources that would allow them to design a culturally responsive learning experience. They might need to spend considerable time outside of their regular duties to source, verify, and adapt materials – a task that becomes daunting in the face of time constraints and workload. Moreover, there is the pivotal issue of training. Not all designers have been equipped with the tools or strategies to design in a culturally responsive manner. Without adequate training, they might either shy away from attempting to be culturally responsive for fear of getting it wrong or, with the best intentions, might inadvertently perpetuate stereotypes or misconceptions.

In multicultural classrooms, significant language differences can pose a considerable challenge. While the content might be culturally tailored, if it is not linguistically accessible, the effectiveness diminishes. Overcoming this might require additional resources like translators, software, tools or bilingual educators, which might not always be feasible.

The utilisation of student data in educational design could raise ethical challenges. While student data can provide valuable insights, it is imperative that ethical guidelines and protocols are adhered to in order to protect the privacy and confidentiality of students. These ethical concerns are magnified when non-teaching staff, such as learning designers, seek access to this sensitive information. Some universities have strict policies about non-teaching staff obtaining/retrieving student data.

Financial constraint is a significant hurdle in the journey of designing for cultural responsiveness. Developing a curriculum, learning modules and assessments that reflect a vast array of cultural perspectives demands intensive research, which necessitates the engagement of experts from various ethnic, linguistic and cultural backgrounds. Employing such a diverse group of experts is a financial commitment that many institutions and companies might find challenging. Furthermore, culturally responsive design often requires the use of diverse resources, such as multicultural textbooks, software tailored to cater to different linguistic groups and interactive tools that honour varied cultural narratives. Procuring or developing these resources involves costs that can quickly escalate. Continuous professional development sessions, workshops on cultural sensitivity and seminars on global pedagogical trends necessitate both time and money. Another financial challenge arises when trying to maintain the relevance of culturally responsive materials. As societal norms, cultural values and global events evolve, educational content must be updated regularly to remain accurate and relevant. This constant updating and revising is not just a pedagogical demand but also a financial strain.

Summary of design for cultural responsiveness

Key Takeaways

What?

Culturally responsive design embraces, deeply values, and celebrates the diverse cultural heritage, knowledge, skills and dispositions that students bring into a learning environment. The design prioritises creating a learning environment that draws on students' inherent cultural backgrounds and experiences as a resource (Taylor & Sobel, 2011). Learners in this environment are provided with opportunities to interact and collaborate with one another to learn from one another and develop multiple perspectives and ways of knowing. This means the foundation of learning and educational design becomes intertwined with students' unique cultural perspectives, frames of reference, language and communication styles (Wages, 2015). Culturally responsive design not only champions academic growth, it also fosters strong interpersonal relationships.

Why?

Learners' engagement and educational performance: Chuang (2016) highlights the positive correlation between culturally responsive approaches and enhanced learner engagement and performance. However, ignoring the cultural backgrounds of learners, or forcing them to conform to dominant sociocultural norms, can result in feelings of alienation, as discussed by White and Lowenthal (2011).

Globalisation: In the face of increasing globalisation and diverse classroom compositions, designing for cultural responsiveness in education becomes very important. Culturally responsive design prepares learners for our globalised world and enhances intercultural competencies that are crucial in today's interconnected societies. The emphasis on cultural responsiveness is not only about equipping learners with knowledge but also about fostering essential life skills like empathy, collaboration and critical thinking.

Decolonial movement: The decolonial movement is gaining momentum. It advocates for educational reforms that accurately represent diverse cultures and histories. This movement challenges the dominant, often Eurocentric narratives, and aims to rectify systemic biases and provide a more balanced educational experience.

How?

Designing for cultural responsiveness begins with foundational groundwork that involves self-awareness and reflection, knowing the learners, and engaging with communities. Learning designers should be aware of our own cultural biases and how these may influence our work. We then get to know the learners, their backgrounds, cultures, and needs. This will help us to create relevant, inclusive, and effective learning experiences. Engaging with the communities assists us to access to valuable cultural capital. By tapping into these resources, learning designers can create a curriculum that both mirrors learners' backgrounds and broadens their horizons and so fosters a sense of belonging and appreciation for diverse cultures.

Once the groundwork is laid, learning designers can focus on key areas to ensure cultural responsiveness: empowerment through representation, assessment and feedback, and active engagement and participation. Empowerment through representation involves integrating diverse voices and perspectives into the curriculum and ensuring learners see themselves reflected in learning materials.

Assessment and feedback strategies should be designed to be culturally responsive. Educational designers

modes of expression and understanding. Choices in assessment that allow learners to demonstrate their achievement and acknowledge diverse life experience and skill sets should be provided for them. Flexible assessment timelines that recognise that significant cultural or religious events might clash with pre-set assessment timelines should be also considered.

Active engagement and participation can be used to foster culturally responsiveness. Some examples of design for active engagement and participation includes:

- Designing learning activities where learners can share their cultural heritage, knowledge, skills and dispositions.
- Adopting teaching strategies that honour different ways of knowing. For example, storytelling might resonate with some cultures more than analytical discussions.
- Using real-world tasks across cultures that encourage learners to dive into cross-cultural scenarios.

References

Biggs, J., & Tang, C. (2011). *Teaching for quality learning at university*. McGraw-Hill Education.

Bishop, R., & Berryman, M. (2010). Te Kotahitanga: Culturally responsive professional development for teachers. *Teacher Development, 14*(2), 173–187. https://doi.org/10.1080/13664530.2010.494497

Boettcher, J. V., & Conrad, R.-M. (2016). *The online teaching* survival guide: Simple and practical pedagogical tips. Jossey-Bass.

Chuang, H.-H. (2016). Leveraging CRT awareness in creating web-based projects through use of online collaborative learning for pre-service teachers. *Educational Technology Research and Development, 64*(4), 857–876. https://doi.org/10.1007/s11423-016-9438-5

Daniels, H., Cole, M., & Wertsch, J. V. (2007). *The Cambridge companion to Vygotsky*. Cambridge University Press.

Gay, G. (2002). Preparing for culturally responsive teaching. *Journal of Teacher Education, 53*(2), 106–116. https://doi.org/10.1177/0022487102053002003

Gay, G. (2018). *Culturally responsive teaching: Theory, research, and practice*. Teachers College Press.

Green, T., Hoffmann, M., Donovan, L., & Phuntsog, N. (2017). Cultural communication characteristics and student connectedness in an online environment: Perceptions and preferences of online graduate students. *International Journal of E-Learning & Distance Education / Revue Internationale du e-Learning et la Formation à Distance, 32*(2), Article 2. https://www.ijede.ca/index.php/jde/article/view/1033

Hargraves, V. (2022). *The principles of culturally responsive teaching*. The Education Hub. https://theeducationhub.org.nz/what-is-culturally-responsive-teaching/

Hindle, R., Savage, C., Meyer, L. H., Sleeter, C. E., Hynds, A., & Penetito, W. (2020). Culturally responsive pedagogies in the visual and performing arts: Exemplars, missed opportunities and challenges. *Curriculum Matters, 7*, 26–47. https://doi.org/10.18296/cm.0133

Kukulska-Hulme, A., Bossu, C., Charitonos, K., Coughlan, T., Deacon, A., Deane, N., Ferguson, R., Herodotou, C., Huang, C.-W., Mayisela, T., Rets, I., Sargent, J., Scanlon, E., Small, J., Walji, S., Weller, M., & Whitelock, D. (2023). *Innovating pedagogy 2023: Open University innovation report 11*. The Open University & University of Cape Town. https://www.open.ac.uk/blogs/innovating/

Kyei-Blankson, L., Blankson, J., & Ntuli, E. (2019). *Care and culturally responsive pedagogy in online settings*. IGI Global.

Ladson-Billings, G. (1995). Toward a theory of culturally relevant pedagogy. *American Educational Research Journal, 32*(3), 465–491. https://doi.org/10.2307/1163320

Ladson-Billings, G. (2021). *Culturally relevant pedagogy: Asking a different question*. Teachers College Press.

Lareau, A. (2011). *Unequal childhoods: Class, race, and family life*. University of California Press.

McGrady, P. B., & Reynolds, J. R. (2013). Racial mismatch in the classroom: Beyond black-white differences. *Sociology of Education, 86*(1), 3–17. https://doi.org/10.1177/0038040712444857

Nguyen, N., & Williams, P. J. (2016). An ICT supported sociocultural approach to improve the teaching of physics. *Asia-Pacific Science Education, 2*(1), 1–21. https://doi.org/10.1186/s41029-016-0008-2

Rogoff, B. (2003). *The cultural nature of human development*. Oxford University Press.

Suarez, C., Anderson, M., & Young, K. (2018). The changing roles and contributions of campus diversity offices and their influence on campus culture. *Metropolitan Universities, 29*(1), Article 1. https://doi.org/10.18060/22178

Taylor, S. V., & Sobel, D. M. (2011). *Culturally responsive pedagogy: Teaching like our students' lives matter*. Emerald.

Wages, M. (2015). *Creating culturally responsive schools: One classroom at a time*. Rowman & Littlefield.

Ware, F. (2006). Warm demander pedagogy: Culturally responsive teaching that supports a culture of achievement for African American students. *Urban Education, 41*(4), 427–456. https://doi.org/10.1177/0042085906289710

White, J. W., & Lowenthal, P. R. (2011). Minority college students and tacit 'codes of power': Developing academic discourses and identities. *The Review of Higher Education, 34*(2), 283–318. https://doi.org/10.1353/rhe.2010.0028

Zajda, J. (2021). Constructivist learning theory and creating effective learning environments. In J. Zajda (Ed.), *Globalisation and Education Reforms: Creating Effective Learning Environments* (pp. 35–50). Springer International Publishing. https://doi.org/10.1007/978-3-030-71575-5_3

About the author

Dr Nhung Nguyen
UNIVERSITY OF TASMANIA
https://www.utas.edu.au/

Nhung Nguyen is a Senior Lecturer in Learning and Teaching at the University of Tasmania with over 19 years of experience in learning design, digital technologies, and science education. Previously, she worked at Auckland University of Technology in New Zealand. Nhung has published over 25 titles and is a sought-after keynote speaker, recognized for transforming educational engagement and inclusive learning experiences.

8. Working with students with lived experience of disability to enhance inclusive and accessible learning

KATIE DUNCAN AND RHIANNON HALL

Introduction

Much work has been done in higher education to create inclusive learning environments and reduce barriers to participation for groups that have historically been excluded. People with disabilities are one such group, and although accessibility is now 'on most people's radar' in universities (Wood et al., 2014, p. 147), more work is needed to ensure staff have adequate knowledge and skills to provide accessible learning environments for all students. Unfortunately, people with disabilities continue to face ableism in the form of barriers that prevent their full participation across all levels of society, with disability rights violations ranging from violence and exploitation, to a lack of services that allow people with disabilities to have autonomy over their lives (Young & Thorne, 2023).

Ableism manifests across the university experience for students in numerous ways, such as: low participation and completion rates, higher levels of student debt than nondisabled students, inadequate resourcing for accessibility accommodations, and frequent reporting of stigmatisation and discrimination (Dolmage, 2017, pp. 20-24). For people with disabilities to have equitable access to higher education, the development and maintenance of accessible learning environments is vital. University staff, both professional and academic, play a crucial role in fostering an inclusive culture that prioritises and provides access for people with disabilities. We define an accessible learning environment as one in which students with disabilities can learn, participate and engage without being hindered by access barriers. While there is crossover in the aims and values guiding our work with those of learning designers and educators, our position is professional staff providing learning and teaching support and guidance to academic staff. Our accessibility projects, especially those involving students, tend to happen in what is often called the 'third space', in which professionals work across the administration/academic threshold (Smith et al., 2021). In the course of this work, we have found that the process of developing effective services for staff often necessitates the input of students, who are able to provide unique insight into existing issues and collaborate with us on solutions. This informs our approach in being facilitators of existing processes, and inviting and encouraging students to be active partners in (re)shaping them.

In our experience, encouraging staff to learn about and adopt accessible practices can be a complex endeavour, yet it also offers additional opportunities to involve and empower students with lived experience of disability. Our approach follows an increasing desire within higher education to collaborate with students. Some of these approaches include **co-design**, Students as Partners (Mercer-Mapstone et al., 2017), inclusive pedagogies (Stentiford & Koutsouris, 2021) and listening to the 'student voice' (Seale, 2010). These are not strictly methodologies, but rather flexible approaches that may significantly vary in their delivery across different institutions. These approaches typically involve a staff and student exchange or collaboration at some stage of the learning or design process, with the aim of using direct feedback from students to inform and enable a better learning experience and to enhance student life more broadly.

Our role as providers of, and advocates for, accessible learning environments and practices has concentrated our efforts on producing instructive content for staff to create and maintain such environments. In this chapter, we explore why accessibility in higher education would greatly benefit from the engagement of university staff at all levels, why collaboration with students who have lived experience of disability is essential for effective results, and we further offer advice drawn from our own experience in collaborating with students for an informative campaign and suite of resources aimed at university staff. We present our project 'Students Explain Digital Accessibility' as a case study and model for working collaboratively with students to incorporate their lived experience into accessibility advice for learning and teaching staff.

Accessibility and social justice

Accessibility comprises many different things, ranging from our legal to our social and ethical obligations. It helps to understand the historical and political context we are building on when working in accessibility.

In 1998, American author and disability rights activist James Charlton published the seminal text, *Nothing about us without us: Disability oppression and empowerment*. The title evokes a clarion call that was beginning to gain prominence within disability rights movements worldwide, capturing the argument that people with disabilities 'know what is best for themselves and their community' (Charlton, 1998, p. 14). In over two decades since Charlton's call, the slogan 'nothing about us without us' has continued to reverberate across activist spaces, despite broader cultural attitudes often being slow to change. For us as professional staff, this framework forms the basis for our approach in advocating for accessible learning environments for students and bolsters our commitment to consultation with students who have lived experience of disability.

For all university staff involved in shaping learning experiences in higher education, inclusive principles are vital for responding to current student demographics, ensuring that curriculum remains relevant for contemporary demands, and improving the learning environment to cater for a diverse (and continuously diversifying) group of students. Beyond the university context, inclusive higher education experiences are an important factor in setting students up for success and graduation, and they contribute to building a more diverse workforce. Students living with a disability report lower rates of satisfaction with tertiary study and are more likely to drop out of university before they complete their studies (Cherastidtham & Norton, 2018; Li & Carroll, 2019). While poor learning experiences may not be the sole cause for student attrition, they are an important factor that can be improved with clear guidelines and adequate resourcing.

Inclusive practice in the context of higher education should be conceived as creating a space for learning that is effective and appropriate for all, and particularly for those who have experienced barriers to education and general social participation. The assertion that such spaces cannot genuinely exist without the involvement of, and consultation with, students who have lived experience is relevant beyond the realms of disability rights and encompasses other marginalised groups who have historically been excluded from higher education. Additionally, while inclusive design practices respond specifically to the requirements of certain groups, in almost all cases, inclusive design holds benefits for everyone, simply by providing a wider range of options and pathways for learners to engage with educational content. This approach also fits within the framework of Universal Design, described by Jay Timothy Dolmage (2017) as a method that, when employed in the context of education, allows 'teachers to structure space and pedagogy in the broadest possible manner', a way of 'building community, building better pedagogy, building opportunities for agency' (p. 118).

In education, this framework is articulated as Universal Design for Learning (UDL) and Universal Design for Instruction (UDI), both of which have been shown to improve accessibility and experience of students with disabilities (Black et al., 2015). While UDL and UDI share common goals with digital accessibility, tensions exist between these approaches, namely that a 'universal' approach does not specifically address accessibility requirements or comply with recommendations for digital accessibility. UDL can provide value for students with disabilities when implemented alongside accessible practices and may reduce the need for individual accommodations (Ableser & Moore, 2018). As our work focuses on the experiences of students with disabilities, our approach is based primarily on digital accessibility practices.

Benefits of working with students with lived experience of disability

Lived experience provides unique insight

Various student experiences in the higher education sphere, whether they take place in person in a physical classroom, in digital spaces via online learning or in the wider university campus, are not necessarily designed inclusively. That is to say, often these experiences are designed to fit assumed social norms. When those doing the designing lack the lived experience of someone who does not fit these norms, crucial elements may be overlooked and present insurmountable barriers for students with disabilities. Working with students who have lived experience of disability can often reveal shortcomings that designers in any field may be completely unaware of.

Rosemarie Garland-Thomson (2011) utilises the concept of the misfit to describe the social positioning of people with disabilities in this context. In arguing for the inherent value of the misfit, Garland-Thomson states that 'the concept of misfitting as a shifting spatial and perpetually temporal relationship confers agency and value on disabled subjects at risk of social devaluation by highlighting adaptability, resourcefulness, and subjugated knowledge as potential effects of misfitting' (2011, p. 592). In developing our project, we purposefully sought out students who identified as having lived experience of disability (noting that these students may not always identify with the terms disabled or person with disabilities), anticipating that the opportunity to hear directly from them about the barriers of inaccessibility they had encountered in their studies would reveal unknown shortcomings of a learning design project.

Student agency

A positive outcome of involving students in the design process for any type of work is that it increases the likelihood that students will endorse the final product. Shelley Wright (2012) argues that 'powerful learning begins to manifest when students take responsibility and ownership for their learning when they become co-creators of their learning experience, rather than their education being something that is done to them. True student empowerment and engagement begins when we cross the threshold of co-creation' (2012). While our project was not a learning design project, this is a valuable approach for design of any element of the university experience.

The students we worked with often expressed a desire to be able to tell their teachers when they encountered problems with inaccessibility (or in some cases, for teachers to respond to and respect their accessibility requirements when they were informed of them). Our goal in the project was to act as facilitators for students and connect their messages with the staff audience – bringing into action the crossing of the threshold discussed by Wright (2012).

Accessibility is crucial

Although the students we recruited for the project were sought after for their accessibility expertise, their contributions also provided important insight into aspects of the student experience unrelated to accessibility. For example, while some members of the group required captions for their learning to be accessible, most appreciated the provision of captions and found them helpful for other reasons. In our discussions, students pointed out the ways that functions often regarded as accessibility features provided important support for many students, and for different reasons (such as the usefulness of captions for students who speak English as a secondary language). Alt text was not only important for students with vision-related disabilities, it also provided information for students who might not be able to load images due to a poor internet connection. The benefits of accessible practices, including overall improvement of digital learning environments for anyone who uses them, form the guiding principle for our messaging on accessibility.

Our project: Students Explain Digital Accessibility

We are part of a learning and teaching support unit at the University of Technology, Sydney. As of January 2023, UTS employed 3,836 full- time equivalent staff members including casual staff, and had 44,615 enrolled students, including international students (UTS, 2023). The main UTS campus is located in Sydney's Central Business District, and courses are taught face-to-face, online and in hybrid formats.

Learning and teaching support for academics at UTS is overseen by the Institute for Interactive Media and Learning (IML), which is in the division of the Deputy Vice-Chancellor (Education and Students). The team consists of academic and professional staff who develop, coordinate, facilitate and advise on a range of projects and initiatives that support and improve the learning and teaching experience. The unit we are part of, the LX.lab, is housed within IML and provides direct support to academics in their learning and teaching, via face-to-face and online consultations, events and workshops, and digital content on our LX at UTS website. As well as timely support, we also aim to upskill academics in using technologies and enhancing the learning experience.

While the LX.lab now has a dedicated Inclusive Practices team which supports and explores accessibility guidelines and assistive technologies, this was not the case when the project was carried out in 2020. Our small team consisted of a learning technologist, a content officer and a media officer. As our experience shows, a specialist role in accessibility is not necessarily required for this kind of project.

This project was developed in response to our observations of student experiences of inaccessible learning environments, and a lack of resources for staff to consult when preparing their subject materials. We had also observed that staff inexperienced with accessibility barriers lacked an understanding of the significant impacts for students. These observations were made in workshops we held, in staff requests for support, in our communication with academics from faculties across the university, and most apparently in requests for accessible alternatives and accommodations from students registered with the UTS Accessibility Service.

Previous training sessions with staff were well-received when we demonstrated an example of poor user experience by showing how a screen reader would interact (or fail to interact) with content that had not been formatted in an accessible way. Colleagues expressed interest in seeing more examples of the different ways that assistive technology users interact with content.

These responses indicated to us that for staff to understand the significance of unmet accessibility requirements for students, they needed a more direct explanation and description of the impacts from a user perspective. While we had been aware of the gap in supportive resources for staff around accessibility, the effectiveness of showing the impacts of inaccessibility from a user perspective reinforced the importance of ensuring that the voices of those most affected should be included in filling that gap. In arguing for the concept of 'nothing about us without us', Charlton (1998) states that the slogan forces 'cultural systems to incorporate people with disabilities into the decision-making process and to recognize that the experiential knowledge of these people is pivotal in making decisions that affect their lives' (p. 25). With our aim to provide clear and comprehensive resources that we hoped would shape the practice of staff, specifically by bringing their attention to the real-world impact of accessibility, it was both an ideal opportunity and essential to work alongside students with lived experience.

Using a co-design approach

Co-design is a collaborative approach to design. It is about designing with, not for, people. It brings the expertise of the designers (or facilitators) together with the expertise of people with lived experience to create and learn about something. Co-design can be adapted and used in many different contexts, for example product design, urban planning, healthcare, technology and software development, social innovation and activism, and education – in short, anywhere that design is being undertaken to create something.

Co-design can be adapted to these different contexts, because it is not a set process. According to McKercher (2020), 'co-design is about how we are being (our mindsets), what we are doing (our methods) and how our systems embrace the participation of people with lived experience (social movements)'. McKercher sets out four key principles for co-design:

- Share power: It is important that lived experience participants are able to make decisions in the co-design process, and that they are not just there in a consultative capacity.
- Prioritise relationships: It is important to build trust and create a safe space so that everyone can bring their authentic self to the process.
- Use participatory means: It is important that lived experience participants are actively engaged and are partners during the process.
- Build capability: It is important that facilitators enable and encourage the participants to be able to engage with the process. 'Everyone has something to teach and something to learn' – and that goes for lived experience participants and the facilitators as well.

The *Students Explain Digital Accessibility* video series is an example of co-design, as we were collaboratively designing the videos together. We shared power with the students, by asking them to write the script based on their own lived experiences. We prioritised relationships, creating a safe space where we listened and valued the experiences of our students. We used participatory methods to ensure they were actively contributing to the process. And finally, we were able to build capacity – both of the students, by teaching them how to create video content, write scripts, write blogs and present on camera, and ourselves because we were able to learn a lot from them about accessible content, which was one of the most rewarding experiences as facilitators.

Our process

There is no set way to do co-design. However, there are several key considerations for implementing a co-design project. In this section we detail the key stages required for a successful co-design process, using the *Students Explain Digital Accessibility* video series as an example.

The key stages for the creation of *Students Explain Digital Accessibility* were:

- planning and setting clear objectives
- recruiting participants
- creating a safe space
- collaborating and designing
- getting feedback.

Planning and setting clear objectives

It is important to have an idea of the goals you are aiming to achieve from the beginning so that you can:

- streamline decision-making by having a clear direction and focus
- align all stakeholders' expectations so that everyone is on the same page
- set your target audience so you can take a user-centred approach
- develop an evaluation strategy to measure if you are successful.

For *Students Explain Digital Accessibility*, our objective was to create a suite of videos targeting academics and learning and teaching staff to build a better understanding of the importance of accessibility in digital learning environments. To do this, we knew we wanted to recruit a number of students with lived experience of disability to help us develop the content and appear in the videos to demonstrate how they are impacted by inaccessible content.

To help communicate this and ensure that the project team was on the same page, we developed a project brief. In our project brief we articulated the overarching principles of our project:

Extract from *Students Explain Digital Accessibility* project brief:

Our project is guided by two overarching principles. The first is a slogan often associated with international disability rights movements, 'Nothing About Us Without Us', which declares that the structural inequities produced by disability oppression cannot be dismantled without the involvement of those with lived experience (Charlton, 1998, p. 3). The alignment of our project with this statement necessitates the involvement of the people who are most severely affected by the issue that we seek to address, being students with disabilities, and positions their voices and experiences as the most essential component of the project. Our second guiding principle, which we often employ in our own accessibility training for academics, is that accessibility benefits all, is critical for some, and should be recognised as a tool for enhancing digital learning environments. This stance is well supported in scholarship on inclusive/universal design (Gilbert, 2019, p. 25).

By setting out the objectives and principles at the beginning, we were able to make decisions easily, provide clear instructions for the students we worked with and map out our project from beginning to end.

Recruiting participants

Compensation for participation

McKercher (2020) argues that in an authentic co-design process, 'co-designers must be recognised for their time and not coerced into volunteering'.

Students should always be paid for work they do, especially students from marginalised groups like those with lived experience of disability. Students should only be involved in projects when they can be appropriately compensated.

For the *Students Explain Digital Accessibility* we originally applied for a UTS Social Impact Grant in 2020. These are $5,000 grants offered annually and administered through the Centre for Social Justice & Inclusion to support researchers and practitioners at UTS to maximise their contribution to positive social change.

While our grant submission was unsuccessful (in part because the work we were proposing was best covered by available institutional funding rather than that particular grant program), we were able to secure funding through the Centre for Social Justice & Inclusion via the Access & Inclusion Plan. This demonstrates that it is worth pursuing accessibility and inclusion projects through multiple avenues and teams should not be discouraged by initial failure – in short, do not give up.

Some ideas for finding funding include:

- small grant programs either within your institution or community grants (check your local council) and
- partnering with other units or organisations that have similar aims as your project.

Writing inclusive expression of interest/job advertisements

It is important to be mindful of appropriate language when you are crafting the job advertisement or expression of interest for your co-design project. This will be the first impression of the project and project team for the person with lived experience, and it will be more effective and trustworthy for potential applicants if recruitment information is written inclusively, with clear expectations set out for the role. To make the process positive and productive for your co-design participants, or students, you need to create a safe space for them to be able to share their own experiences. This starts with the language you use when you are recruiting them, so it is important that you set the correct tone and use person-first language.

Some tips for structuring the expression of interest/job advertisement for your participants include:

- Use person-first language, such as 'person with a disability' rather than 'disabled person', as some people do not identify as being 'disabled'. Appropriate language may differ depending on the context or the people you are working with. People who have the same disability or medical condition might prefer different language, so it is best to start with person-first language or ask people their preference.
- Start with the context of the project and the types of lived experience you need to fulfil the overall objectives of the project.
- Set the expectations of the role beyond their lived experience. For example, have criteria for the person that include the types of lived experience the project requires in addition to other skills or experiences they will need. For example: Will they need to collaborate? Will they need to

be able to share their experiences? Will they need to learn new skills?
- Include the remuneration information and how the successful candidates will be compensated for their time and expertise.
- Include a position description so people are clear on the tasks that are going to be required of them.
- Do not ask people to disclose any medical or personal information. It is none of your business. Even if you need someone with specific lived experience, outline what types of experiences you are looking for, and then ask the candidates to tell you why they would be suitable for the role. This will allow them to disclose as much information as is relevant and/or they are comfortable with.

For example, for the *Students Explain Digital Accessibility* videos in the job advertisement, where we were looking for our Digital Accessibility Ambassadors, we outlined the project thus:

> The LX.lab is looking for current UTS students, with lived experience of disability, to become Digital Accessibility Ambassadors. This is a paid, short-term role to assist the LX.lab to create video resources on digital accessibility for academics across UTS.

We were clear that we were looking for students with experience or some familiarity with using assistive technology, or lived experience of disability, and who had some knowledge of digital access requirements and accommodations. However, they also needed to be capable of working collaboratively, of reflecting on and sharing experiences and opinions, and be willing to be the voice/talent/narrator for video content and to offer feedback and critique on work.

It is also important that you make sure that the recruitment process is accessible for your potential participants, so make sure you ask them if they have any access requirements. Be clear that this is to ensure they have an accessible experience and that the information is not going to be used to inform recruitment decisions.

Privacy is another big part of recruiting people with lived experience. Not all people with disabilities want to disclose details of their conditions or whether they have a disability, and it is vital to respect and understand people's wishes in these circumstances.

Sourcing participants

When the time comes to source your participants, it is helpful to partner with a team or organisation that helps support people with disabilities to help spread the word. In our experience, people in these types of teams/organisations are happy to share information about paid opportunities.

For this project, we were supported by the university's Accessibility Services team who are the central contact point for all students living with one or more disabilities, or ongoing medical or mental health conditions. For *Students Explain Digital Accessibility*, we were able to share our job advertisement for our Digital Accessibility Ambassadors with the Accessibility Services team to send out to students who are registered with the service. We also shared it with the Careers Team, in case there were students with lived experience of disability who were not registered.

Depending on your context, recruitment might look different. If you work in the tertiary sector, you could ask whether your in-house accessibility support staff are able to assist you with distributing job advertisements. If you do not have an in-house accessibility team that you could partner with, you could look into organisations that help support people with lived experience of disabilities. Some Australia-wide organisations include:

- Australian Network on Disability
- Deaf Australia
- Hearing Australia
- Neurodiversity Hub
- Vision Australia.

Creating a safe space

An effective co-design experience requires that all your participants feel psychologically safe, so that they are able to bring their authentic selves and collaborate and engage freely, without the fear of judgement. In order to do that, you need to prioritise relationships with your participants (one of the principles of our co-design approach). This includes giving your participants the space to be heard, and genuinely listening to them.

Some other considerations to be mindful of include:

- modelling inclusive practices (beyond accessibility)
- implementing inclusive practices and everyone's access requirements
- structuring sessions in a way to encourage collaboration.

Modelling inclusive practices (beyond accessibility)

People's lives and experiences are intersectional, and so it is important to model inclusive practices outside of accessibility, while also considering the ways in which intersecting identities can affect a student's accessibility requirements. For example, an Acknowledgement of Country that recognises the traditional owners of the land on which you are holding your sessions is generally a respectful gesture (particularly in an Australian context, though this can also be appropriate in other locations). You can also be inclusive of LGBTQIA+ participants, and if you are comfortable to announce your own pronouns, include pronouns on name tags or on the online platform you are using like Zoom, provide opportunities for participants to specify their own pronouns, and ensure that you use the correct pronouns when communicating with participants.

Implementing inclusive practices

Before the session:

- Create accessible workshop materials.
- Share documents and slides beforehand to give people time to prepare; especially if they use assistive technology, it is good for them to have a copy that they can use with their assistive technology.
- Ensure the room and facilities are accessible, e.g., if you have students who use wheelchairs or other mobility aids.
- Turn on captions (this can be useful in hybrid, face-to-face and online sessions).

During the session:

- Use a microphone for hearing augmentation and to enhance sound clarity.
- Give participants multiple ways of engaging with the session (e.g., by writing/typing as well as verbal).

- Provide opportunities for people to reflect individually before discussing in smaller groups.
- Schedule regular breaks during the session and encourage people to take breaks whenever they need.
- Narrate what is on the screen. Do not assume everyone can see what is happening on your screen and describe essential visual content.
- Provide clear instructions, with unambiguous, specific questions.

Implement access requirements for all participants

Once you have asked participants about access requirements that might impact their participation, take the time to make sure that these requirements are met.

If you know that someone is using assistive technology, make sure you adjust the technology you are using so it will work for all participants. You can also make sure that in their group they have a scribe and/or reader, and that they can also read other people's responses (it will not be enough to only assist with input of information; they will also need to know about other participant contributions to be able to fully participate).

Getting feedback and sense-checking with participants

As co-design is about designing with and not for, it is important that participants are given the opportunity to provide feedback on the final product/service/video that is created.

The structure of the Students Explain Digital Accessibility co-design process

We ran three collaborative sessions where we as facilitators were able to learn from the students, in addition to providing opportunities for them to learn new skills and connect with one another. The following list shows how we structured the sessions and phases of the project:

- Collaborative session one: responding to the accessible content practices
- Project team: content planning
- Collaborative session two: script- writing
- Individual: script- writing and check-ins
- Individual: filming
- Project team: editing
- Collaborative session three: feedback and blog- writing workshop
- Individual: blog-writing
- Launch event

Collaborative session one: Responding to the accessible content practices

During the first session, we ran an icebreaker activity to ensure that our five Digital Accessibility Ambassadors were introduced and felt comfortable working together.

We then provided context for the type of work we do in the LX.lab and our proposed plan for the videos. As we were intending to put the videos on the LX at UTS website, alongside our accessible content practices, we provided participants with an overview of each of the content practices. We then asked them to individually draw on their own experiences, explicitly stating that there were no wrong answers and that they should not feel pressured to come up with answers if they were not sure or did not have any personal experience with a particular practice. This was completed in a shared Google doc.

After allowing ten minutes for individual work and reflection on each accessible practice, we then discussed it as a wider group. This provided the students with multiple ways of engaging in the session, in addition to having time to collect their own thoughts and ideas and prepare for the group discussion.

This section created space for participants to share their expertise based on their own lived experience. We were there to learn from them, to create a safe space and facilitate the conversation. Listening and valuing participants' experiences is a key task for a facilitator.

Project team: Content planning

After the Digital Accessibility Ambassadors shared their thoughts and opinions on the accessible content practices, it was our opportunity to provide our expertise in video creation and online content. The project team used responses from the students to plan and structure the videos – their expertise also helped us to refine our scope. For example, we removed a video from our plans when we found that the topic did not resonate with the participants.

During this time, we created our script template that would remain consistent across the series. This template, or shell, was used as scaffolding for the students to articulate their own experiences.

Collaborative session two: Script-writing

During our second collaborative session we shared the template script with the students. We provided advice on script-writing and allocated time in the session for individual work on scripts. The participants made decisions and were in control of the content of the scripts that would be used in the final videos.

The second session was also adjusted to meet changed access requirements, as one participant needed to attend online. This introduced us to the process of creating an accessible hybrid meeting. While our set-up was not particularly well-suited for the purpose, we were able to make adequate changes to ensure that accessibility requirements of both the online participant and those attending in person were met. Our lesson from the experience was that it is always worth taking the time to explore different ways of providing accessibility.

Learnings from our collaborative sessions

As discussed earlier in this chapter, people with lived experience of disability have insight that can only be gained through that lived experience. While we had knowledge of generally accepted accessibility standards, online learning during the COVID-19 pandemic had revealed further barriers that had perhaps not been fully explored before this time. Some of the issues raised in our discussions throughout the project were:

- the importance of clear, good- quality audio in both recorded lectures and online classes facilitated via platforms like Zoom and Microsoft Teams.
- a typically low usage of captions and transcripts that

impacted learning, not only for students with hearing loss but also for students living with other types of disabilities.
- a feeling of disconnection and lack of engagement with online learning.
- disorganised file management in digital learning management systems, which led to issues in finding tasks and details of assessments.
- poorly formatted documents lacking in readability.

Collaborative session three: Feedback and blog-writing workshop

After filming and editing were completed, we ran our final collaborative session with the students. This involved showing them rough cuts of the videos, soliciting feedback from the group and ensuring that we were representing them in accordance with their personal preferences. This is an important part of the process and is a way to share power with your participants.

During this session we also ran a blog-writing workshop, so that the students could write their own blog posts to promote the video series. This provided further opportunity to amplify their voices and be able to tell their stories to the learning and teaching community in a more flexible format.

Student Digital Accessibility Ambassador blogs

- 'For me, accessibility adjustments equal success', by Ashley Willcox
- Stop speaking into a black abyss, turn on your video, by Bettina Liang
- To the student that's hesitant to disclose, by Elham Hafiz
- Creating accessible and comfortable learning

environments for accessibility students, by Jatin Dhanji
- Why inclusive environments are important for learning, by Jackson Tait

Other ways to enhance inclusive learning

Nothing beats working with people with lived experience and being able to fully immerse yourself in a co-design process – we cannot stress enough the richness that comes from working with people with lived experience. However, it is understandable that not all projects can be given the resourcing (both time and money) for co-design. Co-design may also not be appropriate for all-inclusive practice projects, depending on circumstances like project length, expected output, stakeholders and other factors. Consider the suggestions below as alternative ways to create and engage with accessibility practice:

Familiarise yourself with accessibility standards

Education providers have a legal obligation to take reasonable steps to enable students with a disability to participate in education on the same basis as a student without a disability. The two key state and federal legislation that you need to know about are:

- *Disability Discrimination Act 1992* (Cth)
- *Disability Standards for Education 2005* (Cth)

For learning designers, this includes designing inclusive and accessible learning online learning environments.

The Web Content Accessibility Guidelines (WCAG) are the

international standards when it comes to web accessibility. They are important for learning designers to know. They can be overwhelming when you first encounter them, so if you are new to accessibility you can start with the basics like the UTS Accessible Content Practices.

Try using assistive technology, or your keyboard only to access content

If you have designed a learning experience for students, try accessing it using a screen reader, other type of assistive technology or just your keyboard. While testing with a native user will provide more value, having first-hand experience can give you a better understanding of how they operate.

Screen readers, especially those designed for people with low vision, tend to require a steep learning curve, but they will provide you with a better insight for designing. A user experience that works with a screen reader is likely to work for all your students. NVDA is a free screen reader for Windows, and Mac has many native accessibility features.

Use accessibility checkers and simulators (but don't rely on them alone)

Many programs have an in-built accessibility checker. It is important to use these tools in order to capture accessibility issues that can be checked programmatically, such as missing alternative text on images, colour contrast issues or heading levels not being used sequentially. However, they cannot understand your purpose or context so they will not be able to determine if your alternative text is meaningful, or whether you have structured your document appropriately using heading levels.

There are also a number of simulators available that can simulate different types of disabilities like colour vision deficiency, which can be helpful in selecting colour combinations.

Find information and content from people with lived experience

If you cannot work directly with students, there is still an abundance of online content created by people with lived experience. Seek out, read, and learn more.

Conclusion

Accessibility is a vital part of the big picture of inclusivity and diversity. All people working in higher education play an important role in advocating for and improving accessibility, and ensuring that the voices of people with lived experience of disability are included in planning and design processes makes this practice more effective. Learning designers are particularly well positioned to ensure that accessibility is considered from the outset, and is embedded consistently in university learning experiences. We encourage all learning and teaching practitioners to take the time to learn about accessible practices, look for opportunities to include students with lived experience and make accessibility a permanent priority in their practice.

References

Ableser, J., & Moore, C. (2018). Universal design for learning and digital accessibility: Compatible partners or a conflicted marriage? *Educause Review*. https://er.educause.edu/articles/2018/9/universal-design-for-learning-and-digital-accessibility-compatible-partners-or-a-conflicted-marriage

Black, R. D., Weinberg, L. A., & Brodwin, M. G. (2015). Universal design for learning and instruction: Perspectives of students with disabilities in higher education. *Exceptionality Education International, 25*(2), 1–26. https://doi.org/10.5206/eei.v25i2.7723

Charlton, J. I. (1998). *Nothing about us without us: Disability oppression and empowerment*. University of California Press.

Cherastidtham, I., & Norton, A. (2018). *University attrition: What helps and what hinders university completion?* Grattan Institute.

Dhanji, J. (2021, March 2). Students explain: Creating accessible and comfortable environments for accessibility students. *LX at UTS*. https://lx.uts.edu.au/blog/2021/03/02/enabling-accessible-comfortable-environment-for-students/

Dolmage, J. (2017). *Academic ableism: Disability and higher education*. University of Michigan Press.

Garland-Thomson, R. (2011). Misfits: A feminist materialist disability concept. *Hypatia, 26*(3), 591–609. https://doi.org/10.1111/j.1527-2001.2011.01206.x

Hafiz, E. (2021, April 19). Students explain: To the student that's hesitant to disclose. *LX at UTS*. https://lx.uts.edu.au/blog/2021/04/19/students-explain-student-hesitant-to-disclose/

Li, I. W., & Carroll, D. R. (2019). Factors influencing dropout and academic performance: An Australian higher education equity perspective. *Journal of Higher Education Policy and Management, 42*(1), 14–30. https://doi.org/10.1080/1360080X.2019.1649993

Liang, B. (2021, April 14). Students explain: 'Stop speaking into a black abyss, turn on your video'. *LX at UTS*. https://lx.uts.edu.au/blog/2021/04/14/students-explain-stop-speaking-into-a-black-abyss/

McKercher, K. A. (2020). *Beyond sticky notes: Co-design for real: Mindsets, methods, and movements*. Beyond Sticky Notes.

Mercer-Mapstone, L., Dvorakova, S. L., Matthews, K. E., Abbot, S., Cheng, B., Felten, P., Knorr, K., Marquis, E., Shammas, R., & Swaim, K. (2017). A systematic literature review of students as partners in higher education. *International Journal for Students as Partners, 1*(1), 15–37. https://doi.org/10.15173/ijsap.v1i1.3119

Seale, J. (2010). Doing student voice work in higher education: An exploration of the value of participatory methods. *British Educational Research Journal, 36*(6), 995–1015. https://doi.org/10.1080/01411920903342038

Smith, C., Holden, M., Yu, E., & Hanlon, P. (2021) 'So what do you do?': Third space professionals navigating a Canadian university context. *Journal of Higher Education Policy and Management, 43*(5), 505–519. https://doi.org/10.1080/1360080X.2021.1884513

Stentiford, L., & Koutsouris, G. (2021). What are inclusive pedagogies in higher education? A systematic scoping review. *Studies in Higher Education, 46*(11), 2245–2261. https://doi.org/10.1080/03075079.2020.1716322

Tait, J. (2021, March 31). Students explain: Why inclusive

environments are important for learning. *LX at UTS*. https://lx.uts.edu.au/blog/2021/03/31/students-explain-inclusive-environments/

UTS. (2023, July 4). *Facts, figures and rankings*. University of Technology Sydney. https://www.uts.edu.au/about/university/facts-figures-and-rankings

Willcox, A. (2021, March 17). Students explain: 'For me, accessibility adjustments equal success'. *LX at UTS*. https://lx.uts.edu.au/blog/2021/03/17/accessibility-adjustments-equal-success/

Wood, T., Dolmage, J., Price, M., & Lewiecki-Wilson, C. (2014). Where we are: Disability and accessibility – moving beyond Disability 2.0 in composition studies. *Composition Studies, 42*(2), 147–150.

Wright, S. (2012, September 24). Deep learning isn't about technology. *Powerful Learning Practice*. https://plpnetwork.com/2012/09/24/deeper-learning-technology/

Young, E., & Thorne, L. (2023, September 29). The disability royal commission is over and the recommendations are in: Here are the main takeaways. *ABC News*. https://www.abc.net.au/news/2023-09-29/disability-royal-commission-recommendations-findings-explained/102911410

About the authors

Dr Katie Duncan
UNIVERSITY OF TECHNOLOGY SYDNEY
https://www.uts.edu.au

Katie Duncan is an advocate for inclusivity in higher education, focusing on practical ways to make subjects accessible for all students. She established the Inclusive Practices team at the University of Technology Sydney's LX.lab in 2021, winning two Accessibility in Action Awards. Katie integrates student voices into her work through paid co-design opportunities and leads the Student Learning Advisory Committee, ensuring accessibility improvements are informed by students' experiences.

Rhiannon Hall
UNIVERSITY OF TECHNOLOGY SYDNEY
https://www.uts.edu.au

Rhiannon Hall writes and edits content for LX at the University of Technology Sydney's Education Portfolio. She focuses on learning and teaching, with a strong interest in accessibility and social equity. Rhiannon collaborates with students and co-facilitates projects on accessible practices. She holds a Bachelor of Communication from the University of Newcastle and a Master of Cultural Studies from the University of Sydney.

9. Baking a cake: Engaging staff in inclusive learning design

BRUNA CONTRO PRETERO

Introduction

I find that discussions about accessibility and inclusive learning design are often best illustrated through the analogy of baking a cake. Frequently, especially regarding digital accessibility, learning experiences are designed only for accessibility to be considered as an afterthought. Incorporating accessibility at a later stage can be either impractical or excessively costly. To put it into perspective, with digital products (such as software and websites) as an example, rectifying an accessibility issue in the final product might incur a cost of up to 30 times the investment required for integrating accessibility from the outset (Gualtieri, 2011). This issue persists in the domain of learning design as well. When accessibility isn't a foundational consideration, rectifying problems at a later stage inevitably becomes more costly than if an inclusive design approach had been embraced from the start (Burgstahler & Doe, 2015).

> **Vignette 1: A costly oversight**
>
> Once I was tasked with rendering a large council paper accessible. Unfortunately, accessibility was not prioritised from the document's inception; it was only addressed at the end. What should have taken minutes at the document's outset – e.g., adjusting styles, headings and creating an accessibility plan – resulted in three more days of work. When seen in context, this scenario not only caused delays in other tasks but also inflated the final document's cost far beyond what would have been required had accessibility been incorporated during the planning stage.

Here's where the cake analogy proves invaluable.

Imagine building or creating your accessible learning experience (e.g., an online learning module, a multimedia resource, an alternative assessment) much like baking a cake. Often, accessibility is treated as an optional embellishment during the design phase. Essentially, the learning experience is built, and afterwards, considerations are made for incorporating certain accessible elements (such as checking colour contrast and looking at alternative text) (Burgstahler & Cory, 2010; Burgstahler & Doe, 2015). Using the cake analogy, accessibility in this example would resemble the decorative sprinkles on the top of the cake – something that's added for decoration right at the end. However, for any learning experience to genuinely achieve accessibility, it must be a fundamental ingredient, just like adding baking powder to the cake batter. Without baking powder, the cake may rise and taste okay, but the reality remains that only a limited audience would truly enjoy it. This is how I perceive accessibility – as one of the main ingredients, and not an optional extra.

Similarly, even when the intent to integrate accessibility is present from the beginning, its actual inclusion might get delayed (Beetham & Sharpe, 2013). These setbacks often stem from the complexities of incorporating Universal Design for Learning (UDL), for example, and digital accessibility principles into practice, which demand thoughtful considerations and can momentarily stall projects (Burgstahler & Cory, 2010). The challenge intensifies if designers still haven't fully integrated inclusion and accessibility into their personal approach to learning design.

> **Vignette 2: The rushed decision**
>
> In my role as an educational designer, I once collaborated with an academic seeking to revamp the presentation of biological/biochemical cycles for their students. This request came just a week before their content deadline. While accessibility always formed the bedrock of my design principles, in the urgency of the moment, I overlooked discussing it before delving into the design with the academic. We both found the idea of a drag and drop activity appealing, as it promised immediate feedback and an engaging way for students to test their understanding.

> However, upon reflection during the design process, I realised that drag and drop activities inherently pose accessibility challenges. Such tasks can be exclusionary for visually impaired students or those reliant on keyboard-only navigation. Despite the hours we'd already invested in conceptualising this activity, I decided to supplement the drag and drop with a detailed textual description of the cycle. Both the academic and I recognised the limitations of the activity and committed to revisiting and refining this approach for the course's next iteration.
>
> In hindsight, I could have:
>
> - Enlightened the academic about the accessibility challenges associated with drag and drop activities.
> - Considered alternative engagement tools from the outset.
>
> Thus, when collaborating with academics and other subject matter experts (SMEs) on content and activity design, always ponder:
>
> How can I ensure accessibility and inclusivity are central to this discussion?
>
> Am I unintentionally setting up barriers that might hinder student participation or engagement with this choice of activity?

Baking the cake is only one part of the challenge. Serving the cake is as vital as baking it. Have you ever designed an inclusive learning object that was pedagogically robust and fit for purpose and yet struggled to gain support from fellow learning designers, academics and SMEs to implement it? Unfortunately, this is a more prevalent challenge than one might assume. Often, we focus heavily on the product's design, neglecting the strategy for implementation and adoption. That is, we plan to bake the cake but don't necessarily think about how, when and to whom we might serve it.

> **Vignette 3: The power of relationships**
>
> In one instance, I was tasked with developing and implementing a template for a learning management system (LMS) course site. This template encompassed all the essential elements for an effective and inclusive LMS course site: consistency and clarity in content organisation, accessibility-conscious and user-friendly interactive elements, engaging activities, etc. While academics recognised the template's benefits, its spontaneous adoption was minimal. Those who did embrace it were primarily academics with whom we had established a rapport. Before rolling out the template, we engaged these academics, guiding them through the process and illustrating how its usage would benefit them and their students. The successful adoption of the templates by these academics was only possible because we identified their needs and were able to 'serve them the cake' in a way that seemed meaningful and relevant to them. Drawing from this experience and numerous others, I've become very mindful of how I promote

> the resources I create. These considerations now influence the planning phase of any project I undertake, acknowledging that, much like the cake, how I serve it holds equal importance.
>
> So, when working on inclusive learning design projects, always ask yourself:
>
> - Do I know the needs of the academics and learning designers I am engaging with?
> - How can I align their needs to what this learning experience has to offer?
> - How can I make this learning experience relevant to academics and fellow learning designers involved in the project to increase buy-in?
> - How can I be explicit in demonstrating the value proposition of this new learning object?

This chapter adopts the above-mentioned cake analogy to delve into the planning, creation and implementation stages of an inclusive learning design project. Just as we meticulously plan, bake and serve a cake, we should similarly address each phase of our inclusive learning design projects.

A recipe for success: Planning for inclusive learning design

Baking a cake requires careful planning and consideration of key ingredients. The same is true for the process of designing an inclusive learning experience. In this section, we'll follow the cake recipe analogy – exploring the essential questions of what, who, how and why – to guide us through the crucial planning stages of inclusive learning design. We'll then delve into the ingredients necessary for creating a rich and authentic learning experience that resonates with all learners.

We will use the example of creating an inclusive and accessible online learning module in this chapter to illustrate the cake analogy. Consider the following scenario:

Scenario

You are a member of the learning design team at a prestigious higher education institution. Your task is to collaborate with one or more subject matter experts (SMEs) to develop an online learning module. This module is designed to seamlessly replace a series of traditional lectures, presenting students with a rich and engaging exploration into dermatology and skin conditions. Below, we will dive into the essential steps you, as a learning designer, need to navigate to effectively plan and design this online module. Alongside each section (what, who, how and why), you'll encounter a checklist, detailed much like a well-curated recipe, acting as a concise guide to assist you in creating an online learning experience that is both impactful and inclusive.

What: Defining the online learning module

In the world of inclusive learning design, the 'what' refers to the learning module itself. What are the learning objectives? What content needs to be covered? What are the desired outcomes for learners? Just as a cake has a unique flavour and design, your learning module should have a distinct educational flavour that aligns with your objectives. Outline the key concepts and topics you intend to cover. This stage sets the foundation for everything that follows. Here, you also begin forging meaningful connections with your fellow learning designers, academics and additional SMEs – after all, 'serving the cake' truly commences during its preparation.

In this context, as a learning designer your first step is to hold collaborative meetings with your SMEs to delve into the core of your learning module. Your primary goal in this stage is to identify what students should be able to achieve after completing the module. For instance, should they be able to identify the different layers and structures of the skin? Evaluate skin conditions and recognise potential signs of infections and infestations? Integrate these concepts with others learned in other courses during their degree? Be able to apply diagnostic principles and describe the best course of action? Or all of the above? All these learning outcomes need to be documented.

Once the learning outcomes are fleshed out, it is important to understand what content and scaffolding students would need to achieve these goals. During these preliminary discussions with the SMEs, the objective is to grasp the learning goals and content scope, which shapes the trajectory of the module's development. Additionally, building rapport with your collaborators is vital from the outset. Understanding their perspectives and needs ensures a cohesive approach. Such relationships enhance collaboration throughout the project, allowing you to tailor the module in a manner that resonates with their expectations and expertise.

> **Checklist**
>
> ( ) Schedule initial collaborative meetings with SMEs.
>
> ( ) Clearly define and document the module's learning outcomes.
>
> ( ) Understand the core content to be covered in the module.
>
> ( ) Understand the needs and scaffolding required for learners to achieve the desired learning outcomes.
>
> ( ) Foster initial relationships with collaborators for a cohesive design approach.

Who: Identifying stakeholders

Like determining who will enjoy your cake, in the context of learning design, identifying the 'who' is about recognising the stakeholders you will have to engage with to promote your online learning module. Who are the academics and professional staff who need to buy into this module? Consider their diverse needs, preferences and potential challenges. Just as you would customise a cake to suit the tastes of your guests, tailor your learning module to cater to the needs and expectations of your fellow learning designers and collaborators.

In this phase, your foremost responsibility is to delineate a thorough list of stakeholders invested in the online module's success. Consider the following:

1. **Academics and SMEs:** Their insights are crucial, given their subject expertise and understanding of student learning in this area. For instance, when developing this module, collaboration with a lead academic and several other dermatologists – each with distinct specialisations and teaching roles – might be essential.
2. **Students:** As the main consumers of the content, securing their initial feedback and understanding their learning processes is indispensable. Engaging them as co-designers and/or student casuals in the module creation can be advantageous.
3. **Technical support teams:** These individuals ensure back-end functionality and module accessibility. Recognising their strengths and limitations is key. Collaborations could involve graphic designers, learning technologists and specialists in LMS and accessibility. Engaging them from the onset is crucial to facilitate the module's seamless creation and deployment.
4. **Administration (Leadership, Councils, Committees, Working Groups, etc.):** Their broader institutional objectives can offer alignment insights. Is there a committee overseeing curriculum alterations, like the introduction of new learning modules? Understanding your engagement responsibilities and potential endorsement requirements for the module with such committees is crucial.
5. **External partners:** When the module is crafted in partnership or under the sponsorship of industry figures,

understanding their expectations becomes imperative. For instance, if dermatologists seem eager to leverage the module's content in student placements, they might be another stakeholder group you'd have to engage with.

This comprehensive list becomes invaluable during the module's implementation, providing clarity on stakeholder preferences, aversions and motivations, thus assisting with strategy not only for baking the cake but also serving it later. This knowledge equips you to tailor the module effectively. Just as you'd avoid making a peanut cake for an allergic friend or would cater for different dietary requirements when baking a cake for a birthday party, you can now adapt the module to address each stakeholder's unique requirements.

With your list in hand, initiate stakeholder engagement activities, ranging from focus groups and individual meetings to surveys. As the module evolves, keep stakeholders updated, integrating their feedback. This cyclical feedback mechanism not only refines the module but also nurtures a shared sense of ownership among all participants.

Checklist

( ) Recognise and list all potential stakeholders.

( ) Engage with academics and other SMEs for content expertise.

( ) Gather preliminary feedback from students or work with them as partners.

> ( ) Understand technical requirements and constraints with support teams.
>
> ( ) Align with administrative and institutional goals.
>
> ( ) Factor in expectations of external partners, if any.
>
> ( ) Keep stakeholders updated and involved throughout the process.

How: Designing with universality in mind

The 'how' of the cake analogy translates to the design process in inclusive learning. How will you make your cake? In our context, how will you design your online learning module? This is where the principles of UDL come into play. UDL focuses on creating materials and experiences that are accessible and effective for a wide range of learners by providing multiple means of representation, engagement, and action and expression (CAST, 2018). Just as you carefully select ingredients for your cake, choose the suitable methods, media and interactive elements that accommodate diverse learning preferences and abilities (CAST, 2018).

With this in mind, here are some key considerations:

1. **Research and empathy:** Begin by comprehending the diverse needs of your learners. This could entail surveys tailored for the targeted student cohort, direct interactions with students, or examining recent educational resources developed for this group to identify challenges they might

encounter. For content of a sensitive or explicit nature, especially medical visuals, it's prudent to provide content warnings, ensuring students are forewarned and can plan and prepare before engaging with the topic.
2. **Diverse representation:** It is essential to diversify content delivery. Introduce a blend of text, video, audio and interactive simulations, catering to varied learner preferences or needs (CAST, 2018; Mayer, 2002). Ground your strategies in multimedia and cognitive load theories. While it's advantageous to offer diverse content forms, it's not necessary to replicate the same information across all mediums (Mayer, 2002). For example, when illustrating skin infections, a captioned video case study might suffice, allowing students multiple engagement points: viewing, reading captions, listening or perusing the transcript. However, avoid redundant content like duplicating the case study in text, video and infographic forms. Aim for diverse representation without overwhelming students with repetitive content (CAST, 2018; Mayer, 2002).
3. **Engagement and expression strategies:** Incorporate a diverse array of relevant activities and assessments (CAST, 2018). Though tools like discussion boards, quizzes, peer reviews and project assignments are available, utilise only those that align pedagogically with your learning outcomes and facilitate varied student expressions (CAST, 2018).
4. **Accessibility as a priority:** Commit to making all materials universally accessible (CAST, 2018; W3C, 2022). This commitment could entail, but is not limited to, captioned videos, textual alternatives for images, and ensuring interactive elements are accessible via keyboard commands or screen readers and other assistive technology (W3C, 2022).
5. **Feedback mechanisms:** Champion a culture of ongoing feedback from students, discerning the effective

components and areas of improvement. Such insights are invaluable for module enhancement.

By meticulously embracing these strategies, you guarantee your online learning module is as universally appealing as a masterfully crafted cake, satisfying the diverse tastes and needs of every learner.

Checklist

( ) Anchor the design in UDL principles.

( ) Conduct initial research to understand diverse learner needs.

( ) Ensure diverse content representation (text, video, audio, etc.).

( ) Avoid redundant content across different mediums.

( ) Incorporate varied, pedagogically relevant activities and assessments.

( ) Prioritise accessibility in all materials.

( ) Foster a continuous feedback culture.

Why: Clarifying the purpose and benefits

In the cake analogy, the 'why' signifies the occasion – a

birthday party, for instance. Similarly, the 'why' in learning design encompasses the purpose and desired outcomes. Why are you creating this module? What benefits will it bring to both the students and the institution? Clearly articulate the reasons behind your module's existence. This will not only guide your design decisions, it will also help communicate the value of your module ('serve the cake') to academics and fellow professional staff.

In this context, as a learning designer focusing on establishing the purpose and benefits of your module:

1. **Identify the gap:** Examine the current curriculum and ascertain any deficiencies or omissions. By recognising these gaps, you underscore the significance of the new module.
2. **Articulate the value:** Pinpoint what distinguishes this module from a traditional series of lectures. Whether it's presenting novel insights, offering adaptability and accessibility, or making more space for other equally important content to be covered, emphasise its distinctiveness.
3. **Implement iterative feedback:** Institute a system for ongoing feedback, enabling an understanding of the module's strengths and areas for improvement, which aids in continuous refinement.
4. **Engage in ongoing evaluation:** Post-launch, periodically assess the module's relevance and efficacy. Make requisite modifications to align with evolving goals or learner needs.

By diligently shaping and revisiting the module's underlying 'why', you solidify its value-driven foundation, benefitting both learners and the institution. This deliberate crafting, akin to baking a cake for a special occasion, ensures the module's enduring resonance and appreciation.

Checklist

( ) Engage stakeholders to understand the module's significance.

( ) Identify and document gaps in the current curriculum.

( ) Articulate the unique value proposition of the module.

( ) Implement iterative feedback mechanisms.

( ) Ensure alignment with broader institutional objectives.

( ) Regularly communicate the module's purpose to stakeholders.

( ) Periodically review and refine the module's purpose post-launch.

Selecting the ingredients: Accessibility, pedagogy and technology

Just as a cake requires the right ingredients to taste delightful, an inclusive learning module needs specific components to be effective. Accessibility must be woven into your design's fabric, ensuring all learners can access and engage with the content

(Burgstahler & Cory, 2010; Burgstahler & Doe, 2015; Rose & Meyer, 2002; W3C, 2022). A solid pedagogical framework provides the structure for meaningful learning experiences. Technology serves as the mixing bowl, enabling you to blend various elements seamlessly.

Consider your pedagogical approach – how will you engage learners? What interactive elements will enhance the learning experience? Integrate technology that supports your objectives, ensuring it is user-friendly and aligns with accessibility standards (Beetham & Sharpe, 2013; Rose & Meyer, 2002; W3C, 2022). Just as you fine-tune the balance of flavours in a cake by adjusting the ingredients, designers should find the equilibrium between these elements to create a harmonious learning environment.

Revisiting and drawing upon pedagogical frameworks can inform your practice and help you use technology in a meaningful, critical and accessible way within your learning module (Beetham & Sharpe, 2013). Some examples of these frameworks include TPACK, which helps you integrate technology, pedagogy and content knowledge (Koehler & Mishra, 2008). The SAMR model categorises technology use into stages, from substitution to redefinition, allowing you to understand the role technology will play in your module (Puentedura, 2010). PICRAT is a model that draws attention to the socio-cultural dimensions of technology in education (Kimmons, et al., 2020) and Mayer's multimedia theory delves into cognitive principles in multimedia design (Mayer, 2002). It is important to note that these are just a few examples of the many frameworks available to assist you depending on your pedagogical goals.

For instance, you can leverage Mayer's principles of multimedia learning when considering the integration of various elements into your learning module (Mayer, 2002). Just as adding too much flour can make your cake dense and dry, overwhelming your module with excessive text, videos or activities can lead to cognitive overload for learners (Mayer, 2002). By carefully selecting and balancing your ingredients, much like ensuring the right proportions of flour, milk and baking powder in a cake, you can create a learning experience that is engaging, effective and conducive to meaningful learning (Mayer, 2002).

As you progress through these planning stages, remember that just as a cake's success relies on thoughtful preparation, an inclusive learning module's success hinges on careful planning and consideration. In the following sections, we'll transition from planning to the creation stage, where we'll put these concepts into action, much like mixing the batter and putting the cake into the oven. By the end of this chapter, you'll have a well-structured roadmap for engaging staff in designing inclusive learning experiences that cater to the needs of all learners.

Baking the inclusive learning module: From recipe to prototype

With our planning complete, it's time to transition from the theoretical to the practical – from the recipe in hand to the actual act of baking. Inclusive learning design, like baking, is a dynamic process that involves creativity, precision and attention to detail. In this section, we'll delve into the 'baking' stage of our cake analogy, where we'll transform the ingredients of planning into a tangible prototype of your online learning module, all while utilising UDL as our guiding principle.

Blending the ingredients: UDL as your base

Universal Design for Learning serves as the foundational recipe for your inclusive learning module. Just as a cake requires a well-balanced blend of ingredients, your learning module demands a thoughtful combination of various UDL principles – multiple means of representation, engagement, and action and expression (CAST, 2018). Craft your content in ways that cater to different learning preferences and abilities. Incorporate various formats of content presentation – text, images, audio and video – ensuring that learners have multiple avenues to access and comprehend the material (CAST, 2018; Dalton & Smith, 2019).

When incorporating UDL principles into your learning module, it's important to avoid the pitfall of imbalance. Just like adding too much sugar can make a cake overly sweet or too many eggs can make it dense, neglecting or overloading your module with certain elements can hinder the learning experience. UDL encourages a balanced approach, similar to achieving the right blend of ingredients in a cake recipe. Provide multiple options for engagement, representation, and action and expression, but do so thoughtfully. Ensure that each element serves a purpose, aligns with your learning objectives and doesn't overshadow the others (CAST, 2018; Dalton & Smith, 2019; Rose & Meyer, 2002). In doing so, you'll create a learning experience that respects the diverse needs and preferences of your learners while maintaining a balanced and effective module design, much like achieving the perfect cake texture through a harmonious blend of ingredients.

Checklist

( ) Use Universal Design for Learning as your foundational design principle.

( ) Integrate UDL guidelines to cater to different learning preferences.

( ) Employ diverse content formats like text, images, audio and video.

( ) Aim for a balanced approach, ensuring each element serves a purpose and aligns with your pedagogical goals.

Taste as you cook: The importance of prototyping

Imagine you're using a cake recipe for the first time. Before you present the final product, you likely create a prototype to ensure that the flavours and textures are just right. Similarly, in learning design, prototyping is a crucial step. As you create your online learning module, build a prototype to test its functionality and effectiveness (Brown & Green, 2016). This prototype acts as a working draft that allows you to identify potential challenges and areas for improvement (Brown & Green, 2016).

Just as you could bake a small version of your final birthday cake, or test the batter mixture quickly by baking a mug cake in your microwave or using an air fryer, you can design the outline and skeleton of your learning module with your main ideas and activities (Brown & Green, 2016). By doing so, you can get some early feedback from students and stakeholders before investing in the creation of the entire module (Brown & Green, 2016). This prototype serves as a valuable testing ground, allowing you to make necessary adjustments, refine your approach, and ensure that the final product meets the desired learning objectives (Brown & Green, 2016). Much like tasting a small sample of your cake batter to make adjustments before baking the full cake, prototyping in learning design allows you to fine-tune your module for a more successful and engaging learning experience.

Checklist

( ) Think about simpler ways of representing your ideas for the module (e.g., storyboarding, designing one section of the module, outlining a skeleton for the module).

( ) Discuss these ideas with your stakeholders.

( ) Engage in this process as many times as needed before progressing to building the entire module.

Adjust to taste: Engaging with feedback

Just as you might gather feedback on your cake prototype from taste testers, your learning module prototype needs input from learners, academics and professional staff. Seek feedback on the design and overall user experience. This iterative process ensures that your learning module becomes a finely tuned creation that resonates with its audience and your learners and reflects the needs of your stakeholders. Incorporate suggestions and address concerns to refine your prototype further (Fisher & Wright, 2010).

Much like refining a cake recipe based on feedback from a panel of tasters, incorporating suggestions and addressing concerns raised by students and stakeholders enables you to refine your prototype further. By actively involving a range of individuals in the testing and feedback process, you increase the likelihood of creating a highly effective and user-friendly online learning experience that meets the needs and expectations of all stakeholders (Fisher & Wright, 2010).

Checklist

( ) Gather feedback on the design and user experience of the learning module prototype from students, academics and staff.

( ) Be prepared to engage in consultation more broadly if needed.

( ) Use an iterative feedback process to refine the prototype based on suggestions and concerns.

( ) Make adjustments that align with the needs and expectations of students and stakeholders to create a better online learning experience.

Baking for all tastes: Fine-tuning for accessibility

You adjust to achieve the desired taste and texture as you bake your cake. Similarly, when creating your learning module prototype, pay special attention to accessibility. Ensure that all learners can interact with the content seamlessly, regardless of their abilities (Dalton & Smith, 2019). Incorporate features such as alternative text for images, closed captions for videos, and keyboard-friendly navigational elements. Just as a well-baked cake delights all taste buds, an accessible learning module accommodates all learning needs (Burgstahler & Doe, 2015; CAST, 2018).

Incorporating well-established guidelines, such as the Web Content Accessibility Guidelines (WCAG) 2.2 and the Authoring Tool Accessibility Guidelines (ATAG), can significantly improve the accessibility of your module (W3C, 2022). By revisiting the key accessibility principles and considering these guidelines during the development phase, you can ensure that your module is inclusive and user-friendly for a wider audience (W3C, 2022). It's also essential to be prepared to differentiate and adjust aspects of your module as specific accessibility needs and issues arise during user testing (Burgstahler & Doe, 2015). Like adjusting a recipe to accommodate different dietary preferences and requirements, such as using lactose-free or soy milk when baking a cake for a lactose-intolerant friend, addressing unique accessibility challenges ensures that your online learning experience considers the diverse requirements of your learners (Burgstahler & Doe, 2015). By actively engaging with accessibility principles and guidelines and being adaptable in your approach, you can create a learning module that is accessible and user-friendly for all (W3C, 2022).

Checklist

( ) Embed accessible practices throughout your module (e.g., alternative text, closed captions, transcripts, etc.)

( ) Review well-established guidelines and digital accessibility principles to ensure optimal accessibility.

( ) Be ready to adjust the module according to new or specific needs and access requirements.

Vignette 4: The free fall

A few years ago, I was given the responsibility of finalising a project that aimed to replace traditional lectures with a set of online learning modules. The project was initially assigned to a fellow learning designer who was leaving our team. I received the handover notes and access to the learning modules and was asked to add the finishing touches and elements to each of them. Due to the project's tight deadlines, I had to work quickly and relied heavily on the handover notes and existing resources to complete the modules. Once I finished, I reached out to our SME to gather some final feedback, and that's when I learned that the modules did not achieve the intended outcomes and lacked sufficient content. As a result, a complete redesign was necessary, which inevitably led to a delayed launch date.

This experience taught me the importance of feedback and consultation throughout the design process, from start to finish. Active engagement with stakeholders and careful consideration of their feedback is crucial for ensuring that the module not only meets its intended purpose but also satisfies the needs and expectations of SMEs.

So, when engaging in inclusive learning design process make sure you ask yourself:

- How can I create a prototype of my learning design object that showcases my ideas to all stakeholders?
- Have I considered the goals of the project and the expectations and needs of students and stakeholders?
- How do I best engage with students and stakeholders for feedback?
- Have I consulted with students and stakeholders alike during all steps of the project?

> - Have I addressed their feedback, suggestions and concerns?

Serving the inclusive learning experiences: Strategies for engaging staff

After several rounds of prototyping, testing and refining, your cake is ready for its grand presentation. Similarly, your inclusive learning module, now well-constructed and refined, is ready to be shared with your target audience.

In this section, we'll explore the importance of effectively presenting your inclusive learning module to academic and professional staff. Just as a beautifully decorated cake is a visual delight, a well-designed learning module, when introduced strategically, can capture the attention and engagement of your stakeholders (Brown & Green, 2016).

With your prototype honed through the iterative process and your learning module ready for presentation, you're one step closer to successfully engaging staff in the realm of inclusive learning design. Through the lens of our cake analogy, you've successfully navigated the stages of planning and baking, each contributing to creating a rich and impactful learning experience.

Having successfully baked and refined your inclusive learning module, it's time to shift our attention to the crucial task of serving it. Just as a beautifully baked cake deserves to be presented and appreciated by many, your thoughtfully designed learning module awaits its moment of impact. In this section, we'll explore the intricacies of serving your inclusive learning experience to professional and academic staff, ensuring your creation is acknowledged and embraced.

Tailoring to the audience: An analogy of cake presentation

When serving cake at a birthday party, considerations for guests' comfort and preferences are paramount. Children might require sturdier surfaces, paper plates and utensils that match their dexterity, while adults could probably manage with only a few serviettes. Translating this to your inclusive product, you must adapt your approach to resonate with your target groups. Your online learning module, video content, or alternative assessment may require different modes of presentation to secure the necessary buy-in and usage.

For simplicity, we'll focus on two key audiences: professional and academic staff, often at the forefront of a learning designer's engagement.

Engaging professional staff: Applying a framework

When embarking on the journey of engaging professional staff, a well-constructed framework acts as a steady guide, ensuring a strategic and holistic approach. This proposed framework resembles the carefully constructed recipe one follows to create a culinary masterpiece. Within this framework, every step is orchestrated to foster understanding, collaboration and commitment, ultimately leading to the effective adoption of your inclusive learning module. Let's delve deeper into each facet of this framework:

> A. Scoping research
>
> B. Creating interest, accountability and momentum
>
> C. Offering training and support –- training the trainer
>
> D. Dividing and conquering

A. Scoping research: Understanding the terrain

Imagine embarking on a culinary adventure in an unfamiliar kitchen. Before selecting ingredients and techniques, you explore the kitchen's layout, your tools and the culinary preferences of your audience. Similarly, in the context of engaging professional staff, conducting comprehensive scoping research is the essential groundwork. Dive into their work and identify their specific needs, challenges and aspirations. This research is the foundation for your engagement strategy. Start early and integrate throughout the entire process.

B. Creating interest, accountability and momentum: Igniting the appetite

In the culinary realm, a skilled chef knows that presenting a visually enticing dish ignites diners' appetites. Similarly, in the world of professional staff engagement, capturing attention and interest is paramount. Demonstrate the significance of your inclusive learning module by showcasing its direct relevance to their work. Illustrate how it can elevate their teaching effectiveness and enhance student learning outcomes. Additionally, establish a sense of shared ownership and responsibility by involving them in the decision-making process. As they become co-creators, their engagement naturally deepens, fostering a sense of accountability and investment.

C. Offering training and support –- training the trainer: Nurturing expertise

Just as a seasoned chef imparts culinary techniques to junior chefs, nurturing expertise is critical to your engagement framework. For instance, assemble a subset of fellow learning designers and provide them with comprehensive training on the nuances of your inclusive learning module. This 'train the trainer' approach empowers them to become advocates and ambassadors (Brown & Green, 2016). Armed with knowledge, they can effectively disseminate information, train their peers and provide ongoing support. This strategy not only cultivates a knowledge-sharing culture, it also fosters a collaborative atmosphere where expertise is nurtured collectively.

D. Dividing and conquering: Collaboration with precision

In a bustling kitchen, culinary creations come to life through precise coordination and delegation. Similar precision is needed when engaging professional staff. As you implement your inclusive learning module, break down the journey into manageable and actionable steps. Assign different tasks to various team members based on their strengths and expertise. Encourage collaboration, allowing each individual to contribute in ways that resonate with their skills. This collective effort not only expedites the implementation process but also fosters a dynamic environment where diverse perspectives enrich the overall outcome.

As you apply these steps within the proposed framework, envision yourself orchestrating a culinary symphony, each note harmonising to produce a delightful experience. By the time you've engaged professional staff, the groundwork for the successful integration of your inclusive learning module will be firmly in place. In the forthcoming section, we'll turn our attention to academic staff, exploring how to tailor your approach to garner their enthusiastic participation in creating an inclusive learning environment that caters to the diverse needs of their students. Just as a perfectly executed dish delights the senses, your strategic engagement with staff will create a harmonious and impactful learning experience.

Engaging academic staff: A tailored approach

Navigating the landscape of engaging academic staff requires finesse and customisation, much like crafting an intricate dish to suit varying palates. Just as a skilled chef tailors flavours to different diners, you'll tailor your approach to academic staff by following these proposed steps:

> a. Raising awareness and showcasing relevance
>
> b. Offering small, practical solutions
>
> c. Assisting integration into routine
>
> d. Providing avenues and tools for independence

a. Raising awareness and showcasing relevance: An educational palette

Imagine presenting a sumptuous dish to a connoisseur – your goal is to help them appreciate the nuanced flavours and unique combinations. Similarly, when engaging academic staff, begin by raising awareness about the vital role of inclusive learning design within academic environments (Brown & Green, 2016). Present how your learning module seamlessly aligns with their teaching objectives, enriching the overall learning experience (Brown & Green, 2016). Much like presenting a dish's ingredients, showcase the elements that resonate with their expertise and teaching philosophy. In your approach, bridge the gap between their existing practices and the potential of your inclusive learning module, emphasising how their needs and expectations would be met through the implementation of the designed experience.

b. Offering small, practical solutions: Culinary touches of inclusion

Just as a master chef adds subtle seasonings to elevate a dish, introduce academic staff to small yet impactful solutions that enrich their teaching methods. These solutions are like the delicate seasonings that bring out the best in the main ingredients. Introduce user-friendly tools that seamlessly integrate into their existing routines (Brown & Green, 2016). Or, in our case, introduce ideas of how the designed online module already incorporates some elements which would usually be designed separately, such as formative and summative assessments. These minor adjustments, analogous to culinary garnishes, hold the potential to significantly enhance the learning experience. By aligning these solutions with the academic staff's current practices and pedagogical styles, you're creating an environment where inclusive practices naturally integrate, much like flavours melding in a well-cooked dish.

c. Assisting integration into routine: Guiding the cooking process

Academic staff benefit from support as they integrate inclusive design principles and learning experiences into their teaching routines, much like an apprentice chef benefits from guidance to master complex techniques. Offer workshops, resources and 1:1 opportunities to ease the transition and implementation (Brown & Green, 2016). This process is akin to guiding them through a complex recipe, ensuring every step is executed with precision (Brown & Green, 2016). In your approach, scaffold academic staff's integration of inclusive practices, helping them grow into effective facilitators of inclusive learning experiences.

d. Provide avenues and tools for independence: The art of culinary exploration

Just as a chef equips an aspiring cook with essential tools, empower academic staff to independently implement inclusive strategies and learning experiences such as your online module and to even contemplate creating their own. Provide resources, guidelines and tools that cater to their needs and scaffold their learning process just like you would scaffold student learning (Brown & Green, 2016). This stage is reminiscent of a budding chef taking the skills they've acquired to embark on their culinary explorations. Similarly, provide academics with the avenues and tools to experiment and adapt their practice, ensuring they are confident in their own abilities and know when, how and who to ask for help. As you traverse these steps, remember that just as a perfectly executed dish delights diners' senses, your tailored engagement with academic staff cultivates an inclusive learning environment, fostering growth and enriching not only these relationships but also the overall educational experience of their students.

Conclusion

In this comprehensive chapter, we have embarked on a journey guided by the delightful analogy of baking a cake to explore the intricacies of inclusive learning design. Like baking a cake, creating inclusive learning experiences requires careful planning, thoughtful ingredient selection (considering accessibility, pedagogy and technology), meticulous prototyping and strategic engagement with staff. Through this culinary lens, we've unveiled key strategies and practices for designing, refining and serving inclusive learning modules to academic and professional staff. As we reflect on this journey, several key takeaways emerge.

We have learned that inclusive learning design is a holistic process that goes beyond creating content. It requires active engagement with students and stakeholders alike, ongoing refinement and a commitment to ensuring that the designed modules truly meet the needs of all learners drawing from **UDL** and digital accessibility principles. Most importantly, we have discussed and demonstrated the importance of considering **accessibility** and inclusive design from the beginning, not as an afterthought. Just as the quality of ingredients affects the taste of a cake, the inclusivity and accessibility of your learning design projects profoundly impact the learning experience. By prioritising inclusion and accessibility in your practice, you ensure you create experiences that are not only pedagogically sound, robust and engaging but that are also welcoming and inclusive of student diversity, regardless of their abilities.

If you are a new learning designer embarking on your inclusive journey, consider these questions: How can you actively involve students and stakeholders throughout the design process to ensure their needs are met? How will you integrate accessibility principles and inclusive design from the very beginning? And how can you continually refine and improve your practice to create truly inclusive learning experiences? Remember, like a well-baked cake, the journey of inclusive learning design is both a science and an art, and with dedication and thoughtful practice, you can create educational experiences that embrace diversity and enrich the educational experiences of all learners.

References

Beetham, H., & Sharpe, R. (2013). *Rethinking pedagogy for a digital age: Designing and delivering e-learning.* Routledge.

Brown, A, & Green, T. (2016). *The essentials of instructional design: Connecting fundamental principles with process and practice.* Routledge.

Burgstahler, S. E., & Cory, R. C. (Eds.). (2010). *Universal design in higher education: From principles to practice.* Harvard Education Press.

Burgstahler, S., & Doe, T. (2015). *Universal design in higher education: Promising practices.* DO-IT, University of Washington.

CAST. (2018). *The UDL guidelines* (version 2.2). https://udlguidelines.cast.org/

Dalton, E. M., & Smith, D. S. (2019). Universal design for learning: Guiding principles to reduce barriers to digital & online education. *Information Technology & Libraries, 38*(4), 28–39. https://doi.org/10.23860/JMLE-2019-09-02-02

Fisher, E. A., & Wright, V. H. (2010). Improving online course design through usability testing. *Journal of Online Learning and Teaching, 6*(1), 228–245.

Gualtieri, M. (2011, February 11). The seven qualities of wildly desirable software. *Forrester.* https://www.forrester.com/blogs/11-02-11-the_seven_qualities_of_wildly_desirable_software/#:~:text=Forrester%20defines%20the%20seven%20qualities,adaptability%2C%20security%2C%20and%20economy.

Kimmons, R., Graham, C. R., & West, R. E. (2020). The PICRAT model for technology integration in teacher preparation. *Contemporary Issues in Technology and Teacher Education, 20*(1), 176–198.

Koehler, M. J., & Mishra, P. (2008). Introducing TPCK. In AACTE Committee on Innovation and Technology (Eds.), *Handbook of technological pedagogical content knowledge (TPCK) for educators* (pp. 3–29). Routledge.

Mayer, R. E. (2002). Multimedia learning. *Psychology of Learning and Motivation, 41*, 85–139. https://doi.org/10.1016/S0079-7421(02)80005-6

Puentedura, R. (2010). *SAMR and TPCK: Introductory remarks* [Lecture presentation]. ISTE 2010 Conference and Exposition. http://hippasus.com/resources/sweden2010/SAMR_TPCK_IntroToAdvancedPractice.pdf

Rose, D. H., & Meyer, A. (2002). *Teaching every student in the digital age: Universal design for learning.* ASCD.

W3C. (2022). *Web content accessibility guidelines (WCAG) 2.2.* https://www.w3.org/TR/WCAG22/

About the author

Bruna Contro Pretero
CANBERRA INSTITUTE OF TECHNOLOGY
https://cit.edu.au/

At the time of writing, Bruna Contro Pretero was a Digital Accessibility Specialist at the Australian National University with 15 years of experience in various educational roles. She holds Bachelor's degrees in Sciences and Teaching, and in Translation and Interpreting Services, along with multiple postgraduate diplomas in education and accessibility. Bruna's expertise includes Technology-Enhanced Learning, Critical Pedagogy, Diversity and Inclusion, and Digital Accessibility. As a queer and disabled advocate, she is dedicated to transforming education and society through inclusive and accessible practices.

10. Conclusion

MAIS FATAYER

Not just another textbook

In writing this book our primary aim was to provide a practical resource for the use of learning designers in higher education. We concentrated in particular on:

- Addressing the existing gap by providing an open textbook that focuses on diversity in learning design within the Australasian region.
- Different conceptual frameworks for learning designers for designing diverse learning environments, considering the challenges prevalent in higher education.
- Providing practical examples, evidence-based solutions, and draw from educational theory to shape socially just learning experiences.

The process of creating this book was intrinsically rewarding. By choosing to produce an open textbook, we implicitly convey our commitment to ongoing development. The shared characteristics between designing for learning and authoring open textbooks are their iterative, collaborative, and diverse nature. Although this is the first edition of the book, we envision its potential for growth, both within its chapters and beyond, utilising the **5Rs**.

A glimpse of each chapter

In each chapter, we aimed to explore the implications of the conceptual approach presented for fostering inclusivity and diversity in learning design, and provide practical examples and guidelines that learning designers can immediately apply to their work.

Making socially just pedagogy a reality

In this chapter, Keith and Camille emphasise the importance of inclusivity, going beyond just accessibility. They argue that it's vital to create an inclusive learning environment by actively involving students in the learning process, rather than focusing solely on individuals or specific groups. They suggest that learning designers should consider incorporating students as active partners in the learning ecosystem to facilitate genuine inclusivity and diversity. To do so, they introduce a framework that combines **Fraser's three dimensions of social justice** with **Universal Design for Learning (UDL)** principles and **David Wiley's 5 Rs of Open Education**. While Keith and Camille acknowledge the complexity of these three layers, they stress the importance of an ongoing and iterative approach to developing inclusive and socially just learning. Practical examples are provided to demonstrate how this approach can be put into practice, with a focus on authentic learning and student involvement in alignment with the framework.

Designing inclusive learning experience through open educational practices

Moving forward, Mais delves into **Open Educational Practices (OEP)** as a catalyst for designing inclusive and socially just learning environments. In her chapter she presents practical approaches for the adoption of OEP in higher education, offering insights from Australia and other places around the world. The chapter emphasises that learning designers must embrace OEP in the design processes, and develop an understanding of open education fundamentals. Further, the chapter highlights the benefits of OEP in empowering academics to update biased curricula, offer opportunities to decolonise education and foster inclusivity amidst disruptions.

Negotiating the assumptions and identity tensions surrounding third space academics/professionals

The next chapter in this sequence, delve deeper into the professional identity of a learning designer. Through the lens of Bhabha's concept of ambivalence, the notion of liminal space and reflecting on her own experience, Puva P Arumugam, the author of this chapter, sheds light on the challenges and tensions confronted by **third space practitioners** in higher education. These challenges Puva find them arising in the context of contrasting expectations and assumptions held by traditional institutional and discipline academics. Key tensions include the struggle to define the role of learning designers (LD) within the academic framework versus their professional identity, which is influenced by cultural factors. Additionally, this chapter explores the polymathic nature of third space practitioners' roles, a concept presented by Manoharan (2020). Being polymathic involves transcending singular specialisation and operating with a multifaceted expertise. Third space practitioners, due to their involvement in diverse teaching and learning projects, often possess in-depth knowledge across multiple domains of specialisation. This chapter provides a dynamic and interactive experience, with Puva's voice serving as a guide through the multifaceted realm of learning designers. It delves into their professional identity and the diverse array of skills they contribute to tertiary education.

Indigenous-led learning design: Reimagining the teaching team

Chapter 5 of this book highlights the remarkable collaboration between academic subject matter experts, learning design team, instructional designer and Centre for the Advancement of Indigenous Knowledges (CAIK) scholars to design and develop the microcredential, Supervising Indigenous Higher Degree Research. This exceptional partnership fostered mutual understanding and a high degree of collegial respect. Reflecting on the collaboration, Katrina, Shaun, Susan, highlighted three key factors emerged as driving forces: trust, iterative discussions, and the combined skills of scholars and learning designers. The authors further illustrate their design decisions they made during the process by offering concrete examples from the subject. These examples showcase their commitment to presenting content knowledge in compelling format, their attention to cultural sensitivity, and their skills in creating online learning experiences that enhance student engagement and the learning outcomes.

This chapter exemplifies the guiding principle of 'Nothing about us without us' as the team actively engaged in co-designing the subject with consultations from the Director of CAIK. Furthermore, the team wholeheartedly embraced the responsibility of preserving and sharing crucial cultural knowledge, however, their crucial design decisions are thoughtfully shared, with the intention of aiding fellow learning designers undertaking similar projects.

Designing for Equity in Learning

In this chapter, John took us back to his personal learning experience in such an interesting and insightful way to then introduce a range of innovative pedagogical strategies aimed at fostering inclusive and engaging educational environments. The strategies discussed – Notice and Wonder, the 4Hs of Belonging Centred Math Instruction, Ingenious Influencers, and the collaborative online platform Virtual Math Teams (VMT) – collectively offer practical avenues for educators and learning designers to enhance teaching practices. Throughout the chapter, John offers engaging examples that illustrate the instructional steps for implementing activities. He follows these with real-life situations from the classroom, demonstrating how these activities promote inclusivity.

Designing for cultural responsiveness

Chapter 7 is another lively chapter written with a personal touch by Nhung Nguyen. Nhung emphasis that culturally responsive design in education entails deeply valuing and celebrating students' diverse cultural heritage, knowledge, skills and languages. By fostering interactions, collaborations, and multiple perspectives, this approach intertwines educational design with students' unique cultural perspectives, frames of reference, language, and communication styles, ultimately nurturing both academic growth and strong interpersonal relationships.

The importance of culturally responsive design is underscored by several key factors: Learners' Engagement and Educational Performance, globalisation and the Decolonial Movement.

The process of implementing culturally responsive design

involves laying the groundwork by promoting self-awareness, understanding the learners, and engaging with communities. Furthermore, it requires empowering learners through representation, implementing culturally sensitive assessment and feedback, promoting active engagement and participation, and adopting a multilingual approach to enhance the educational experience.

Working with students with lived experience of disability to enhance inclusive and accessible learning

In chapter 8, Katie and Rhiannon call for university staff particularly learning designers to pursue the requisite knowledge and skills for crafting accessible learning environments. They firmly believe that Ableism serves as a primary barrier, contributing to low participation and completion rates, increased student debt among disabled students, insufficient resourcing for accessibility accommodations, and frequent reports of stigmatisation and discrimination.

They posit that University staff, including learning design teams, play a pivotal role in providing accessible learning environments. Despite acknowledging the intersection between the accessibility and learning design teams, Katie and Rhiannon highlight that both teams need to be working hand in hand to support academics and guide them in creating inclusive learning environments.

While recognising the challenge of upskilling academic staff in accessibility, Katie and Rhiannon stress the imperative of engaging students in developing effective services, as they can provide unique perspectives and collaborate on solutions.

Emphasising their approach to designing for accessibility, they underscore the danger of excluding students with disabilities from the learning experience design. They advocate strongly for a **co-design** approach, positioning students with disabilities as active partners in the design process, as these students can reveal shortcomings that designers may be unaware of.

This is a call for learning designers to acknowledge the crucial role of students with lived experience in shaping an inclusive learning environment and fostering socially just education. Katie and Rhiannon follow with practical examples, echoing the call made by Keith and Camille in Chapter 2 that designing with accessibility in mind means designing for everyone. Additionally, they present a project focused on developing resources that shape practices, providing guidelines for learning designers to implement accessibility practices effectively.

Baking a cake: Engaging staff in inclusive learning design

In Chapter 9, Bruna sheds light on a pressing issue in learning design— the tendency to relegate **accessibility** to an afterthought. She stresses that this neglect leads to significant challenges—impracticality and increased costs. Using a baking analogy, Bruna asserts that accessibility is as vital to learning design as baking powder is to a cake, yet it's often treated as a discretionary embellishment, akin to cake decoration.

Strategically positioned after Chapter 8, this chapter offers valuable insights for learning designers. Through personal vignettes, Bruna underscores the importance of considering accessibility and inclusivity throughout the learning design process. The chapter not only imparts practical advice but also provides checklists guiding designers from initial stages to feedback. Bruna introduces a structured approach by outlining four stages of the learning design process—what, how, who, and why. Weaving in the Universal Design for Learning (UDL) framework, consistently emphasised throughout the book, she reinforces UDL's pivotal role in creating inclusive and accessible learning environments. Throughout the narrative, Bruna engages readers, prompting reflection on their experiences as learning designers. Thought-provoking questions encourage a reevaluation of design decisions, processes, stakeholder communication, and overall outcome quality.

This chapter issues a call to action, compelling us to reassess our approach to learning design. It prompts deliberate consideration of inclusivity as an integral, non-negotiable element rather than an optional feature. This introspection is crucial for steering the learning design process toward a genuinely inclusive process.

Where to go from here

As the authors of this open textbook, we maintain an open-minded stance towards receiving and responding to feedback. We view feedback as a catalyst for initiating constructive conversations that, ideally, result in the sharing of knowledge and the creation of new insights for our learning design community.

In this collaborative project, all chapters of our book are accessible for viewing and comments through Hypothesis. This streamlined approach allows for the prompt receipt of constructive feedback without the need to directly contact the authors. Upon receiving notifications regarding the feedback, authors will diligently review and thoughtfully incorporate any necessary updates into the respective chapters, ensuring a dynamic and responsive learning resource.

Final message to the learning design community

As learning designers, we stand at the forefront of influencing the learning process. The framework and the practical approaches presented in this book provide an exciting opportunity for us to initiate change. While we can certainly begin implementing the practical solutions suggested, it's crucial to delve deeper and understand how these strategies function in real-world educational settings. We must consider whether these approaches are equally effective for both diverse and more homogeneous groups of learners. Are there instances where customisation or alternative strategies might be more appropriate for specific cohorts for example, where the learners are from diverse ethnicities, races or religious backgrounds? By critically examining the practical impact of these ideas, we can tailor our approaches to ensure that our efforts lead to greater inclusivity in learning, irrespective of the learner's background or characteristics.

About the author

Dr Mais Fatayer
UNIVERSITY OF TECHNOLOGY SYDNEY
https://www.uts.edu.au

Mais Fatayer is an educational technology specialist, learning designer with extensive experience in higher education and open education advocate. As of the publication of this book, she was the Learner Experience Design Manager at the University of Technology Sydney (UTS). Mais specialises in creating engaging learning materials and leading transformative projects and initiative in learning design and open education. She has received the 2023 UTS Vice Chancellor's Professional Staff Excellence Award and the 2018 Blackboard Catalyst Award for Student Success. Her PhD research focused on developing a sustainable open educational resources development model.

Versioning History

This page provides a record of changes made to this textbook. Each set of edits is acknowledged with a 0.01 increase in the version number. The exported files for this toolkit reflect the most recent version.

If you find an error, please contact utsepress@uts.edu.au

Version	Date	Change
1.01	31 December 2023	Published chapters 1-6
1.02	26 July 2024	Published all chapters
1.03	8 August 2024	Updated contributor profiles
1.04	20 August 2024	Minor updates: accessibility, metadata, formatting
1.05	30 August 2024	Minor updates: formatting, removing duplicated section 'About the Authors' from the Introduction

Review Statement

UTS ePress is committed to publishing high-quality open textbooks which meet the needs of students and educators. This book has been peer-reviewed by two subject experts from two higher education institutions. Each chapter received a single-blind review from academics with specialist knowledge and experience in learning design and higher education.

Reviews were structured around considerations of the intended audience of the book and examined the comprehensiveness, accuracy and relevance of the content. Reviews were also focused on relevance longevity, clarity, consistency, organisation, structure flow, grammatical errors and cultural relevance.

The author and the publication team would like to thank Associate Professor Henk Huijser and Associate Professor Leanne Ngo for the time, care, and commitment they contributed to reviewing the project. We recognise that peer reviewing is a generous act of service on their part. This book would not be the robust, valuable resource that it is were it not for their feedback and input.

Feedback and corrections

If you'd like to report a problem, share feedback or request corrections, please contact utsepress@uts.edu.au.

Thank you for your help!

Glossary

Accessibility

Accessibility focuses on ensuring that environments, services, and tools are usable by everyone, particularly students with disabilities. It involves removing barriers to participation and making sure that everyone can engage with educational materials and activities on the same basis as their peers. This includes providing resources in accessible formats, such as screen reader-compatible documents or videos with captions, to comply with legal obligations under acts like the *Disability Discrimination Act 1992*.

Artificial Intelligence (AI)

UNESCO World Commission on the Ethics of Scientific Knowledge and Technology, COMEST (2019) defines Artificial Intelligence (AI) into two distinct aspects: theoretical or scientific AI and pragmatic or technological AI. The theoretical aspect explores AI concepts and models to answer questions about human beings and other living things, intersecting with disciplines like philosophy, logic, linguistics, psychology, and cognitive science. It addresses questions about intelligence, distinguishing natural from artificial intelligence, the role of symbolic language in thought processes, and the possibility of achieving "strong AI" comparable to human intelligence. On the other hand, pragmatic or technological AI is engineering-oriented, leveraging branches of AI such as natural language processing, knowledge representation, machine learning, deep learning, computer vision, and robotics. It aims to create machines or programs capable of independently performing tasks that typically require human intelligence. The success of pragmatic AI is evident in its integration with information and communications technology (ICT), leading to widespread applications in areas like transport, medicine, communication, education, finance, law, military, marketing, customer services, and entertainment (COMEST, 2019).

COMEST (2019), "Preliminary study on the ethics of artificial intelligence", Paris, SHS/COMEST/EXTWG-ETHICS-AI/2019/1.

From https://unesdoc.unesco.org/ark:/48223/pf0000367823

Co-design

The co-design process in learning design is a collaborative approach that involves various stakeholders, including educators, students, learning designers, and sometimes industry partners, in the creation and development of learning experiences and educational materials. This process emphasises partnership and shared decision-making to ensure that the learning solutions are effective, relevant, and engaging for the learners.

Inclusivity

Inclusivity goes beyond providing access. It requires intentional and deliberate efforts to ensure that everyone, including students with disabilities, feels a sense of belonging at the university. Inclusivity encompasses designing resources and learning experiences from the outset in a way that considers diverse needs and perspectives. It's about creating an environment where all students feel valued and included, not just accommodated.

Nancy Fraser three dimensions of social justice

Nancy Fraser outlines three dimensions of social justice in her work: redistribution, recognition, and representation. These dimensions are designed to address different forms of social injustices and inequities:

Redistribution: Focuses on the economic aspect of social justice, aims to address inequalities in the distribution of resources and wealth and seeks to correct economic disparities by redistributing wealth, income, and opportunities to ensure a fairer allocation.

Recognition: Concentrates on the cultural and social aspect of social justice, addresses issues of misrecognition or cultural domination where certain groups are devalued or disrespected based on their identity (e.g., race, gender, ethnicity) and calls for the affirmation and respect of diverse identities and cultural practices to combat discrimination and promote equal respect.

Representation (or **Political Justice**): Pertains to the political aspect of social justice, deals with issues of political voice and participation, ensuring all individuals and groups have equal opportunities to be heard and influence decision-making processes and seeks to address political marginalisation and ensure fair representation in political institutions and public life.

Fraser argues that a comprehensive approach to social justice must consider all three dimensions, as focusing on only one can lead to incomplete or even counterproductive outcomes. Redistribution without recognition, for example, may fail to address the deeper cultural injustices that perpetuate economic inequalities, and vice versa. Similarly, without proper representation, marginalised groups may lack the political power needed to achieve both economic redistribution and cultural recognition.

Open educational practices

Open educational practices are a set of activities around instructional design and implementation of events and processes intended to support learning. They also include the creation, use and repurposing of Open Educational Resources (OER) and their adaptation to the contextual setting. They are documented in a portable format and made openly available.

Open Educational Quality Initiative. (2011). Beyond OER: Shifting the focus to open educational practices. The 2011 OPAL Report. http://duepublico.uni-duisburg-essen.de/servlets/DerivateServlet/Derivate-25907/OPALReport2011_Beyond_OER.pdf

Open Educational Resources

Open Educational Resources (OER) are learning, teaching and research materials in any format and medium that reside in the public domain or are under copyright that have been released under an open license, that permit no-cost access, re-use, re-purpose, adaptation and redistribution by others.

Open License

Open license refers to a license that respects the intellectual property rights of the copyright owner and provides permissions granting the public the rights to access, re-use, re-purpose, adapt and redistribute educational materials.

Social justice

Social justice is the fair and just treatment of all people, regardless of their race, ethnicity, gender, sexual orientation, disability or other personal characteristics. It is about ensuring that everyone has the same opportunities to succeed in life.

The 5Rs of Openness

– Retain – the right to make, own, and control copies of the content
– Reuse – the right to use the content in a wide range of ways (e.g., in a class, in a study group, on a website, in a video)
– Revise – the right to adapt, adjust, modify, or alter the content itself (e.g., translate the content into another language)
– Remix – the right to combine the original or revised content with other open content to create something new (e.g., incorporate the content into a mashup)
– Redistribute – the right to share copies of the original content, your revisions, or your remixes with others (e.g., give a copy of the content to a friend)

Third space practitioner

A "Third Space Practitioner" in higher education refers to individuals who operate in the hybrid and often innovative spaces between traditional academic and administrative roles. They play a crucial role in bridging the gap between these areas to facilitate collaboration, enhance student experiences, and drive institutional change.

Universal Design for Learning (UDL)

The UDL Guidelines are a tool used in the implementation

of Universal Design for Learning. These guidelines offer a set of concrete suggestions that can be applied to any discipline or domain to ensure that all learners can access and participate in meaningful, challenging learning opportunities.